BASIC EVANGELISATION

Dedicated to the members of the New Springtime Community

'Holy Spirit, Comforter, Advocate and Guide,
inspire a new springtime of holiness and apostolic zeal
for the chuch in Ireland'
— Pope Benedict XVI, Prayer for the Church in Ireland

Pat Collins CM

Basic Evangelisation

GUIDELINES FOR CATHOLICS

First published in 2010 by
the columba press
55A Spruce Avenue, Stillorgan Industrial Park,
Blackrock, Co Dublin

Cover by Bill Bolger
Origination by The Columba Press
Printed in Ireland by ColourBooks Ltd, Dublin

ISBN 978 1 85607 696-8

Contents

Abbreviations Used For Church Documents

AG Decree: *Ad Gentes* (The Church's Missionary Activity)
CCC *Catechism of the Catholic Church*
CCL *Code of Canon Law* (1993)
CD Encyclical Letter: *Christus Dominus* (The Bishop's Pastoral Office in the Church.)
CL Apostolic Exhortation: *Christifideles Laici* (The Lay Members of Christ's Faithful)
CT Apostolic Exhortation: *Catechesi Tradendae* (Catechesis in Our Time)
CV Encyclical Letter: *Caritas in Veritate* (Love in Truth)
DM Encyclical Letter: *Dives et Misercordia* (Rich in Mercy)
DeV Encyclical Letter: *Dominum et Vivificantem* (Lord and Giver of Life)
DV Dogmatic Constitution: *Dei Verbum* (On Divine Revelation)
EE Apostolic Exhortation: *Ecclesia in Europa* (The Church in Europe)
EN Apostolic Exhortation: Evangelii Nuntiandi (Evangelisation in the Modern World)
EV Encyclical Letter: *Evangelium Vitae* (Gospel of Life)
FC Apostolic Exhortation: *Familiaris Consortio* (The Christian Family in the Modern World)
FR Encyclical Letter: *Fides et Ratio* (Faith and Reason)
GS Pastoral Constitution: *Gaudium et Spes* (The Church in the Modern World)
IM Decree: *Inter Mirifica* (Instruments of Social Communication)
LG Dogmatic Constitution: *Lumen Gentium* (The Church)
NA Declaration: *Nostra Aetate* (On the Relationship of the Church to Non-Christian Religions)
NMI Apostolic Letter: *Novo Millennio Inuente* (At the Beginning of the New Millennium)
PO Decree: *Presbyterorum Ordinis* (Ministry and Life of Priests)
PP Encyclical Letter: *Populorum Progressio* (On the Development of Peoples)
RM Encyclical Letter: *Redemptoris Missio* (Mission of the Redeemer)
RP Apostolic Exhortation: *Reconciliatio et Paenitentia* (Reconciliation and Repentance)
RVM Apostolic Exhortation, *Rosarium Virginis Marie* (Rosary of the Virgin Mary)
SC Constitution: *Sacrosanctum Concilium* (The Sacred Liturgy)
SS Encyclical Letter: *Spes Salvi* (The Hope of Salvation)
TMA Apostolic Letter: *Tertio Millennio Adveniente* (As the Third Millennium Approaches)
UR Decree: *Unitatis Redintegratio* (On Ecumenism)
UUS Encyclical Letter: *Ut Unum Sint* (That they May be One)
VS Encyclical Letter: *Veritatis Splendor* (Splendour of the Truth)

Introduction

In November 2009 an ecumenical group asked me to give a talk in Ferns, Co Wexford, on the topic, 'Are Irish Christians a Dying Breed?' At a time when some people speak about the church as a spent force, such a question was understandable and well worth asking. In order to answer it, one can refer to the fact that in modern religious circles there is an on-going debate about the related notions of secularisation and secularism. Secularisation can be understood in positive and in negative terms. Speaking about the former, Pope Paul VI observed in par 55 of his Apostolic Exhortation, *Evangelii nuntiandi* (hereafter EN), 'secularisation is the effort, in itself just and legitimate and in no way incompatible with faith or religion, to discover in creation, in each thing or each happening in the universe, the laws which regulate them with a certain autonomy, but with the inner conviction that the Creator has placed these laws there.' Understood in mainly negative terms, secularisation is a complex phenomenon that has some of the following characteristics:

- A decline of the prestige and influence of religion as an institution and an increasing emphasis on personal spirituality.
- An increased focus on 'this world' and abandonment of a supernatural perspective, e.g. notions such as the devil or hell.
- A privatisation of religious practice and a move away from community-based religious activity.
- A shift towards 'scientific' and rational explanations for phenomena, which leads to a desacralisation of the world.
- A move from objective religious authority to subjective religious experience.

Secularisation, both good and bad, can lead to secularism. Pope Paul VI noted in EN 55 that, 'secularism is a concept of the world according to which the latter is self-explanatory, without any need for recourse to God, who thus becomes superfluous and an encumbrance. This sort of secularism, in order to recognise the power of man, therefore ends up by doing without God and even by denying him.'[1] Speaking about this tendency shortly before his death, John Paul II said in par 9 of the Apostolic Exhortation, *Ecclesia in Europa* (hereafter EE), 'European culture gives the impression of "silent apostasy" on the part of people who have all that they need and who live as if God does not exist.'

I would suggest that during the last twenty five years or so, Christian Ireland has experienced a process of secularisation both good and bad, which has tended to evolve into secularism. While I realise that church attendance is not necessarily a sign of deep Christian conviction, all things being equal, it is an important if imperfect indicator of how religious people are. When Pope John Paul II came to the Republic of Ireland in 1978 about 94% of the population was Catholic. Surveys at that time, conducted by the European Economic Community, indicated that about 87% of Catholics in the Republic attended weekly Mass.[2] Ten years later the figure was about 85%.[3] On the website of the Irish Bishops there is a report entitled, *The European Social Survey: A Review of 2005 Religious Practice Data*, which indicates that 63% of Catholics were going to weekly Mass at that time.[4] Those figures for weekly Mass attendance no longer ring true for two reasons, especially in urban areas. Firstly, sociologists have found a tendency among people who are polled to say they are going to church more frequently than is actually the case. Secondly, there is reason to believe that the percentage of those going to church in Ireland has dropped considerably between 2005 and 2009, due in part to the publication of the Ferns report on clerical sex abuse (2005), the Ryan Report on institutional abuse (2009), and the Murphy Report on the handling of clerical sex abuse in the Archdiocese of Dublin (2009). A Red C

1. EN 55.
2. *Irish Values and Attitudes: The Irish Report of the European Values Systems Study*, eds Fogarty, Ryan, Lee (Dublin: Dominican Publications, 1984), 134.
3. *Values and Social Change in Ireland*, ed Christopher Whelan (Dublin: Gill & MacMillan, 1994), 22.
4. http://www.catholicbishops.ie/research (accessed 20 Nov. 2009)

poll for the Iona Institute confirmed this impression. It was conducted between 19 and 21 October 2009. It found that weekly church attendance had dropped to 46% while monthly attendance was 65%.[5] I have heard a senior cleric say that it was estimated that the practice rate in the Archdiocese of Dublin in 2009 was about 17%.[6] There are some parishes where it is less than 10%.

There are clear indications, therefore, that church practice in Catholic Ireland has probably halved since John Paul's historic visit in 1979. This has been due to a multiplicity of factors such as growing prosperity, increased education, urbanisation, clerical scandals, a rejection of Christian sexual ethics, influence of the media, pluralism, a move from institutional religion to personal spirituality and the like. However, critics overdramatise the situation when they say that Ireland is a post-Catholic or post-Christian country. It is worth remembering that it is estimated that only 30-40% of Catholics in pre-famine Ireland attended weekly Mass.[7]

It is also worth noting that vocations to the priesthood and religious life have fallen dramatically in recent years. For example, only 15 men were ordained for the priesthood for the whole of Ireland in 2004,[8] whereas during that same year about 160 priests died. There are currently 4,752 priests in Ireland; in 2028 it is estimated that there will be about 1,500.[9] The current statistics indicate that Ireland is still one of the most religious coun-

5. Patsy McGarry, 'Mass Attendance in Ireland is Up', *Irish Times*, 2 November 2009.

6. I have found it hard to get accurate figures for the Protestant churches in Ireland. Apparently the number of Presbyterians attending church regularly has dropped from just under 50% in 1989 to 40% in 2004, and in the Church of Ireland it fell from 40% in 1989 to 35% in 2004. Harold Millar, Bishop of Dromore, whose diocese includes Belfast, says that weekly church attendance in his area has dropped to 17%. See http://www.christiantoday.com/article/ireland.survey.reveals.sharp.drop.in.church.attendance/4600.htm

7. Michael P. Carroll, 'Rethinking Popular Catholicism in Pre-famine Ireland', *Journal for the Scientific Study of Religion* (1995): 354.

8. Philip Jenkins, *God's Continent: Christianity, Islam and Europe's Religious Crisis* (New York: Oxford University Press, 2007), 33.

9. David Sharrock, 'Catholic Church faces new crisis – Ireland is running out of priests', *Irish Times*, 27 February 2008.

tries in the Western World.[10] But it won't be for long if present trends continue. What is clearly needed is an all Ireland commitment to renewal in the Holy Spirit and a new evangelisation.

When the Irish bishops made an *Ad Limina* visit to Rome in 1999 Pope John Paul II spoke repeatedly to them about the need for a new evangelisation.[11] During a subsequent *Ad Limina* visit in Oct 2006, Pope Benedict said to the bishops: 'The present time brings many new opportunities to bear witness to Christ and fresh challenges for the church in Ireland. You have spoken about the consequences for society of the rise in prosperity that the last fifteen years have brought. [The Celtic Tiger was still in our midst at that time!] After centuries of emigration, which involved the pain of separation for so many families, you are experiencing for the first time a wave of immigration. Traditional Irish hospitality is finding unexpected new outlets. Like the wise householder who brings forth from his treasure "what is new and what is old" (Mt 13:52), your people need to view the changes in society with discernment, and here they look to you for leadership. Help them to recognise the inability of the secular, materialist culture to bring true satisfaction and joy. Be bold in speaking to them of the joy that comes from following Christ and living according to his commandments. Remind them that our hearts were made for the Lord and that they find no peace until they rest in him.'

The boom of the early twenty first century, to which Pope Benedict referred, has been followed by the end of the property bubble, a banking crisis and severe economic downturn. These in turn have led to rising unemployment, falling living standards, increased emigration, and massive borrowing by the government. We are living through a time of national crisis (i.e. a decisive turning point for better or worse). The choice is largely ours. In this context it is worth remembering that Pope John Paul II anticipated, in a prophetic way, the advent of a new springtime for Christianity, which would be inaugurated by a

10. France is sometimes referred to as the eldest daughter of the church. According to *The Tablet* (9 Jan 2010), 31, in 1952, 27% of French Catholics attended Mass regularly, in 2006 attendance had fallen to 4.5%.

11. *Ad limina* literally means 'to the threshold', i.e. of the apostles.

new evangelisation.[12] Speaking about the latter he said, 'The new evangelisation begins with the clear and emphatic proclamation of the gospel, which is directed to every person. Therefore it is necessary to awaken again in believers a full relationship with Christ, mankind's only Saviour. Only from a personal relationship with Jesus can an effective evangelisation develop.'[13]

Now, a word about the title of this book. As chapter four will indicate, although there are many forms of evangelisation, this study will focus on basic, or kerygmatic evangelisation, namely, the 'clear and unequivocal proclamation of the person of Jesus Christ.'[14] Speaking to the German bishops in August 2005, Pope Benedict XVI said, 'We must reflect seriously on how we might carry out a true evangelisation today, not just a new evangelisation, but often *a true first evangelisation* [my italics]. People don't know God, they don't know Christ. A new paganism is present, and it is not enough just to maintain the community of believers, although this is very important. I believe that together we must find new ways of bringing the gospel to today's world by preaching Christ anew and by establishing the faith.'[15] Speaking to priests in July 2007 Pope Benedict clarified what he meant by first, or basic evangelisation: 'Christianity is not a highly complicated collection of so many dogmas that it is impossible for anyone to know them all; it is not something exclusively for academicians who can study these things, but it is something simple: God exists and God is close in Jesus Christ. Thus, to sum up, Jesus Christ himself said that the kingdom of God had arrived. Basically, what we preach is one, simple thing. All the dimensions subsequently revealed are dimensions of this one thing and all people do not have to know everything but must certainly enter into the depths and into the essential. In this way, the different dimensions also unfold with ever increasing joy.'

It seems obvious in the light of the decline of the Irish church

12. cf Pat Collins, 'Intimations of a New Springtime', *Gifted and Sent* (Luton: New Life Publishing, 2009), 25-37.
13. Ad Limina visit of Bishops of Southern Germany, 4 December 1992, *L'Osservatore Romano* (English ed) 23-30, December 1992, p 5.
14. Pope John Paul II, par 66, *The Church in America*.
15. Pope Benedict has borne eloquent testimony to the Lord in his book, *Jesus of Nazareth* (London: Bloomsbury, 2007).

that we need to engage in the new evangelisation called for by Popes John Paul II, and Benedict XVI. John Paul wrote in par 40 of his apostolic letter, *Novo millennio inuente* (hereafter NMI), 'Over the years, I have often repeated the summons to the new evangelisation.'[16] When many priests and lay people hear the word evangelisation they think in a slightly complacent way that it is something in which they are already involved, in many different ways. There is a vague assumption which says, 'everything we do is a form of evangelisation.' That may well be true, but when the popes speak about a *new* evangelisation they have something specific in mind. As the American *National Directory for Catechesis*, explains, 'the new evangelisation is primarily the clear and unequivocal proclamation of the person of Jesus Christ, that is, the preaching of his name, his teaching, his life, his promises and the kingdom which he has gained for us by his Paschal Mystery.' It involves the active participation of every Christian in the proclamation and demonstration that the Christian faith is the only full and valid response to the problems and hopes that life poses to every person and society.'[17] The new evangelisation focuses on people who still go to church but who are not yet fully evangelised and also on the unchurched and unbelievers. Judged by that particular understanding of the new evangelisation, very few priests and lay people are currently carrying it out in the way the church expects.

This book is not intending to say exactly how the new evangelisation *should* be conducted. Rather it intends to offer some guidelines about how it *might* be progressed. The *Merriam Webster Dictionary* explains that the word *guideline* is derived from the custom by which one is led along a path by means of a cord or rope which either helps a passerby over a difficult point or permits him or her to retrace their steps. The book will involve an interplay of theory and praxis. The English word theory is derived from Greek meaning, 'contemplation, spectacle, or mental conception.' As Raymond Williams has pointed out, the word *theory* unlike the word *speculation*, involves a practical

---

16. cf. Pat Collins, 'What is the New Evangelisation?' *The Gifts of the Spirit and the New Evangelisation* (Dublin: Columba, 2009), 16-36.
17. (Washington: UCCB, 2005), 60.

component.[18] The English word *praxis,* is also derived from Greek, meaning 'practice or action.' So it could be said that praxis is a theory in action. There is a reciprocal relationship between the two. Theory informs practice, but theory can be modified in the light of praxis when it is evaluated in a reflective way.

Throughout the book, besides quoting many scripture texts, I intend to refer to the church's official teaching on evangelisation, such as the documents of the Second Vatican Council; the 1983 *Code of Canon Law* (hereafter CCL), the *Catechism of the Catholic Church* (hereafter CCC), and the relevant teachings of recent popes. Although, the many quotations may lead to a rather awkward and staccato prose style, I do not apologise, because such quotations are not only authoritative, wise and reliable, they can act as a resource for all those who are interested in the Catholic Church's thinking on evangelisation.[19] Three papal documents in particular will be referred to repeatedly.

Firstly, there is Paul VI's post-synodal apostolic exhortation, *Evangelii nuntiandi* which was published in 1975.[20] It is interesting to note that as relator of the 1974 synod of the bishops on evangelisation, Cardinal Wojtyla, later Pope John Paul II, wrote the final draft report. Commenting on Paul VI's apostolic exhortation in *Crossing the Threshold of Hope,* he wrote, 'It is not an encyclical, but in its great importance it perhaps surpasses many encyclicals. It can be considered the interpretation of the Council's teaching on the essential duty of the church: "Woe to me if I do not preach the Gospel!"'[21]

---

18. 'Theory', in *Keywords: A Vocabulary of Culture and Society* (London: Fontana, 1980), 266-8.

19. cf Francis A. Sullivan, *Magisterium: Teaching Authority in the Catholic Church* (New York: Paulist Press, 1983). Because apostolic exhortations do not define the development of doctrine, they are lower in formal authority than encyclical letters. Paul VI's *Evangelisation in the Modern World,* and John Paul's *Church in Europe* were apostolic exhortations, whereas John Paul II's *Mission of the Redeemer* was an encyclical. See also, Avery, Cardinal Dulles, 'Teaching Authority in the Church,' in *Church and Society: The Lawrence J. McGinley Lectures, 1988-2007* (New York: Fordham University Press, 2008), 16-26.

20. *Vatican Council II: More Post Conciliar Documents,* ed Austin Flannery (Dublin: Dominican Publications, 1982), 711-61.

21. *Crossing the Threshold of Hope,* (London: Jonathan Cape, 1994), 114

- The first section of the document highlights the connection between Christ the evangeliser and the church which, by Christ's mandate is commissioned to evangelise.
- The second section is the centre of the apostolic exhortation. In it, Paul VI deliberately proposes a true definition of evangelisation in contrast to a false or inadequate one.
- The third section describes the content of evangelisation in all its breadth.
- The fourth sets out the methods of evangelisation.
- The fifth speaks of the beneficiaries of evangelisation.
- The sixth says something about the different people and groups engaged in evangelisation.
- The seventh dwells on the spirit of evangelisation, namely, the Holy Spirit.
- The conclusion speaks about the Blessed Virgin Mary who is referred to as the Star of evangelisation.

Secondly, in 1990 Pope John Paul II published an Encyclical Letter entitled, *Redemptoris missio* (hereafter RM). According to his biographer, George Weigel, it is the most consequential of John Paul's many encyclicals for both the church and the world.[22] Commenting on it, John Paul said that it 'represents a new synthesis of the church's teaching about evangelisation in the contemporary world.'[23] Clearly, it is a companion to Paul VI's exhortation. It contains the following sections,

- Firstly, Jesus Christ is the only Saviour.
- Secondly, the kingdom of God.
- Thirdly, the Holy Spirit is principal agent of evangelisation.
- Fourthly, the vast horizon of the mission to the nations.
- Fifthly, the paths of missionary activity.
- Sixthly, leaders and workers in the service of evangelisation.
- Seventhly, co-operation in missionary activity.

Thirdly, in 2003 John Paul wrote a post-synodal apostolic exhortation entitled, *Ecclesia in Europa*. Section three entitled, 'Proclaiming the Gospel of Hope,' is specifically about the need

22. *Witness to Hope: The Biography of John Paul II 1920-2005* (London: Harper/Collins, 2005), 637.
23. *Crossing the Threshold of Hope*, 114.

for a new evangelisation in our continent.[24] It is divided into three main sections.

- Firstly, proclaiming the mystery of Christ;
- Secondly, bearing witness in unity and dialogue;
- Thirdly, evangelising the life of society. Section three ends with a strong recommendation to read the scriptures on a regular basis.

In EN 78 Pope Paul VI wrote, 'Men of learning – whether you be theologians, exegetes or historians – the work of evangelisation needs your tireless work of research, and also care and tact in transmitting the truth to which your studies lead you but which is always greater than the heart of man, being the very truth of God.' Years later John Paul II wrote in EE 52, 'There is an intrinsic and inseparable link between evangelisation and theological reflection, since theology, as a science possessed of a proper status and methodology, draws its life from the church's faith and stands at the service of the mission.' Please God, this book will make a small but useful contribution to the kind of research and reflection called for by the two pontiffs. It is intended to be a companion volume to *The Gifts of the Spirit and the New Evangelisation*.[25] Those who think that this book fails to deal with important aspects of evangelisation at sufficient length, or that it has virtually ignored important subjects such as the theology, psychology and sociology of conversion, are in all likelihood correct. Given the constraints of space it was not possible to cover every topic or to devote sufficient space to those that are covered. Even so, it is my hope that this volume, which is written like a manual or textbook will be used by, (1) Lay people and clergy who want to evangelise; (2) By those attending courses on the new evangelisation; (3) By schools of evangelisation in the English speaking world. Hopefully, it will be one of the positive outcomes of the first ever year of evangelisation in Ireland

24. On the New Evangelisation see John Paul II, 'What is the New Evangelisation?' *Crossing the Threshold of Hope*, 105-17; Avery Dulles, 'John Paul II and the New Evangelisation', in *Church and Society: The Lawrence J. McGinley Lectures, 1988-2007*, 87-102; Pat Collins, 'What is the New Evangelisation?' in *The Gifts of the Spirit and the New Evangelisation*, 16-36; 'The New Evangelisation', *Gifted and Sent*, 165-76.
25. (Dublin: Columba, 2009).

which has been called for by the Archbishop of Dublin.[26] Speaking about it, Dr Diarmuid Martin said, 'The Year of Evangelisation begins in these days. It is not a process of self celebration. It is not a once-off event. It is to be a real call to conversion, to renewal of the church, of continual conversion of those who belong actively to the church communion and a missionary reaching out towards new members on the path of Christian discipleship.'[27]

I want to thank a number of people who have taught me a lot about the theory and practice of evangelisation. Firstly there are the clerical and lay members of the Vincentian Ember Mission Team with whom I gave parish missions in the past. Secondly, there are those who collaborate with Alpha Ireland who have devoted so much time and effort to basic evangelisation in this country. Thirdly, there are the members of the New Springtime Community, to which I belong, who are dedicated to evangelising and to the training of evangelisers. Fourthly, I want to thank the many friends in the Charismatic Renewal, in Ireland, Britain and Italy who have faithfully promoted basic evangelisation for nearly half a century. Fifthly, I owe a deep debt of gratitude to the staff and students of Sacred Heart Major Seminary in Detroit where I studied for an STL degree in the New Evangelisation between 2006-2008. Sixthly, there are the members of Aid to the Church in Need who have promoted the Rekindle the Faith campaign here in Ireland while seeking to support the work of evangelisers in needy parts of the world where the church is sometimes persecuted.[28] Among other things it encourages its donors to recite the following prayer:

> Lord, we thank you for the countless blessings you poured out on Ireland in the past. We thank you for the many ways in which your grace found expression in generous and loving lives. We are also thankful for the times of prosperity we have enjoyed. However, like the prodigal son, we regret that sometimes we allowed the flame of the Spirit to be quenched

26. From June 29th 2009, to Advent 2010.
27. http://www.dublindiocese.ie/index.php?option=com_content&task=view&id=1595&Itemid=372 Archbishop Martin also established the first office for evangelisation in an Irish diocese.
28. http://www.acnirl.org

within us by an idolatrous pursuit of power, pleasure, popularity and possessions. We confess, Lord, that many of us have gone astray, and selfishly rewritten the commandments to suit ourselves. We believe that you came to cast fire on the earth, and long to renew your wonders in our day as by a new Pentecost. Help us to turn back to you with all our hearts, and to fan the smoldering embers of our faith into a lively flame, especially by self-denial, together with regular periods of personal and family prayer. Mary Mother of Jesus we entrust Ireland to your motherly care. In the past our people remained faithful to your Son in times of persecution. We now pray that we may witness to his abiding love in these testing times. Amen.

SECTION ONE

Evangelisation in Context

CHAPTER ONE

Spiritual Renewal and Evangelisation

This opening chapter will take a brief and impressionistic look at the reciprocal relationship that has existed throughout Christian history between renewal and evangelisation in the power of the Holy Spirit. There is something fascinating about beginnings. As T. S. Eliot wrote in his *Four Quartets,* 'We shall not cease from exploration and the end of all our exploring will be to arrive where we started and know the place for the first time.'[1] That is especially true about the numinous beginnings of the Christian Church.

The scriptures tell us that Christianity came to birth on Pentecost Sunday about two thousand years ago when the promised Holy Spirit was poured out on Mary, the apostles and the other disciples gathered in the upper room. Having been renewed, they endeavoured to share the grace they had freely received, by means of evangelisation. We are told that as a result of their efforts, 'the Lord added to their number daily those who were being saved' (Acts 2:47). Luke tells us that the members of this community, 'devoted themselves to the apostles' teaching and to the fellowship, to the breaking of bread and to prayer. Everyone was filled with awe, and many wonders and miraculous signs were done by the apostles' (Acts 2:42). Before it was ever a doctrine, the new religion was an intense religious experience which was based on the acceptance of the kerygma or core teachings of Christianity, which could be encapsulated in the words, 'Jesus is Lord' (1 Cor 12:3). Later on, the first disciples tried to express the nature and implications of their paradigmatic experience in conceptual terms. Within a generation or so they had written the New Testament which not only gave inspired expression to Christian belief and ethics, it defined the parameters of orthodoxy for future generations.[2] In this chapter ref-

1. 'Little Gidding,' sec 5, line 240 (London: Faber, 1968), 59.
2. The word *dogma* is derived from Greek and literally means 'opinion,'

erence to spiritual renewal is mainly preoccupied with learning from that seminal experience with a view to recreating it within the very different circumstances of contemporary culture by means of Christian transformation and evangelisation.

Apostolic Fathers on Renewal

When one reads the Apostolic Fathers it is very interesting to see how the early Christians began to separate themselves from their original Jewish context and how they also distanced themselves from the pagan cultures in which they found themselves living. The following extended extract was written by the anonymous author of *The Epistle to Diognetus* (c 150 AD), which has been described by J. B. Lightfoot as, 'the noblest of early Christian writings.'[3] The treatise contains a striking description of the way the early Christians rejected pagan ways: 'They live in their own countries, but only as non-residents; they participate in everything as citizens, and endure everything as foreigners. Every foreign country is their fatherland, and every fatherland is foreign. They marry like everyone else, and have children, but they do not expose their offspring. They share their food but not their wives. They are in the flesh, but they do not live according to the flesh. They live on earth, but their citizenship is in heaven. They obey the established laws; indeed in their private lives they transcend the laws. They love everyone, but by everyone they are persecuted. They are unknown, yet they are condemned; they are put to death, yet they are brought to life. They are poor, yet they makes many rich; they are in need of everything, yet they abound in everything. They are dishonoured, yet they are glorified in their dishonour; they are slandered, yet they are vindicated. They are cursed, yet they bless; they are insulted, yet they offer respect. When they do good, they are pun-

---

that which seems good. It was applied by classical authors as a technical term to refer to the tenets of philosophers or public authorities. In Christian terms it refers to a religious truth established by Divine Revelation and defined by the Church. cf. 'Dogma' in *The Oxford Dictionary of the Christian Church*, ed F. L. Cross (Oxford: OUP, 1984), 415.

3. Quoted by Michael Holmes, *The Apostolic Fathers in English*, (Grand Rapids: Baker Academic, 2006), 288.

ished as evildoers; when they are punished, they rejoice as though brought to life. They are assaulted as foreigners and persecuted, yet those who hate them are unable to give a reason for their hostility.'[4]

Over a long number of years the early Christians developed the implications of New Testament belief and ethics, such as the dogma of the Trinity,[5] and the notion of the two ways of life and death, as outlined in the *Didache* and *The Shepherd of Hermas*. However, it is noticeable that even during this early historical period something of the primordial Christian experience was already being compromised and weakened. For instance, it is evident reading the Apostolic Fathers that charismatic activity was already declining. James D. G. Dunne has noted that this trend may have begun as early as the apostolic era. He points out that although the charisms were highlighted in Paul's early letters, such as 1 Corinthians, the later pastoral epistles highlighted the offices and ministries of bishops, deacons, and elders. The 'later theology of the church,' he points out, 'has been determined primarily by the Pastoral Epistles, with Paul's theology of the church as the body of Christ either passed over quickly or conformed to the structures envisaged in the Pastorals and developed by subsequent church Fathers like Ignatius and Cyprian.'[6] Later in the fourth century, it is clear from the writings of St John Chrysostom that the gifts of the Spirit were no longer in evidence. For example, he said with great candour, 'This whole passage in 1 Cor 12:8-12, is very obscure; but the obscurity is produced by our ignorance of the facts referred to, and by their cessation, being such as then used to occur, but now no longer take place.'[7]

Although some Jews and pagans were deeply impressed by the witness of the first Christians, there were others who persec-

4. *The Apostolic Fathers in English*, ed Michael W. Holmes, 295-6.
5. cf. par 9 of *The Letter of Ignatius to the Ephesians*; par 13 of *The Letter of Ignatius to the Magnesians*; Introduction to *The Letter of Ignatius to the Philadelphians*, *The Apostolic Fathers in English*, 99, 106, 117.
6. James D. G. Dunne 'The Body of Christ in Paul,' *Pastoral Review* (Nov/Dec 2008): 9.
7. Homily, XXIX on 1 Corinthians, http://www.newadvent.org/fathers/220129.htm (accessed May 2nd 2008).

uted them. That antagonism was evident for the first time when the Apostles Peter and John were imprisoned by the Jewish authorities. Later they were released in a miraculous way. When they returned to the Christian community they recounted what had happened. Then they prayed, 'Now, Lord, consider their threats and enable your servants to speak your word with great boldness. Stretch out your hand to heal and perform miraculous signs and wonders through the name of your holy servant Jesus.' After they prayed, the place where they were meeting was shaken. And they were all filled with the Holy Spirit and spoke the word of God boldly' (Acts 4:29-31). Notice how these verses link the notions of renewal in the power of the Holy Spirit, and the proclamation of the gospel. One of the main ways in which the early followers of Christ bore heroic witness to their crucified Lord was martyrdom. For instance, not only was Stephen persecuted, he gave his life for Christ (cf Acts 7:59-60). Some years later, Bishop Polycarp was arrested and told to deny Christ or be burnt at the stake. He was executed when he refused to betray the Lord: 'Eighty and six years,' he testified, 'have I served Christ, and he has done me no wrong. How then can I blaspheme my King and my Saviour?'[8]

When the persecutions ended, Christians wondered how they could continue to live the gospel in a heroic and faithful way. It was this desire to recover the integral spirituality of the first Christians that eventually led to the emergence of the monastic movements, which amounted to a renewal movement that took the form of a living martyrdom. At first, some people devoted themselves to lives of consecrated celibacy and poverty within the local Christian community. This was followed by the eremitical phase when people like St Anthony lived austere lives, alone in the desert. Eventually, monks banded together to form religious communities. For instance, St Pachomius (290-346) started to organise his followers in Egypt in what was to become the first Christian monastery. St Martin of Tours (335-397) did much the same in France. Soon, similar institutions spread throughout the Egyptian desert as well as the rest of the eastern and western parts of the Roman Empire. These were among the

8. 'The Martyrdom of Polycarp,' *Early Christian Writings: The Apostolic Fathers* (London: Penguin Classics, 1975), 158-9.

first significant attempts to engage in spiritual renewal, by recovering the pristine experience of the New Testament church within the cultural context of the times in which they lived. Later on the monastic movement was developed by orders such as the Cistercians, Carmelites, Benedictines, Carthusians and Premonstratensians.

Post-Patristic Renewal and Evangelisation

Notable among these evangelising founders of monasteries was St Patrick (390-460), the apostle of Ireland. As he testified in his *Confessions,* having been renewed in the Spirit himself, he became the evangelist of the country where he had once been a captive. 'How, then, does it happen' he asked in par 41 of his autobiography, 'that in Ireland a people who in their ignorance of God always worshipped idols and unclean things in the past, have now become a people of the Lord and are called children of God? How is it that the sons and daughters of Irish chieftains are seen to be monks and virgins dedicated to Christ?'[9] In a book entitled *The Celtic Way of Evangelism: How Christianity Can Reach the West Again,*[10] author George G. Hunter maintains that the Celtic church founded by Patrick not only converted Ireland from paganism to a genuine form of Christianity, his successors then proceeded to send missionaries throughout Europe where they converted many people during the dark ages.[11] He argues that the genius of the Patrician and Celtic approach to evangelisation was its ability to enculturate the message, even in the barbarian societies of northern Europe which had been avoided by earlier evangelists who had adopted the Roman way of evangelisation.

In the medieval era the gifted founders of religious orders such as the Dominicans and Franciscans tried to recreate the *vita apostolic,* (i.e. an apostolic way of life) while also engaging in energetic evangelisation. St Dominic Guzman (1170-1221) established an order of mendicants. In 1220 the General Chapter of the new Order of Preachers stated that its primary aim was the

9. Joseph Duffy, *Patrick in His Own Words* (Dublin: Veritas, 1975), 30.
10. (Nashville: Abingdon Press, 2000).
1. cf Thomas Cahill, *How the Irish Saved Civilisation* (New York: Anchor Books, 1996).

salvation of souls through preaching. St Thomas Aquinas (1225-74), one of the most notable followers of St Dominic stated, 'The apostolic life consists in this, that having abandoned everything, they should go throughout the world announcing and preaching the gospel, as is made clear in Mt 10:7-10.'[12] St. Bonaventure tells us that St Francis of Assisi (1181-1226) who, like Dominic, tried to recreate the life of the early church, 'went forth through divers regions, boldly preaching the gospel, the Lord working with him and confirming his word by signs following.'[13] Like their Christ-like founder, members of the order of Friars Minor engaged in popular preaching and missionary activity. In the fifteenth century St Vincent Ferrer (1350-1419), another eminent Dominican, felt commissioned by the Lord, who was accompanied by Sts Dominic and Francis in a vision, 'to go through the world preaching Christ.' In response he spent a quarter of a century preaching to huge crowds all over Europe. What was notable about his approach was his focus on the imminence of the last judgement and his success in converting many Jews and Moslems. Sometime later, the Bothers of the Common Life, who had been founded in the Netherlands in the fourteenth century, promoted the *Devotio Moderna* (Modern, or New Devotion) and sought to live the evangelical ideal described in the New Testament, while responding to the urgent and unmet needs of their time. For example, deacon Gerard Groote (1340-84) promoted the New Devotion, travelled through the country urging Church reform and repentance of life while preaching against clerical abuses.

The Reformation had the same ideal in mind. Ever since that time, Protestants have tended to speak more of revival than renewal and refer to texts such as Hab 3:2, 'O Lord, I have heard of your renown, and feared, O Lord, your work. In the course of the years revive it, in the course of the years make it known.'[14]

12. *Contra impugnantes Dei cultum et religionem* quoted by Jordan Aumann in *Christian Spirituality in the Catholic Tradition* (London: Sheed & Ward, 1985), 128.
13. St Bonaventure, *The Life of St Francis of Assisi* (Rockford: Tan, 1988), 117.
14. Charles G. Finney, *Revivals of Religion* (Albany: AGES Software Version 2.0, 1996, 1997).

Some Protestants see revival as an outpouring of evangelising grace which brings about the conversion of many people within a relatively short period of time, such as occurred with the rise of Methodism in eighteenth century Britain and the 'great awakening' in New England in the 1740s.[15] The Council of Trent inaugurated a great Counter Reformation renewal movement in the Catholic Church. New religious orders came into existence such as the Capuchins, Barnabites, Ursulines, Jesuits, Vincentians and Redemptorists as instruments of that reform. They not only promoted Christian renewal, they also engaged in evangelisation by means of popular and foreign missions. For instance, St. Francis Xavier (1506-52), one of the first Jesuits, was an apostle of India and Japan. His burning zeal for souls was obvious not only in those countries of the East, but also when he lamented the lack of renewal and evangelisation in centres of learning at home. 'I have often had the notion,' he wrote, 'to go round the universities of Europe, and especially Paris, and to shout aloud everywhere like a madman, and to bludgeon those people who have more learning than love, with these words, 'Alas what an immense number of souls are excluded from heaven through your fault and thrust down to hell!'.'[16] If he were alive today, would he want to make similar comments about our contemporary European universities?

Vatican II, Renewal and Evangelisation

The Counter Reformation finally came to an end when John XXIII was elected Pope in 1958. He realised that the church has to constantly seek to renew its evangelical spirituality and witness. He referred to it as *aggiornamento,* which literally means, 'bringing up to date'. In a speech he delivered to the assembled bishops at the beginning of the Council he linked the notions of renewal and evangelisation when he said: 'In this assembly, under the guidance of the Holy Spirit, we wish to enquire how

---

15. Jonathan Edwards, 'An Account of the Revival of Religion in Northampton 1740-1742,' *Jonathan Edwards on Revival* (Edinburgh: Banner of Truth, 1987), 148-60.

16. Extract from the letters of St Francis Xavier to St Ignatius, bk, 4, letters 4 & 5 in Office of Readings, 3 December, *The Divine Office,* vol 1, (Dublin: Talbot, 1974), 11*.

we ought to renew ourselves, so that we may be increasingly faithful to the gospel of Christ. We shall take pains to present to the men of this age God's truth in its integrity and purity that they may understand it and gladly assent to it.'[17] He also said, 'Today the Spouse of Christ prefers to use the medicine of mercy rather than severity. She considers that she meets the needs of the present age by showing the validity of her teaching rather than by condemnations.'[18] Is it any surprise that Pope John prayed before the council met, 'Renew your wonders in this our day, as by a new Pentecost.' His successor, Paul VI observed, 'The church needs her perennial Pentecost: she needs fire in her heart, words on her lips, prophecy in her outlook.'[19] As many of us remember, when the Council ended, we had wonderful blueprints for spiritual and ecclesial renewal and our hearts were full of enthusiasm and hope. But very quickly, ardent desire gave way to dissentions, divisions, disillusion, and apparent decline.

In 1966, shortly before he left the priesthood, British theologian Charles Davis highlighted something that was lacking in the post-Vatican II church: 'Much speaking in different places on themes of renewal has brought me into contact with many people seeking to revivify their faith. I have found a sense of emptiness, but together with it a deep yearning for God. There is an emptiness at the core of people's lives, an emptiness waiting to be filled. They are troubled about their faith; they find it slipping. I am not speaking of those who are worried about recent changes. These people are not. But they are looking for something more; they are looking for something to fill the void in their lives, and what they hear does not do that. The more perceptive know they are looking for God … Who will speak to them quite simply of God as of a person he intimately knows, and make the reality and presence of God come alive for them once more?'[20] Around the same time Pope Paul VI observed,

17. John XXIII, 'Message to Humanity,' *The Documents of Vatican II,* ed Austin Flannery, 3-4.
18. Peter Hebblethwaite, *John XIII: Pope of the Council* (London: Geoffrey Chapman, 1985), 433.
19. 'The Church's Greatest Need,' *Pope Paul and the Spirit,* ed Edward O'Connor (Notre Dame: Ave Maria Press, 1978), 183.
20. *America,* 29 January 1966.

'Many people have directed interest in renewal toward an external and impersonal transformation of church structure ... rather than toward that primary and principal renewal sought by the Council: one that is moral, personal and interior ... There is no true ecclesial reform without interior renewal.'[21] Clearly, what was needed was spiritual renewal. As Ps 127:1 reminds us, 'Unless the Lord builds the house, in vain do the labourers build.'

Spiritual Renewal in Context

The subject of spiritual renewal is a large one. Firstly, a few comments about the context in which it has to take place. Par 5 of the pastoral constitution, *Gaudium et Spes* (hereafter GS) made the important observation that humankind had substituted, 'a dynamic and more evolutionary concept of nature for a static one.' In other words we have moved from stressing *being* to stressing *becoming*.[22] This major shift has had a big impact on Christianity. The centre of gravity has moved from the experience of religious authority to the authority of religious experience. Spirituality based on authority tends to be essentialist and programmatic in nature. It sees Christian perfection principally in terms of obedience, of conforming in a docile way to a programme of living recommended by the church. Despite its undoubted merit, in our fast changing world the programmatic approach to spirituality is being replaced by a more experiential one. It stresses the importance of such things as religious experience, personal and collective discernment, together with committed action for justice and the new evangelisation called for by Popes Paul VI, John Paul II, and Benedict XVI.

Contemporary Christians are motivated not so much by a static notion of perfection, as by a heartfelt desire for ongoing spiritual transformation (cf 2 Cor 3:18). They long to move away from negative influences of an environmental and unconscious

21. *Pope Paul and the Spirit*, 4-5.

22. cf. Bernard Lonergan's insightful distinction between classical consciousness (*being*) and historical consciousness (*becoming*), 'The Transition from a Classicist World-view to Historical-mindedness,' *A Second Collection*, eds William J. Ryan SJ and Bernard Tyrrell SJ (Philadelphia: Westminister Press, 1974), 1-9.

kind in order to develop an intimate relationship with God, and through God with their deeper selves, other people, and creation. Thomas Merton was one of the most articulate exponents of this existentialist approach to Christianity. He was aware that, for better or for worse, the self had displaced objective truth as the focal point of contemporary spirituality where psychology and religion, nature and grace intersect. In a conference he gave to novices in the monastery of Gethsemane, Merton asked the question, 'Who am I? and replied, 'My deepest realisation of who I am is – I am one loved by Christ ... The depths of my identity is in the centre of my being where I am known by God.'[23] In saying this he was echoing a point which was repeatedly made by Pope John Paul II. For example, in par 25 of the Apostolic Exhortation, *Rosarium virginis Marie* (hereafter RVM) he said, 'Anyone who contemplates Christ through the various stages of his life cannot fail to perceive in him the truth about man. This is the great affirmation of the Second Vatican Council which I have so often discussed in my own teaching since the Apostolic Letter, *Redemptoris missio*, "It is only in the mystery of the Word made flesh that the mystery of man is seen in its true light".' In this context the Holy Father often referred to the following words in GS 24: 'For Jesus implied a certain likeness between the union of the divine Persons, and in the union of God's sons in truth and charity. This likeness reveals that man, who is the only creature on earth which God willed for itself, *cannot fully find himself except through a sincere gift of himself* [my italics].'[24]

Some Key Aspects of Spiritual Renewal

At this point eight key aspects of spiritual renewal will be proposed. Needless to say, the choice of topics is subjective and does not pretend to be comprehensive.

---

23. John Higgins, *Thomas Merton on Prayer* (NY: Image Books, 1975), 62.
24. In his profound book, *Man and Woman He Created Them: A Theology of the Body*, trs & ed Michael Waldstein (Boston: Pauline Media, 2006), John Paul II reflected on marriage as a primordial way of giving the sincere gift of oneself and thereby enjoying communion with one's deepest self as a result of communion with one's spouse and God whose presence is mediated by him or her.

1) Holy Desires

In Jn 6:44 Jesus says, 'No one can come to me unless the Father who sent me draws him.' People experience that drawing of the Father in the form of transcendental desires. There is no blessing or growth in the Christian life without such preceding desires. The deeper and stronger the desires, the greater the openness to subsequent blessing and growth. That is why St Augustine said: 'The things you desire you cannot see yet. But the desire gives you the capacity, so that when it does happen that you see, you may be fulfilled ... This is our life, to be motivated by holy desire. But we are motivated by holy desire only in so far as we have cut off our longings from the love of the world. I have already pointed out – empty that which is to be filled. You are to be filled with good, pour out the bad.'[25] God can excite desires for spiritual renewal by means of such things as personal suffering, moral failure, or the good example of others. We have the scriptural assurance that once a person has a God prompted desire for grace it will be granted. For instance, in Deut 4:29 we read, 'If from there you seek the Lord your God, you will find him if you look for him with all your heart and with all your soul.' Again in Jer 33:3 we are promised, 'Call to me and I will answer you and tell you great and unsearchable things you do not know.'

2) Experiencing the Unconditional Mercy of God

Consciously or unconsciously, spiritual renewal is rooted in a desire for divine mercy for one's sins. We come to know that amazing grace as a result of experiencing the power of the kerygma. Some time after my ordination I came to see that I had been sacramentalised without being fully evangelised. Deep down my belief that God was merciful was offset by an unholy fear of God's justice. I was greatly helped by reading St Thérèse of Lisieux. She discussed this very issue with an elderly companion called Sr Febronie. While the ailing Carmelite was not afraid of dying, she was very much afraid of the judgement that would follow. Thérèse tried in vain to reassure her by stressing the mercy of God. Eventually, she said to Sr Febronie, 'If you

25. 'Treatise on the First Letter of St John,' *Divine Office*, vol 1 (Dublin: Talbot, 1974), 537-8.

want divine justice, you will get divine justice. The soul gets exactly what it expects from God.'[26] Implicit in the saint's reply, was the following axiom: 'If you look into the eyes of God's mercy expecting only mercy, you will receive only mercy, now and at the moment of your death.'

Convinced of this truth herself, Thérèse would say whenever she failed to do what God expected of her, 'If I had been faithful I would have received the reward of merit by appealing to God's justice. I was unfaithful, I am humiliated, I am going to receive the reward of my poverty and humiliation by appealing to God's mercy.'[27] What a remarkable insight into the loving kindness of the heart of God the Father. Presumably Thérèse's failures were small compared to our own. Nevertheless, the principle she enunciated remains the same. Indeed, it could be argued that the greater and the more humiliating the failure, the greater the graces that are lavished upon the grieving heart. God does not react in accordance with what we deserve but in accordance with the Divine nature which loves us unconditionally (cf Rom 9:15-16). Arguably Thérèse's notion of saving trust in God's mercy is similar to what was said about justification in the Reformed and Roman Catholic International Dialogue (1984-90): 'We recognise that our justification is a totally gratuitous work accomplished by God in Christ. We confess that the acceptance in faith of justification is itself a gift of grace. By the grace of faith we recognise in Jesus of Nazareth … the one who saves us and brings us into communion of life with God. To rely for salvation on anything other than faith, would be to diminish the fullness accomplished and offered in Jesus Christ.'[28] Experiential conviction about the saving merits of Christ's death and resurrection is the foundation stone of all genuine spiritual renewal. It prompts the desire to lead a holy and compassionate Christian life while providing the ability to do so.

26. Pierre Descouvemont, Helmuth Nils Loose, *Thérèse and Lisieux* (Dublin: Veritas, 1996), 186.
27. Marie-Eugene of the Child Jesus, *Under the Torrent of His Love* (New York: Alba House, 1995), 28.
28. Footnote 4 in *Evangelicals and Catholics Together in Ireland* (Belfast: ECT, 1998), 5.

3) Experiencing the Unconditional Love of God

Many contemporary Christians maintain that baptism in the Spirit, which is variously referred to as the 'release, infusion, or infilling of the Spirit' is a key constituent in any genuine spiritual renewal. It is a religious experience which initiates a decisively new sense of the powerful presence and working of God in one's life, which is usually associated with one or more of the charismatic gifts. Speaking about this phenomenon Karl Rahner wrote: 'We cannot doubt that in this life we can experience grace in such a way that it gives us a sense of freedom and opens up horizons that are entirely new, making a profound impression on us, transforming and molding in us, even over a long period of time, a more inward Christian attitude. There is nothing that prevents us calling that kind of experience a baptism in the Spirit.'[29] For many people, baptism in the Spirit is a mystical event which fulfills the prayer of Paul: 'I pray that out of his glorious riches he may strengthen you with power through his Spirit in your inner being, so that Christ may dwell in your hearts through faith. And I pray that you, being rooted and established in love, may have power, together with all the saints, to grasp how wide and long and high and deep is the love of Christ, and to know this love that surpasses knowledge – that you may be filled to the measure of all the fullness of God' (Eph 3:16-19). Conscious awareness of the love of Jesus kick starts an ongoing process of conversion which enables people to go beyond the confines of mere statements about the love of God to experience its transforming power in their innermost selves. The effect of repeated in-fillings of the Spirit is that, 'with unveiled faces all reflect the Lord's glory, and are being transformed into his likeness with ever-increasing glory, which comes from the Lord, who is the Spirit' (2 Cor 3:18).

4) God as Abba Father

When people experience God's merciful love as a result of receiving the free gift of an outpouring of the Holy Spirit, they move from knowing about the distant and apathetic God of the philosophers to have an intimate, personal relationship with the

29. 'Erfahrung des Heiligen Geistes,' in *Schrifen zur Theologie*, vol 13 (Zurich: Einsiedeln-Koln, 1978), 232.

empathetic God revealed in Jesus Christ. As St Paul said in Rom 8:15-16: 'For you did not receive a spirit that makes you a slave again to fear, but you received the Spirit of sonship. And by him we cry, "Abba, Father". The Spirit himself testifies with our spirit that we are God's children.' As adopted sons and daughters of the Father we are co-heirs with Christ to all the heavenly blessings (cf Rom 8:17). We know that God our Father has not only a plan for our collective and individual lives, he provides what we need to carry it out. Once Christians have a firm trust in the God of the promises, they rely with confidence on the promises of God. This kind of expectancy is the key to effective prayer. As Jesus promised: 'If you then, who are evil, know how to give good gifts to your children, how much more will your Father who is in heaven give good things to those who ask him!' (Mt 7:11-12).

5) The Imitation of Christ

In 2 Cor 13:5, Paul asked rhetorically, 'Do you not realise that Christ lives within you?' Whenever people experience the liberating power of the kerygma, and are filled with the Holy Spirit, they become aware that Christ is living in their hearts (cf Eph 3:17). As a result they realise in an experiential way what the CCC 521 means when it says: 'Christ enables us to live in him all that he himself lived and he lives it in us.' In one of his writings St John Eudes (1601-1688) quoted a well known Pauline text, 'I make up what is lacking in the sufferings of Jesus Christ for the sake of his body the church' (Col 1:24). He went on to observe that what Paul says about our sufferings can be extended to all our other actions as well. Here is an extended quotation from Eudes's book *The Life and Kingdom of Jesus in Christian Souls*: 'We can say that any true Christian, who is a member of Jesus Christ, and who is united to him by his grace, *continues* and *completes* [my italics] through all the actions that he carries out in the spirit of Christ, the actions that Jesus Christ accomplished during the time of his temporary life on earth. So that when a Christian prays, he continues and fulfils the prayer that Jesus Christ offered on earth. Whenever he works, he continues and fulfils the laborious life of Jesus Christ. Whenever he relates to his or her neighbour in a spirit of charity, then he continues and fulfils the relational life of Jesus Christ. Whenever he eats or rests in a Christian manner, he continues and fulfils the subjection that Jesus Christ wished to have to have to these necessities. *The same can be said of any other action that is carried out in a Christian manner* [my italics].'[30] Although Eudes did not refer to the exercise of the charisms in 1 Cor 12:8-10, the logic of his remarks implies that Jesus can enable us to live in him all of his charismatic activities, even to the point of performing healings and miracles.

Needless to say, Christians are called to be for others what Christ is for them. In other words, they are called to express to others the unconditional mercy and love that God has shown to them in Christ. There are many ways of understanding this. Two texts in the Beatitudes are particularly helpful. In the first Jesus said: 'Be merciful, just as your Father is merciful. Do not judge, and you will not be judged. Do not condemn, and you will not be condemned. Forgive, and you will be forgiven. Give, and it will be given to you' (Lk 6:36-37). There is a very important spiritual principal of reciprocity involved here. If we wish to experience a continuing sense of God's mercy, we must offer that same unconditional mercy to others without criticism or fault finding. Indeed that same principle applies, by extension, to all the graces we receive from God. Paradoxically, nothing we do not give away will ever be truly ours.

In a second text Jesus said: 'Do to others as you would have them do to you' (Lk 6:31). This Golden Rule, which is the key to Christian love, presupposes two things: goodwill and insight. Christian love is benevolent. It desires what is best for the other person. But given the fact that we are all so different, we need the kind of empathy that senses in an understanding way how the other person's needs differ from our own. Once we stand in that person's shoes, so to speak, we can respond in a benevolent manner to his or her needs in an appropriate emotional and practical way. As Paul said in Rom 13:9-10: 'The commandments, Do not commit adultery, Do not murder, Do not steal, Do not covet, and whatever other commandment there may be, are summed up in this one rule: "Love your neighbour as your-

30. *Berulle and the French School: Selected Writings,* ed W. Thompson (New York: Paulist Press, 1989), 296.

self." Love does no harm to its neighbour. Therefore love is the fulfilment of the law.'

6) Prayer and Renewal in the Spirit

Spiritual renewal is not possible without regular prayer and contemplation. As one church document observes, the 'contemplative dimension is the real secret of renewal for every religious life. It vitally renews the following of Christ because it leads to an experiential knowledge of him.'[31] *Lectio Divina* takes pride of place in this dynamic. A twelfth-century writer called Guido the Carthusian, described its purpose in these succinct words: 'Reading you should seek; meditating you will find; praying you shall call; and contemplating the door will be opened to you.'[32] In *Lectio Divina* the word of God takes pride of place. In the Hebrew Bible the term for word is *dabar*. It can be used as a noun and as a verb. As a noun it is objective. It refers to the word of God which is true in itself. The Bible contains that word between its covers. As a verb it is subjective. It refers to the word of God which is true for the individual. It is the revelatory word which is spoken by the Lord to a particular person in specific circumstances.

When the Old Testament was translated into Greek, the scholars of the time acknowledged this distinction. When the Hebrew text referred to the word in itself, they tended to use the Greek term *logos*. When the text referred to the word that is spoken, they often used the Greek term *rhema*. The relationship between *logos* and *rhema* can be expressed in the following statements: *rhema* takes the eternal *logos* and injects it into time. *Rhema* takes the heavenly *logos* and brings it down to earth. *Rhema* takes the general *logos* and makes it specific. *Rhema* takes a portion of the total *logos* and presents it in the form that a person can assimilate. The scriptures make it clear in a number of places that such revelation is possible. It could be said that one of the main purposes of *Lectio Divina* is to allow the word of God

31. 'The Contemplative Dimension of Life' par 30, *Vatican Collection II: More Post Conciliar Documents*, ed Austin Flannery OP, 258.

32 *'Scala Claustralium,'* in *The Companion to the Catholic Church: A Compendium of Texts Referred to in the Catechism of the Catholic Church* (San Francisco: Ignatius Press, 1994), 921-8.

to leap off the page, alive with meaning and relevance into the heart (cf Heb 4:12-13). Once the inspired and inspiring word of God is heard within, it can be proclaimed by means of preaching, teaching, and verbal witness; and demonstrated by means of works of mercy, action for justice, and charismatic deeds of power. As Is 55:11 assures us, 'my word that goes out from my mouth: It will not return to me empty, but will accomplish what I desire and achieve the purpose for which I sent it.'

7) Guided by the Spirit

We know that Jesus was not only filled with the Spirit, he was also prayerfully led by the Spirit (cf. Mt 4:1). Jesus himself testified to the fact that he led his life on the basis of revelation. Here are a number of instances. In Jn 5:19 he said: 'Very truly, I tell you, the Son can do nothing on his own, but only what he sees the Father doing; for whatever the Father does, the Son does likewise.' Again in Jn 5:30 he said: 'I can do nothing on my own. As I hear, I judge; and my judgement is just, because I seek to do not my own will but the will of him who sent me.' Some time later he said in Jn 12:49: 'For I have not spoken on my own, but the Father who sent me has himself given me a commandment about what to say and what to speak.' These verses and similar ones indicate that everything Jesus said and did in the course of his evangelisation was a manifestation of the action of the Father in and through him. Is it any wonder, therefore, that St Paul said in Gal 5:18, 25, 'Be led by the Spirit.' This injunction is the key to Pauline ethics.[33] Commenting on it, George Montague says, 'This little statement is theological dynamite. The Christian life is not a list of things to do and to avoid. It is not virtue acquired by practice. It is the gift of being moved by the Spirit of God, and the key to life is to allow the Spirit to lead ... A crucial point: When confronted by any moral decision, great or small, the Christian's first question should be, "Where does the Spirit lead me in this?".'[34] It is interesting in this context to note that St Faustina Kowalska wrote in her diary, 'faithfulness to the

33. cf Jordon D. Fee, *God's Empowering Presence: The Holy Spirit in the Letters of Paul* (Peabody, Mass: Hendrickson, 1994), 429.

34. *The Holy Spirit: Growth of a Biblical Tradition* (New York: Paulist Press, 1976), 200.

inspirations of the Holy Spirit – that is the shortest route to holiness.'[35]

8) Empowered by the Spirit
Because of divine providence, the Lord not only reveals the divine will, God also empowers believers to carry it out. As Paul said in Phil 2:13: 'It is God who works in you to will and to act according to his good purpose.' The power that the apostle spoke about is the power of the Holy Spirit which raised Jesus from the dead. For instance, in Eph 1:19-20 he talked about, 'his incomparably great power for us who believe. That power is like the working of his mighty strength, which he exerted in Christ when he raised him from the dead and seated him at his right hand in the heavenly realms.' Not only does that immanent power enable a believer to embrace the will of God, it also empowers him or her to carry it out. As St Paul testified: 'I can do everything through him who gives me strength' (Phil 4:13).

Renewal and Evangelisation
As has already been noted, a study of church history shows that there has always been a reciprocal relationship between renewal and evangelisation. Communities and individuals who have been genuinely renewed in the power of the Holy Spirit invariably engage in evangelisation. As Pope John Paul II said in RM 77: 'The Second Vatican Council invited all to a profound interior renewal, so that having a lively awareness of their personal responsibility for the spreading of the gospel, they may play their part in missionary work among the nations.' That activity helps to renew those who accept the Good News with faith, while strengthening renewal in the lives of the evanglisers. That was obvious in the Acts of the Apostles. No sooner had the disciples been baptised in the Holy Spirit at Pentecost than they began to evangelise. The same was true a little later when the disciples prayed for a second outpouring of God's renewing Spirit. They said: 'Now, Lord, consider their threats and enable your servants to speak your word with great boldness. Stretch out your

35. *Diary of St Maria Faustina Kowalska: Divine Mercy in My Soul* (Stockbridge, Mass.: Marian Press, 2003), 291.

hand to heal and perform miraculous signs and wonders through the name of your holy servant Jesus' (Acts 4:29-30).

That passage has two vital implications. For an effective evangelisation to take place a new outpouring of the Spirit is always needed. We have already noted how Pope John XXIII said in 1959 that the church needed updating and renewal in order to be able more effectively to do its work of preaching the gospel. Sometime after the Council ended Pope Paul VI said: 'There is no salvation for humanity except in a new outpouring of the gift of God. May the Creating Spirit come, then, to renew the face of the earth.'[36] On yet another occasion he said rather eloquently: 'The Holy Spirit is he who animates and sanctifies the church. He is her divine breath, the wind in her sails, the principle of her unity, the inner source of her light and strength. He is her support and consoler, her source of charisms and songs, her peace and joy, her pledge and prelude to blessed and eternal life.'[37]

The Spirit was first poured out in a mighty and renewing way upon the first Pentecostals in Azusa Street in 1906.[38] In 1966 Catholics also began to experience a new Pentecost when they were baptised in the Spirit and received the charismatic gifts listed in par 12 of the Dogmatic Constitution, *Lumen Gentium* (hereafter LG). What was noticeable about both renewal movements was the fact that they immediately expressed themselves in a desire to evangelise. The early Pentecostals fanned out, firstly in the United States and then across the world, in order to bring the message of the gospel to people. The same was true of the Catholic Charismatic Movement which quickly spread across America and around the world.[39] Bert Ghezzi has explained that in its early days the leaders of the Catholic Charismatic Renewal were aware that there was need for a sort of catechumenate which would teach people about the kerygma. In 1969 the Word of God Community in Ann Arbor, Michigan, devised what were

36. *Pope Paul and the Spirit*, 218.
37. Ibid., 183.
38. 'Azusa Street Revival,' *The New International Dictionary of Pentecostal and Charismatic Movements*, eds Stanley Burgess, Eduard van der Mass (Grand Rapids: Zondervan, 2002), 344-50.
39. Peter Hocken, *The Glory and the Shame: Reflections on the 20th Century Outpouring of the Holy Spirit* (Guildford: Eagle, 1994).

known as the Life in the Spirit Seminars.[40] They involved a seven week long course that aimed to teach the core Christian truths with a view to enabling people to experience a Pentecostal infilling of the Holy Spirit.[41] As chapter ten will explain, the seminars have become a powerful means of basic evangelisation and renewal in the Catholic Church, especially in English speaking countries.

Pope Benedict XVI said in his inaugural homily: 'The church as a whole and all her pastors, like Christ, must set out to lead people out of the desert, towards the place of life, towards friendship with the Son of God, towards the One who gives us life, and life in abundance ... There is nothing more beautiful than to be surprised by the gospel, by the encounter with Christ. There is nothing more beautiful than to know him and to speak to others of our friendship with him.'[42] So the impetus to evangelise is a characteristic of a renewed community. It is not only a way of bringing renewal to other people's lives, it deepens and strengthens it in the lives of the evangelisers. As Jesus promised in Lk 6:38: 'Give, and it will be given to you. A good measure, pressed down, shaken together and running over, will be poured into your lap. For with the measure you use, it will be measured to you.' No wonder Pope John Paul II reminded us in RM 2: 'Faith is strengthened when it is given to others!'

When people are evangelised, they enter the Christian community. As Pope John Paul II pointed out in RM 47: 'They would be greatly disappointed if, having entered the ecclesial community, they were to find a life lacking fervour and without signs of renewal! We cannot preach conversion unless we ourselves are converted anew every day.' Pope John Paul II believed that the new ecclesial communities, which will be mentioned in greater detail in chapter eight, are reservoirs of both renewal and evangelising zeal. They 'help to make the mystery of Christ and his saving grace present in the world.'[43] Thus they 'represent a true

---

40. *Build With the Lord* (Ann Arbor: Word of Life, 1976), 62-79.
41. Therese Boucher, *The New Life in the Spirit Seminars Team Manual* (Locust Grove: National Service Committee, 2003).
42. 24th April 2005.
43. Pope John Paul II, par 5, 'Message,' *Proceedings of the World Congress of the Ecclesial Movements* (Rome, 27-29 May 1998).

gift of God both for new evangelisation and for missionary activity properly so-called.'[44] For this reason, the Holy Father recommended 'that they be spread, and ... used to give fresh energy ... to the Christian life and to evangelisation, within a pluralistic view of the ways in which Christians can associate and express themselves.'[45]

Some Implications of Spiritual Renewal

A number of years ago there were bizarre reports about weeping and moving statues in Ireland. Such experiences could be interpreted in a Jungian way as day-dreams. As such they could be understood in a symbolical manner as expressions of wishful thinking. For example, if one looks up the entry on 'religious statues' in Tom Chetwynd's insightful and well researched *Dictionary for Dreamers*, it says that when inanimate figures are seen to move in a life-like way it is a sign that 'what was a dead theoretical concept suddenly has new inner meaning for the dreamer' and that 'new potentialities are awakening in the dreamer.'[46] As we know, a dry doctrinal approach to religion does very little for people. Evidently, what the supporters of popular devotion are looking for are doctrines that come alive with experiential meaning. In this context it is interesting to recall something Jung wrote: 'Today Christianity is devitalised . . . "God" has in fact become unconscious to us. This is what always happens when things are interpreted, explained, and dogmatised until they become so encrusted with man-made images and words that they can no longer be seen.'[47]

In this context it is worth remembering that St Thomas Aquinas wisely observed: 'The object of faith is not the statement, but the reality.'[48] Centuries later, St Ignatius of Loyola said something similar in the second annotation of his *Spiritual Exercises*: 'It is not knowing much, but realising and relishing things interiorly, that contents and satisfies the soul.' The kind

44. RM 72.
45. Ibid.
46. (London: Paladin, 1979), 171.
47. Carl Jung, *Psychology and Western Religion* (London: Ark, 1988), 289; 229.
48. *Summa Theologiae*, I-II, q. 1, a. 2, ad 2.

of spiritual renewal briefly described in this chapter enables individuals and communities to go beyond thought and talk about God, to have, 'an intimate knowledge of Jesus, who became human for us.'[49] This kind of mystical awareness, which is made possible by the inward activity of the Holy Spirit, helps to revivify, and if needs be, to reform every aspect of the Christian life. Meropolitan Ignatios of Latakia gave poetic expression to this idea at a meeting of the Ecumenical Council of Churches at Uppsala in 1968:

> Without the Holy Spirit, God is far away,
> Christ stays in the past,
> the gospel is a dead letter,
> the church is simply an organisation,
> authority a matter of domination,
> *evangelisation a matter of propaganda* [my italics],
> the liturgy no more than an evocation,
> Christian living a slave morality.
> But in the Holy Spirit:
> The cosmos is resurrected and groans with the birth-pangs of the kingdom,
> the risen Christ is there,
> the gospel is the power of life,
> the church shows forth the life of the Trinity,
> authority is a liberating service,
> *mission is a Pentecost* [my italics],
> the liturgy is both memorial and anticipation,
> human action is deified.[50]

---

49. *Spiritual Exercises*, par 233.
50. Leon Joseph Suenens, *A New Pentecost?* (London: Darton, Longman & Todd, 1975), 19-20.

Recommended Reading

- Peter Hocken, *The Glory and the Shame: Reflections on the 20th Century Outpouring of the Holy Spirit* (Guildford: Eagle, 1994).
- Jordan Aumann, *Christian Spirituality in the Catholic Tradition* (London: Sheed & Ward, 1985).
- Leon Joseph Suenens, *A New Pentecost?* (London: Darton, Longman & Todd, 1975).
- Mary Ann Fatula, *Thomas Aquinas: Preacher and Friend* (Collegeville: The Liturgical Press, 1993).
- Jim McCormack, *St Patrick: The Real Story: As Told in His Own Words* (Dublin: Columba, 2008).
- Yves Congar, *I Believe in the Holy Spirit* (New York: Crossroad, 2000).
- Pat Collins, *He Has Anointed Me* (Luton: New Life 2005); *Gifted and Sent* (Luton: New Life, 2009).

CHAPTER TWO

Aspects of Contemporary Culture and The New Evangelisation

One of the distinctive aspects of the teaching of Pope Paul VI was his emphasis on the cultural dimension of evangelisation. In EN 20, he wrote: 'The split between the gospel and culture is without doubt the drama of our time ... Therefore every effort must be made to ensure a full evangelisation of culture.' This chapter will look at some important characteristics of contemporary culture with a view to understanding what kind of evangelisation will be needed to Christianise it. Needless to say, the topic is vast and the treatment here is necessarily brief and impressionistic rather than extended and detailed.[1] This may be a difficult chapter for those who are not well acquainted with philosophy, psychology and modern science. If so, do feel free to skip it.

The emergence of the notion of the autonomous self in Western culture has been noted by many commentators.[2] This reflection attempts to situate that important and complex phenomenon within a wider historical context, in the belief that it can aid our understanding of the current cultural milieux in which the new evangelisation has to be conducted. The approach is necessarily synthetic and general rather than particular. However, there will be an attempt to support generalisations by reference to authors who tend to mention them in their writings.

From the Greeks onwards, there seem to have been two complementary ways of looking at the material world. One was mainly static and essentialist in nature and stressed the primacy

1. cf Anthony J. Carroll, *Evangelisation, Culture and Catholic Identity* http://www.margaretbeaufort.cam.ac.uk/research/carroll.pdf (Accessed 9 Nov 2009)

2. Charles Taylor, *Sources of the Self: The Making of the Modern Identity* (Cambridge: CUP, 1989); *A Secular Age* (Cambridge, Ma: The Belknap Press, 2007); *Varieties of Religion Today: William James Revisited* (Cambridge, Ma: Harvard University Press, 2002).

of *being*. Parmenides and Aristotle advocated this point of view. The other tended, to a greater or lesser extent, to be more dynamic and existentialist and stressed the primacy of *becoming*. Heraclitus was the outstanding advocate of this perspective. It tended to see everything that existed as interconnected parts in an integrated world which was governed by God-given affinities. The Pythagoreans talked of the harmony of the spheres, and the Hippocratics maintained that there is one common flow, one common breathing, and that all things are in sympathy.

These two points of view remained in tandem in Christian Europe in the form of the Medieval synthesis of philosophy, science and theology. As late as 1550 Pico Mirandola could write in *Heptaplus:* 'Firstly there is the unity in things whereby each thing is at one with itself, consists of itself, and coheres with itself. Secondly there is the unity whereby one creature is united with the others and all parts of the world constitutes one world. The third and most important (unity) is that whereby the whole universe is one with its Creator, as an army with its commander.'[3] This quotation holds together the notion that every creature asserts its own separate identity while transcending itself by means of its integrative tendencies.[4]

Breakdown of the Unitary Worldview

The unitary worldview was broken by three great historical movements, the Reformation, the rise of science and the way capitalism harnessed the new technologies to exploit nature. One could argue that these movements meant the triumph of left brained activity, namely, rational, objective thinking, over right brained activity of an intuitive and affective kind, and the victory of the typically detached male outlook over the more relational, female one. In spite of their strongly patriarchal tendencies, Catholic and Orthodox forms of Christianity, as the late Sir Kenneth Clark pointed out,[5] offset some of the more extreme implications of the male notion of God by incorporating the

3. VI proem, in *Collected Works*, (Basel 1557), 40.
4. In his book, *The Ghost in the Machine* (London: Pan, 1970), 62-76, Arthur Koestler referred to holons, an idea which is similar to Mirandola's. It refers to the self-assertive and integrative tendencies evident throughout nature.
5. *Civilisation: A Personal View* (London: BBC/John Murray, 1971), 177.

feminine principle in two ways. Firstly, they encouraged the cult of the Virgin Mary. Secondly, they believed that, just as God had become flesh in the womb of the Blessed Mother and the church she epitomises, so the divine presence is mediated by mother nature as well.

However, all that began to change with the Reformation. As H. G. Wells pointed out, communities of obedience (i.e. stable societies of the South such as Catholicism and Orthodoxy), which stressed the virtues of contemplation, were challenged by communities of will, (i.e. the restless nomads of the North), who stressed the importance of dynamic action, such as the Calvinists, and to a lesser extent the Lutherans. They focused on the male characteristics of religion and virtually abolished Marian devotion. They maintained, in an iconoclastic way, that revelation came solely through the word of God, while denying that mother nature could mediate the presence of the Beyond who is in her midst. In this way a masculine notion of revelation tended to predominate over a more feminine one. God could only be mediated to rational consciousness by the conceptual *logos* or word. God could not be mediated in a more feminine way by means of pre-rational religious experiences such as dreams and sacramental symbols. Rupert Sheldrake has indicated in *The Rebirth of Nature: The Greening of Science and God* how the disenchanted worldview of the reformers was conducive to the emergence of the mechanistic perspectives of the Enlightenment.[6] Furthermore, the Reformers, in contrast to the Catholic and Orthodox churches, proposed a very individualistic notion of salvation (i.e. 'accepting Jesus in faith as my personal Lord and Saviour).'[7]

It was the rise of science in particular that shattered the unitary worldview. Men such as Roger Bacon (1220-1292), Nicolaus

6. (New York: Bantam Books, 1991), 20-21.

7. In EN 18 Pope Paul VI described the much more inclusive Catholic notion of salvation: 'If it had to be expressed in one sentence the best way of stating it would be to say that the church evangelises when she seeks to convert, solely through the Divine Power of the Message she proclaims, *both the personal and collective consciences of people* [my italics], the activities in which they engage, and the lives and the concrete milieux which are theirs.'

Copenicus (1473-1543), Galileo Galilei (1564-1642), and Isaac Newton (1642-1727) replaced the medieval conviction that nature was an organism with the notion that it was an inanimate machine. About the same time, Rene Descartes (1596-1650) articulated the implications of the new scientific worldview. He undermined the intimate connection between mind and body when he wrote: 'I consider the human body as a machine, my thought compares a sick man to an ill made clock and a healthy man to a well made clock.'[8] He also undermined the intimate connection between human beings and the world. So by the end of the seventeenth century nature had ceased to be feminine at all. Indeed man's conquest of nature is inseparable from rapacious sexual imagery. As one feminist writer has noted: 'By reconceptualising reality as a machine rather than a living organism, science which was conducted by men and which reflected an exclusively male point of view, sanctioned the domination of both nature and women.'[9]

For their part, sociologists and historians like Max Weber and Richard Tawney have shown how capitalism was able to grow and to thrive within the cultural ethos created by the Reformation and the scientific revolution.[10] By desacralising the world of nature and stressing the importance of the work ethic, both movements paved the way for capitalism. However, it could be argued that modern capitalism had begun to emerge before the Protestant Reformation, (e.g. when commercial centres emerged in the fifteenth-century such as Venice, Florence, and Flanders). We know that in the fifteenth century bankers, such as the Fugger family, were providing capital for different projects such as mining.[11] According to this view, it was capitalism that gave rise to Protestantism and the scientific revolution because it needed a new religious ethic and a new worldview.

8. Quoted in Fritjof Capra, *The Turning Point: Science, Society and the Rising Culture* (London: Flamingo 1982), 62.

9. Carolyn Merchant, *The Death of Nature* (New York: Harper & Row, 1980), xvii.

10. Richard Tawney, *Religion and the Rise of Capitalism*, (New Brunswick: Hesperides Press, 2006); Max Weber, *The Protestant Ethic and the Spirit of Capitalism* (London: Routledge, 2001).

11. J. Russell Major, 'The Fuggers,' *The Western World: The Renaissance to the Present* (London: Frederick Muller, 1967), 149-50.

Protestantism and the scientific revolution provided both in a kind of reciprocal manner.

One way or the other, instead of feeling scrupulous about their desire to dominate and exploit nature, capitalists saw it as their goal in a world where nothing was intrinsically sacred. By applying the best technological insights of the new sciences they learned to master, subdue and exploit the earth's resources. This became increasingly true with the advent of the industrial revolution in the nineteenth century. Not only did it tend to sever the intimate connection between people and nature, it subordinated people, their relationships and their rights, to the abstract and uncaring imperatives of market forces such as profit and loss, supply and demand while stressing competition rather than co-operation. These attitudes were, and still are corrosive as far as community solidarity is concerned.

Those of us who live in the twenty-first century have to cope with the consequences of this form of unfettered capitalism. Not only are we facing an ecological crisis of dangerous proportions, human beings are in trouble too. As we continue to endure the unacceptable face of capitalism, the gap between rich and poor continues to widen. As a result, increasing numbers of people join the ranks of the 'new poor', to use Blessed Teresa of Calcutta's phase. In spite of being economically well off, some of these people are poor in so far as they often suffer from a famine of understanding love. As a consequence they are afflicted by all kinds of psycho-spiritual problems. For more on this see chapter six. In 1985 Joseph Ratzinger echoed what his predecessor Paul VI had already said in par 26 of his Encyclical Letter, *Populorum progressio* (hereafter PP): 'It is becoming an increasingly obvious fact of economic history that the development of economic systems which concentrate on the common good depends on a determinate ethical system, which in turn can be born and sustained only by strong religious convictions. Conversely, it has also become obvious that the decline of such discipline *can actually cause the laws of the market to collapse* [my italics].'[12] More

12. 'Church and economy: Responsibility for the future of the world economy,' *Communio*, 13 (Fall 1986): 199-204. See also, *Salt of the Earth: The Church at the End of the Millennium* (San Francisco: Ignatius, 1997), 274.

recently Benedict XVI has expressed similar views on capitalism in his encyclical letter, *Caritas in Veritate* (hereafter CV).

Some Results of the breakdown of the Holistic Worldview

As a result of the Reformation, science, unfettered capitalism and aspects of the Enlightenment and post-Enlightenment thought, the umbilical cord that connected people to the realm of created and uncreated meaning has been severed with negative knock-on effects. I'd suggest that they can be encapsulated, in a rather arbitrary way under seven A's, those of absurdity, alienation, anxiety, anomie, apathy, agnosticism and atheism. We will take a brief look at each.

Newtonian science, together with Cartesian and Kantian idealism have tended to set human beings adrift in an alien world devoid of any ultimate meaning. This modernist approach has given rise to the postmodern, nihilistic belief that, despite all appearances to the contrary, reality is ultimately absurd. Novelist Andre Malraux had one of his characters echo the views of Jean Paul Sartre in *Nausea* and Albert Camus in *The Outsider* when he said: 'In the depths of European man, where it dominates the great moments of his life, there resides an essential absurdity.'[13]

Not surprisingly, the extent to which people lose touch with a sense of meaning, is the extent to which they suffer from a sense of alienation which can be understood in philosophical and psychological terms of an interrelated kind. Psychologist Karen Horney described it as, 'the remoteness of the neurotic from his own feelings, wishes, beliefs, and energies. It is the loss of the feeling of being an active, determining force in his own life.'[14] Erich Fromm has written: 'Alienation as we find it in modern society is almost total; it pervades the relationship of man to his work, to the things he consumes, to his fellows, and to himself.'[15] It could be added that many, many people also feel alienated from God. St Thérèse of Lisieux bore poignant testi-

13. *La Tentation de L'Occident*, 1926.
14. Quoted by Josephson, 'Introduction,' *Man alone: Alienation in Modern Society*, (New York: Dell, 1962), 16.
15. Eric Josephson and Mary Josephson, 'Alienation Under Capitalism', *Man Alone*, 59.

mony to this desolate feeling in the account of her temptation to atheism. 'It is all a dream,' she wrote when she was ill with tuberculosis, 'this talk of a heavenly country, bathed in light, scented with delicious perfumes, and of a God who made it all, who is to be our possession in eternity! ... All right, all right, go on longing for death! But death will make nonsense of your hopes; it will only mean a darker night than ever, the night of mere non-existence and annihilation.'[16] Writers such as Erik Fromm and Viktor Frankl have shown how these forms of estrangement can be reinforced by bureaucracy and consumerism.

As more and more people lose touch with the meaning of life, they experience deep down anxiety. Paul Tillich has shown how it can manifest itself in neurotic and ontological forms.[17] In fact this phenomenon has become so widespread that poet W. H. Auden described the twentieth century as 'the age of anxiety.' The word *anxiety* comes from the Latin *angustus* meaning 'to narrow'. One would be tempted to suspect that anxious people have a tendency to be mistrustful and to become narrow minded and defensive. They often try to escape from their inner pain by an idolatrous pursuit of power, pleasure and status. As Gerald May has indicated, the attempt to flee from anxiety and inner pain also leads to all kinds of addictions and obsessions.[18]

Emile Durkheim maintained that alienation and anxiety in modern society can lead to what he called anomie. He used the word to describe a state of normlessness, the collapse of rules of conduct, and a loss of values and purpose. The concept can be understood in either psychological or social terms. In his book, *Love and Will*, psychologist Rollo May has suggested that many normless people suppress their anxiety, thereby becoming apathetic. They avoid close relationships and suffer from an inability to feel deeply about anything. They tend to be cold, detached, and superior in their attitude. 'Apathy and lack of feeling,' May wrote, 'are defence mechanisms against anxiety. When a person is continuously facing dangers he is powerless to overcome, his final line of defence is at last to avoid even feeling the

16. *Autobiography of a Saint* (London: Harvill Press, 1958), 255-6.
17. Paul Tillich has a very good analysis of both forms of anxiety in his book *The Courage to Be* (London: Fontana, 1969), 41-88.
18. *Addiction and Grace* (New York: Harper/Collins, 1991).

dangers.'[19] In sociological terms, lack of a social ethic produces moral deregulation, an absence of legitimate aspirations and an increasing number of suicides.[20]

The Radical Cause of the current Religious-Cultural Crisis

It looks as if growing secularism in Western societies is due to the masculinisation of culture. Incidentally, the words masculine and feminine are being used here as metaphors or ciphers for archetypal characteristics which are culturally conditioned. As has already been mentioned, the male principle tends to be rational, detached, and objective, whereas the female principle tends to be intuitive-affective, relational and experiential. Henri Bergson, who was very critical of rationalistic approaches to reality, wrote, 'intuition is a sympathy whereby one carries oneself into the interior of an object to coincide with what is unique and therefore inexpressible in it. Analysis, on the other hand, is an operation which reduces the object to elements that are known and that the object has in common with others.'[21] In an important book entitled, *The Flight From Woman*, psychiatrist Karl Stern talked about scientific (male) knowledge and poetic (female) knowledge.[22] Stern argued very persuasively that many of the architects of modern Western thought were men who were excessively left brained thinkers who were not at all at ease with the feminine principle. Among them, he mentions Descartes, Schopenhauer, Kierkegaard, Goethe and Sartre. Stern wrote: 'Rationalism and positivism have influenced our Western civilisation during the past three centuries, to an extraordinary degree ... And if we equate the one-sidedly rational and technical with the masculine, there arises the ghastly spectre of a world impoverished of womanly values.'[23]

It could be argued that many of the men who were the architects of the contemporary worldview, such as Isaac Newton, Rene Descartes, Immanuel Kant, Gottfried Leibniz, Charles

19. (London: Fontana, 1972), 28.
20. See Emile Durkheim, *Suicide* (New York: Free Press, 1951).
21. *Introduction to Metaphysics* (New York: G. P. Putnam's Sons, 1912), 181.
22. (New York: Farrar, Straus & Giroux, 1965), 41-58.
23. Ibid., 6.

Darwin, Albert Einstein, Kurt Gödel, Paul Dirac and Ludwig Wittgenstein manifested some of the characteristics of ASD, (i.e. autism spectrum disorder), especially Asperger Syndrome. In their book, *Genius Genes: How Asperger Talents Changed the World,*[24] authors Michael Fitzgerald and Brendan O'Brien have shown how those who suffer from this form of abnormality are loners with narrow, obsessive interests, who seek to assuage their anxiety by trying to control their experience by means of obsessive routines. They are often naïve, lacking a sense of humour, physically un-coordinated and are poor at empathising with others.

We can look at two brief examples. Rene Descartes was an instance of someone who might have had Asperger's syndrome. He was a loner, never married, and was obsessive and detached. Like many autistic people the world scared him. To Descartes the universe did not represent a sacramental word of God which could be trusted, but rather the expression of the divine will which was unfathomable at best, and arbitrary and threatening at worst. In a typically autistic way he looked for a certainty he could rely on. He wrote: 'I realised that it was necessary, once in the course of my life, to demolish everything completely and start from the foundations if I wanted to establish anything at all in the sciences that was stable and likely to last.'[25] He found the answer, not in relationship but rather in his own subjectivity when he said, 'I think, therefore I am.' The only way that Descartes could avoid being hopelessly shipwrecked in his solipsistic isolation was to propose a version of the ontological argument for God's existence.[26] If God exists he argued, the deity would act as the guarantor for the apparent existence of the external world and one's own body. Sometime later Kant disproved the legitimacy of the ontological argument, and later still Ludwig Feuerbach argued that God was merely a projection of the infinite potential of human subjectivity.

24. (Shawnee Mission, Kansas: APC, 2007).

25. Meditations on First Philosophy 1, in *The Philosophical writings of Descartes* (Cambridge: CUP, 1985) Vol II, 12.

26. One version goes as follows. (1) Whatever I clearly and distinctly perceive to be contained in the idea of something is true of that thing. (2) I clearly and distinctly perceive that necessary existence is contained in the idea of God. (3) Therefore, God exists.

Immanuel Kant also seems, to a greater or lesser extent, to have suffered from Asperger's syndrome. He too mistrusted the world and took refuge in subjectivity. He maintained that we cannot know reality in itself, but only phenomenal appearances as they are perceived by means of categories of the mind such as causality, quality, quantity, relation, and modality. In the *Critique of Pure Reason*, he wrote in a characteristically autistic way: 'We have now not merely explored the territory of pure understanding, and carefully surveyed every part of it, but have also measured its extent, and assigned to everything its rightful place. This domain is an island, enclosed by nature itself with unalterable limits. It is the land of truth – enchanting name! – surrounded by a wide and stormy ocean, the native home of illusion, where many a fog bank and many a swiftly melting iceberg give the deceptive appearance of further shores, deluding the adventurous seafarer ever anew with empty hopes.'[27] Notice that Kant presumes that the world of reality surrounding his subjectivity threatens him because it refuses to yield to his human control.

Clearly, both Descartes and Kant advocated the hermeneutics of suspicion. They espoused the notion that intelligibility, where everything has its rightful place, is not something discovered in external reality but something imposed in a Faustian way on a chaotic world by the thinking subject. This extremely influential, but questionable point of view, may not be the result of some kind of demonic pride, but rather the effect of autistic pathology.

Simon Baron-Cohen has written a very interesting book, *The Essential Difference: Male and Female Brains and the Truth About Autism*, in which he clearly indicates that excessive masculinity tends to be autistic.[28] He quotes something that Hans Asperger said in 1948: 'The autistic personality is an extreme variant of male intelligence. Even within the normal variation, we find typical sex differences in intelligence ... In the autistic individual, the male pattern is exaggerated to the extreme.'[29] People

27. Trs Normon Kemp Smith (New York: St Martin' Press, 1929), 257.
28. Simon Baron-Cohen, *The Essential Difference* (London: Penguin, 2004), 133-54.
29. Quoted by Simon Baron-Cohen, *The Essential Difference*, 149.

with this condition, he argues, show an extreme of the typical male profile. They have much less ability to empathise together with a greater ability to systematise. As has already been noted, it is striking to see how many extremely bright and creative philosophers and scientists of this extremely male kind have influenced our Western worldview. One could say, with some justification, that such a worldview is at least mildly autistic in nature, rooted in anxiety, detached, and dysfunctional.

As the typical powers of the male psyche have predominated in Western culture, people have lost touch with their deeper feminine identities. In so doing, they have lost contact with the archetypal powers of the *anima* and the deeper spiritual self, to use a Jungian term, which can only be fulfilled by an awareness of the transcendent Other. Alienation from the *anima* has been reinforced by the fact that that cultural conditioning has separated many women from their own feminine depths. Indeed Freud said that the aim of successful analysis was a 'repudiation of femininity'[30] in the lives of men and women. The crisis of the feminine is one of the main reasons for the religious crisis of our time. The admittedly widespread incidence of the so called, 'autonomous self' is a symptom rather than the true cause of our religious and cultural problems. The extent to which men and women lose touch with the feminine archetype, is the extent to which they lose touch with that power of the self, which alone can bind them in an intimate way to one another, to nature, and through both to God. The decline of the feminine, contemplative dimensions of the human psyche have led almost inevitably to the virtual eclipse of God, and therefore to agnosticism and even atheism.

It is well worth noting that at the conclusion of his book, *The Passion of the Western Mind*, Richard Tarnas expressed a view which is similar in some respects to the one expressed in a very sketchy way in this chapter. Here are some quotations from what he says: 'The evolution of the Western mind has been driven by a heroic impulse to forge an autonomous rational human self by separating it from the primordial unity with nature …

30. Sigmund Freud, 'Analysis terminable and interminable,' *The Standard Edition of the Complete Works of Sigmund Freud*, vol. 23 (London: The Hogarth Press, 1953-74), 252.

the perspectives of Western culture have all been affected by this decisive masculinity ... to do this, the masculine mind has repressed the feminine ... The Western mind has been founded on the repression of the feminine – on the repression of the undifferentiated unitary consciousness, of the participation mystique with nature: a progressive denial of the *anima mundi*, of the soul of the world, of the community of being, of the all-pervading, of mystery and ambiguity, of imagination, emotion, instinct, body, nature, woman ... the masculine heroic quest has been pressed to its utmost one-sided extreme in the consciousness of the late modern mind, which in its absolute isolation has appropriated to itself all conscious intelligence in the universe (man alone is a conscious intelligent being, the cosmos is blind and mechanistic, God is dead) ... *The crisis of modern man is essentially a masculine crisis*, and I believe that its resolution is already occurring in the tremendous emergence of the feminine in our culture.'[31]

Acknowledging God-given Affinities

If my contention that masculinisation is the underlying problem in modern and postmodern culture, and that capitalism rather than the Reformation or the rise of science is its fundamental cause, there will be no fundamental change until a sense of the feminine is restored and honoured, and an effective critique of the excesses of unfettered capitalism and its corrosive effects upon people and their relationships is undertaken. Hopefully the world banking crisis which began in 2008 will lead to an overhaul and modification of the excesses of capitalist economics. Tarnas and others suggest that there is also reason to believe that the worst effects of exaggerated masculinisation are already beginning to come to an end. This cultural change is being brought about by a number of modern developments, such as feminism, which promise to activate a paradigm shift in the form of fundamental change in perspective. Fritjof Capra described many instances in his influential book, *The Turning Point: Science, Society, and the Rising Culture*.[32] We can draw attention to a number of them.

31. (New York: Ballentine Books, 1991), 441-2.
32. (London: Flamingo, 1983).

Firstly, unlike Newtonian science, quantum physics stresses the interconnectedness of created reality. As Bede Griffiths OSB wrote: 'In physics, there has recently been the discovery that the material universe is essentially a field of energies in which the parts can only be understood in relation to the whole. A related and most profound idea which has been introduced in physics is that the whole is in some way present in every part and, further, that every part is interconnected with every other part.'[33] This is demonstrable in holography where each part of a holographic plate contains the whole image imprinted on its surface. It would also be true to say that Chaos and Complexity Theory deals with disorder and order in the universe. It has called Newton's notion of the invariable predictability of the laws of nature, understood as a giant mechanical clock, into question. Chaos theory is associated with people such as Edward Lorenz, Mitchell Feigenbaum, and Benoit Mandelbrot who discovered fractals.[34] The holistic perspective which is evident in quantum physics is also reflected in contemporary ecology and meteorology which acknowledges the interconnectedness of everything in the cosmos. This would account for the popularity of James Lovelock's controversial notion of Gaia. The same is happening in psychology (e.g. of the transpersonal kind),[35] which is increasingly going beyond the mechanistic and behaviouristic views of people like Freud and Skinner to a more holistic perspective that integrates the realms of mind, body and spirit. As a result of the work of scholars like Carol Gilligan, author of, *In A Different Voice: Psychological Theory and Women's Development*,[36] there is an increasing appreciation of the distinctive dynamics and value of feminine psychology and how it differs from the male variety. There is also a widespread acknowledgement that

33. *A New Vision of Reality: Western Science, Eastern Mysticism and Christian Faith* (London: Collins, 1989), 17. I believe that a new epistemology will emerge as a result of the new physics, one that will sweep away the radical Cartesian/Kantian dualism between subjective and objective reality which has bedevilled our theories of knowledge for hundreds of years.
34. cf James Gleick, *Chaos: Making a New Science* (London: Penguin, 1988).
35. Pat Collins 'Transpersonal Psychology and Spirituality,' *Mind and Spirit: Spirituality and Psychology in Dialogue* (Dublin: Columba, 2006), 35-56.
36. (Cambridge: Harvard University Press, 1993).

Jung was probably correct when he talked about the complementarity of the *animus* (male) and the *anima* (female), not only in the self and interpersonal relationships, but within the whole culture.

It is my belief that the New Age movement not only understands many of the shortcomings in contemporary culture, it is offering, albeit in a pagan manner, a way forward that is not only attractive to many people but posing a real challenge to the Christian church. It tackles the problem of the masculinisation of culture and the autonomy of the self. It stresses the importance of the feminine archetype and its contemplative abilities. It breaks down the subject-object dichotomy, which is so characteristic of modernist and post-modernist thinking, and replaces it with a mystical sense of the inter-connectedness of all things. Added to that, the New Age has interesting things to say about such topics as ecology and holistic healing.

The document, *Christ the Bearer of the Water of Life: A Christian Reflection on the New Age* offers a well-informed and surprisingly sympathetic description of the worldview informing the New Age movement.[37] For example, referring to its core beliefs, it says succinctly:

1) The world, including the human race, constitutes an expression of a higher, more comprehensive divine nature.
2) Hidden within each human being is a higher divine self, which is a manifestation of the higher, more comprehensive divine nature.
3) This higher nature can be awakened and can become the centre of the individual's everyday life.
4) This awakening is the reason for the existence of each individual life.

Although the Pontifical document does not accept New Age beliefs, it makes a number of positive comments about them. Firstly, it sees the New Age movement as a laudable reaction to the materialism and rationalism of a good deal of western culture. Secondly, it is well attuned to the importance in contemporary culture of experience in general, and religious experience in

37. Published in 2003 by the Pontifical Council for Culture and the Pontifical Council for Inter-religious Dialogue.

particular. Thirdly, it is attracting many people who are keen to have a meaningful spiritual life but who are disillusioned with the institutional churches. Fourthly, rather than being a new phenomenon, it sees the New Age as a reappearance of ancient Gnosticism which talked about achieving salvation solely through higher states of consciousness. But just as Gnostic beliefs were not acceptable in early Christianity, so New Age beliefs are unacceptable in modern Christianity.

Christ the Bearer of the Water of Life also indicates why New Age beliefs are not acceptable from a Christian point of view. Firstly, God is not an impersonal energy but a Trinity of persons, Father, Son and Holy Spirit. Secondly, when the New Age says that Jesus Christ is not uniquely divine, but one of the many historical manifestations of the cosmic and universal Christ, it is quite mistaken. Thirdly, whereas the New Age movement believes that we save ourselves by raising our levels of consciousness by using human effort and psycho-technologies, Christians believe that we are justified by grace through faith in Christ and not by our own unaided efforts. Fourthly, Christians reject the New Age notion of sin as merely an imperfect form of knowledge which can be alleviated by means of New Age methods.[38]

Evangelisation in the contemporary cultural milieux

I do not think that Christians will be able to evangelise effectively unless they have an in-depth understanding of contemporary culture. In RM 25, John Paul II cited the example of St Paul, 'The speeches in Lystra and Athens (cf Acts 14:15-17; 17:22-31) are acknowledged as models for evangelisation of the Gentiles. In these speeches Paul enters into 'dialogue' with the cultural and religious values of different peoples. To the Lyconians, who practiced a cosmic religion, he speaks of religious experiences related to the cosmos. With the Greeks he discusses philosophy and quotes their own poets (cf Acts 17:18, 26-28).' Because space is limited I want to draw brief attention to a number of points that I think are important.

Because of the rapidity of change and the postmodern critique

38. For a critique of New Age spirituality see Joseph Ratzinger, *Truth and Tolerance: Christian Belief and World Religions* (San Francisco: Ignatius, 2003), 126-31.

of mega-narratives and their truth claims,[39] the centre of gravity in our culture has shifted from authority to experience. For more on this see chapter twelve. One reason for the success of the worldwide Pentecostal and Charismatic Movements, as Harvey Cox pointed out in *Fire from Heaven: The Rise of Pentecostal Spirituality and the Re-shaping of Religion in the 21st Century*, is the fact that there is a big experiential component in their approach to evangelisation (e.g. the emphasis on Baptism in the Spirit, expectant faith, and the healing power of prayer). I also believe that in an experiential age like ours, a knowledge of psychology, about the nature and dynamics of such things as neurosis, addiction, stress, anxiety and depression is often more helpful in pastoral and evangelistic terms, than the fine points of Cartesian and Kantian epistemology.[40]

Science has had a tremendous effect on modern culture. The Newtonian worldview saw the universe as a closed system governed by inexorable physical laws. For many educated people, science precludes in an *a priori* way, the possibility of miracles or answers to petitionary prayer because both would involve a *deus ex machina*[41] type intervention. Prayer only makes sense, in this worldview, when it merely asks God to help people to make the best use of the available resources by means of their own human efforts. As a result, there has been a decline in the sense of the supernatural. Christians can do two things about this. Firstly, they need apologists who are familiar with modern science who can point out that, as a result of the findings in quantum physics such as the principle of indeterminacy and a-causal reactions in accordance with Bell's theorem, it is no longer necessary to espouse a completely closed worldview. There are many

39. Deconstruction by means of hermeneutics which uses things such as linguistics and depth psychology. See John Paul II on hermeneutics in pars 95-6 of his encyclical, *Faith and Reason*.
40. I agree with Pope John Paul II's critique of post-modernism in FR 84; 90; 91 & 96 and his insistence that we need to reaffirm St Thomas's confidence in a realistic epistemology and a return to metaphysics.
41. Latin meaning 'God from the machine.' It refers to the convention in Greek tragedies, when a crane was used to lower actors playing a God or Gods onto the stage. In other words it is the arbitrary introduction of God into a situation.

excellent books currently available on the changing relationship of science and religion.[42] Secondly, we need to demonstrate the presence of the supernatural realm by exercising the charisms, especially those of power such as faith, healing/exorcism and miracle working (cf 1 Cor 12:9). St Paul referred to them, quite rightly, as *phanerosis,* namely, manifestations of the transcendent presence and power of God (cf 1 Cor 12:7).

Bernard Lonergan once observed that in contemporary culture there is not a crisis of faith, rather there is a crisis of faith expression.[43] A story can be told to illustrate the point. Three children from central Europe came to live in Ireland. When local kids played with them, one of them asked, 'Have your parents found a home yet?' 'We have a home already,' responded the eldest immigrant child, 'but our parents have not yet found a house to put it in!' By analogy, the Christian faith is our home, but many of us believe that we have not yet found a linguistic house to put it in. Currently, Christian doctrine is often articulated in the static and rationalistic categories of the Greco-Roman worldview. The classical mentality is deductive. It emphasises universal abstract principles and necessary conclusions. It tends to be *a priori* (i.e. from the former, knowledge independent of experience). It examines the nature of things and draws logical conclusions in regard to particular instances depending on whether or not they correspond to stated principles. The historical mode of thinking tends to be practical and *a posteriori* (i.e. from the latter, knowledge proven through experience). It emphasises changing circumstances and contingent conclusions. It begins with concrete data, employs an empirical method, stresses hermeneutics, and draws its conclusions inductively from its sources. If Christian teaching is not to appear anachronistic and irrelevant, it will have to be expressed in the dynamic, evolutionary categories of the age in which we live (cf GS 5).

---

42. John Polkinghorne, *Belief in God in an Age of Science* (New Haven: Yale University Press, 1998); Keith Ward, *Divine Action,* (London: Collins, 1990); Francis S. Collins, *The Language of God: A Scientist Presents Evidence for Belief* (New York: Free Press, 2006); John F. Haught, *Christianity and Science: Toward a Theology of Nature* (New York: Orbis, 2007).
43. 'The Transition from a Classical World-View to Historical-Mindedness,' *A Second Collection,* 1-10.

We have to attempt in our day what the early Fathers of the church, such as Justin Martyr, Irenaeus, and Tertullian achieved in their day. They expressed the insights of the Bible in the language of the Greco-Roman world. Would-be evangelists need to do something similar nowadays by finding contemporary language to express the perennial Christian truths. For example, as chapter twelve will point out, the word 'sin' may not resonate for many people nowadays, but equivalent words such as inauthenticity, alienation, missing the mark and addiction might be used as effective synonyms. If evangelists engage in the kind of theological reflection which seeks to relate personal experience and different forms of secular wisdom to the scriptures and church teaching, they will be more likely to speak in meaningful, relevant terms.[44]

A good deal of research has been done on the dynamics of human development. It has shown that there are different stages involved in cognitive growth (e.g. Jean Piaget); ego development (e.g. Jane Loveinger); psychosocial development (e.g. Ekik Erickson); moral development (e.g. Lawrence Kohlberg); faith development (e.g. James Fowler); male/female development (e.g. Daniel Levinson). Given that 'the grace of God does not replace nature but fulfils it,'[45] evangelists need to attend to their own human development as part of their growth in holiness. We know from research that when people without religious faith are evangelised, they usually end up at a level of faith development equivalent to the stage of their own human development. If the evangelist is a person of some psycho-spiritual maturity and self-awareness, it is more likely that s/he will have something meaningful and relevant to say to the spiritual 'questors' or pilgrims of our day.[46] It can be noted in passing that the psychology of religion contains, like the other human sci-

44. Pat Collins 'Experience and Belief in Theological Reflection', *The Broken Image: Reflections on Spirituality and Culture* (Dublin: Columba, 2003).

45. St Thomas Aquinas, Timothy Mc Dermott ed, *Summa Theologiae: A Concise Translation* (Notre Dame: Ave Maria/Christian Classics, 1991), 3.

46. A word used by C. D. Batson, & P. Schoenrade (1991b), 'Measuring Religion as Quest: Reliability Concerns', *Journal for the Scientific Study of Religion* 30: 430-7.

ences, many valuable insights which can help those who want to evangelise effectively.[47]

Conclusion

When Pope John XXIII convened the Second Vatican Council he said in his opening speech: 'The greatest concern of the ecumenical Council is that the sacred deposit of Christian doctrine should be guarded and taught more effectively ... the church should never depart from the sacred treasure of truth ... But at the same time, *she must ever look to the present, to the new conditions and the new forms of life introduced into the modern world* [my italics].' George Weigel has pointed out in his biography of Pope John Paul II that the Holy Father believed that two paragraphs (GS 22, 24) were the theological linchpins of Vatican II.[48] They maintain that we can only know our deepest selves in and through relationship with God in Christ. Par 24 goes on to draw out the humanistic consequence of this assertion when it adds: 'People can only discover their true selves in a sincere giving of themselves.' That is why he warned in par 38 of the encyclical letter *Fides et Ratio* (hereafter FR): 'When God is forgotten the creature itself grows unintelligible.' In par. 90 he spoke about some of the likely consequences of this theistic amnesia: 'It in turn makes it possible to erase from the countenance of men and women the marks of their likeness to God and thus leads them little by little either to a destructive will to power or to a solitude without hope.' The new evangelisation, which he repeatedly called for, seeks, by every possible means, to counteract the theoretical and practical atheism of our time. It will do this by demonstrating that, instead of being the enemy of man, as many unbelievers maintain, it is only in the knowledge of God made man that human potential can be truly fulfilled.[49] If a postmodern

47. cf Hood, Spilka, Hunsberger & Gorsuch, *The Psychology of Religion: An Empirical Approach* (New York: The Guilford Press, 1996); David M. Wulff, *Psychology of Religion: Classic and Contemporary Views* (NewYork: John Wiley & Sons, 1991); Michael Argyle, *Psychology and Religion: An Introduction* (London: Routledge, 2000).

48. *Witness to Hope: The Biography of Pope John Paul II*, 224; 846.

49. cf Pat Collins, 'Atheism and the Father of Lies,' *The Broken Image*, 208-20. It includes an examination of what Pope John Paul II said about atheism in DeV 37; 38 & 56.

person wants to know who he or she is, he or she needs to know Whose he or she is. As St Irenaeus famously observed, 'Life in man is the glory of God; the life of man is the vision of God.'[50]

Recommended Reading

- *Secularity and the Gospel: Being Missionaries to our Children,* ed Ronald Rolheiser (New York: Crossroad, 2006).
- John F. Haught, *Christianity and Science: Toward a Theology of Nature* (New York: Orbis, 2007).
- Michael Fitzgerald and Brendan O'Brien, *Genius Genes: How Asperger Talents Changed the World* (Shawnee Mission, Kansas: APC, 2007).
- Fritjof Capra, *The Turning Point: Science, Society, and the Rising Culture* (London: Flamingo, 1983).
- Richard Tarnas, *The Passion of the Western Mind* (New York: Ballantine Books, 1991).
- Karl Stern, *The Flight From Woman* (New York: Farrar, Straus & Giroux, 1965).

50. *Against Heresies* (Lib. 4, 20, 5-7; SC 100, 640-642, 644-648)

CHAPTER THREE

Three Models of Evangelisation

Some Christian writers make a useful distinction between professed spirituality, i.e. what we think and feel about God at a conscious level, and operative spirituality, i.e. our primal feelings and gut instincts about God which are largely unconscious, and usually formed in childhood. For example, Dr Ana-Maria Rizzuto, a Catholic psychoanalyst from Argentina, has described how a parish priest came to see her.[1] His presenting symptoms were chronic fatigue and insomnia which inhibited his ability to serve his parishioners in an effective way. A thorough examination revealed that there was nothing wrong with him physically. However, when Rizutto asked the priest about his family it became clear from his tone of voice that, although he admired his father, he also feared him because he was stern and strict disciplinarian. When she asked the priest about his relationship with God his reply was equally ambiguous. As Rizutto observed, the God of the priest was loving, patient and gentle (i.e. professed spirituality). However, the God of the man was critical, distant and demanding (i.e. operative spirituality). The God of the priest was positive (i.e. professed spirituality), but the God of the man was negative (i.e. operative spirituality). Dr Rizutto went on to describe how she helped the priest to consciously recognise the conflict between his professed idea and his operative image of God, and how the former was the fruit of his education and the latter a result of his childhood experience of paternal authority. As soon as he became aware of these conflicting aspects of his relationship with God, he was able to revise his image of the Lord.[2]

This distinction between professed and operative spirituality

1. 'The Psychological Foundations of Belief in God', in *Toward Moral and Religious Maturity* (New Jersey: Silver Burdett Company, 1980), 118.
2. cf Pat Collins, 'False Images of God and Resistance to Change,' *Goodnews* (Jan/Feb 2010): 6-7.

is relevant where evangelisation is concerned. Although the word evangelisation is defined in the dictionary as preaching the gospel and covers a number of different but interrelated activities, as the next chapter will indicate, the way in which the word is understood by different people is often influenced by unconscious factors. Models of evangelisation can help to bring unconscious assumptions to the level of conscious awareness, thereby making it easier for people to dialogue in a constructive way about issues to do with evangelisation. The notion of models can be understood in two distinct senses. Firstly, it can be interpreted as an example or instance of a particular kind of evangelisation (e.g. how St Anthony of the desert modelled one way of evangelising, while St John Vianney modelled another). While that approach has undoubted validity and value, it will not be used here. Secondly, the notion of theological models has been borrowed from the worlds of science and engineering. Many years ago it was adopted and adapted to great effect by Avery Dulles SJ in his book, *Models of the Church*. This ground breaking work explained how, in spite of the fact that Christians use the word church in conversation, nevertheless it can mean different things for different people. This is due to the fact that they are usually influenced by unconscious assumptions about the Church. Dulles suggested that there were five possible models current in Catholic circles:

1. As institution (including a hierarchy of ministries to continue Christ's mission, and reflecting a need for order, unity and consistency of teaching).
2. As mystical communion (including our mysterious and intimate spiritual union with God and each other through the Body of Christ).
3. As sacrament (including the responsibility to be the visible presence of God on earth).
4. As herald (including the mission of proclaiming God's Word at home and abroad to the churched, unchurched and unbelievers).
5. As servant (including dialogue with society and assisting persons in a variety of needs).[3]

3. Dulles added a sixth model of church some time later, i.e. as a community of disciples (including the sense of always being learners, being

He maintained that, for all sorts of reasons, believers tended to unconsciously identify predominately with one particular model while usually augmenting it with admired elements from the others. Following the publication of his book, a questionnaire was produced which helped respondents to identify which model of church was the one to which they mainly adhered. Subsequent models theory has also been used to throw light on important Christian topics such as faith, revelation, spirituality and christology.[4] This chapter will focus on the second understanding of models.

Models are ideal cases, organising images which give a particular emphasis, enabling one to notice and interpret certain salient aspects of experience. Having written about models of the church, Avery Dulles has shown in a number of his other writings how models can be used to understand other important theological ideas. Speaking about such models, Dulles said: 'In constructing types on the basis of the expressed views of individual theologians one is moving from the particular to the universal, from the concrete to the abstract, from the actual to the ideal. The type does not exactly correspond to the thought of the theologians whom it allegedly includes … As an ideal case, the type may be called a model. That is to say, it is a relatively simple, artificially constructed case which is found to be useful and illuminating for dealing with realities that are more complex and differentiated.'[5] Because theological models represent ideal types, an individual person or group would rarely conform

---

formed by the scriptures, acting lovingly, sharing in Jesus' mission and service, and being co-responsible for the church's mission and identity).

4. Avery Dulles, *Models of the Church* (New York: Doubleday, 1974); *Models of Revelation* (Dublin: Gill & Macmillan, 1983); 'The Meaning of Faith Considered in Relationship to Justice' *The Faith that Does Justice*, ed J. C. Haughey (New York: Paulist Press, 1977); *The Assurance of Things Hoped For: A Theology of Christian Faith* (New York: Oxford University Press, 1994); John C. Haughey, 'Contemporary Spiritualities and the Spirit,' *The Conspiracy of God: The Holy Spirit in Us* (New York: Image, 1976), 78-93; John F. O'Grady, *Models of Jesus* (New York: Image, 1982); David L. Fleming, 'Models of Spiritual Direction,' *The Christian Ministry of Spiritual Direction*, ed David L. Fleming (St Louis: *Review for Religious*, 1988), 106-12.

5. *Models of Revelation*, 30.

exactly to any of them. However, they would predominantly belong to one or other, while incorporating characteristics of the other models in their outlook. It is also important to stress that models are descriptive rather than evaluative. All of them are valid up to a point, and have their own distinctive strengths and weaknesses. Ideally, models should be clear and precise.[6]

In a wonderful book on the Holy Spirit, John C. Haughey adverted to the fact that there were many disagreements and divisions in the Post Vatican II Church. He made the important observation that, 'Underneath these tensions there is the key difference: how one images God, approaches him, experiences him, and articulates this experience to oneself.'[7] In other words, conflicts in theology are often rooted in conflicting spiritualities. He suggested that there were three models of spirituality operative in the church, the programmatic, the pneumatic and the autogenous. Space does not allow me to say much about these terms or to give examples.[8] Suffice it to say that programmatic spirituality believes in the God who is beyond. Advocates of this spirituality obediently follow an authoritative programme proposed by the church. Pneumatic spirituality believes in the God who is within, whose presence is revealed in the personality by the Spirit. Advocates of this spirituality seek to be guided by the Spirit in all things. Autogenous spirituality believes in Emmanuel, the God who is among us. Advocates of this spirituality seek meaning in and through merciful deeds, and action for justice. In other words, Haughey suggested that models of theology are usually influenced by people's adherence to one or other of the models of spirituality. For example, those who are programmatic in spirituality usually adopt a model of church as sacrament or institution; those who are pneumatic usually adopt a model of church as herald or mystical communion; those who are autogenous usually adopt a model of church as servant.

6. cf Sharon Callaghan, 'Shifting Images of Church Invite New Leadership Frames,' *Journal of Religious Leadership*, vol 1, no 1 (Spring 2002): 55-82. http://arl-jrl.org/Volumes/CallahanSP02.pdf (accessed Jan 18, 2010).
7. 'Contemporary Spiritualities and the Spirit,' *The Conspiracy of God*, 97
8. See Pat Collins, 'Models of Spirituality,' *Spirituality for the 21st Century* (Dublin: Columba, 1999), 13-36.

Some years after the publication of his groundbreaking book on models of church, Avery Dulles suggested that there are three models of faith: intellectualist, (i.e. as mental assent to truths taught by the church); fiducial, (i.e. as deep trust in the person and promises of the Lord); and performative (i.e. as action that liberates oneself and others from human and spiritual forms of oppression). These three models are based on the fact that faith can be seen as trust, assent and action. Dulles described them in these words: 'Faith includes three elements: a firm conviction regarding what is supremely important, dedication or commitment to that which one believes in, and trustful reliance on the power and goodness of that to which one stands committed. The three components of faith are thus conviction, commitment and trust.'[9] It seems to me that Dulles's models of faith correlate with Haughey's three models of spirituality. Programmatics usually espouse the intellectalist model of faith; pneumatics usually espouse the fiducial model of faith; and the autogenous usually adopt the performative model of faith.

Ever since reading and reflecting upon such studies, I have suspected that like the church, spirituality and faith, there are different but unacknowledged models of evangelisation at work in the present day church. If they could be discerned, then each one of us could seek to identify the one to which we primarily adhere. This would not only help us to appreciate the fact that other people adhere primarily to alternative models of evangelisation, it would help us to see that our understanding of evangelisation is not the only valid way of doing so. This mutual recognition could bring greater clarity and tolerance to our discussions and evangelising activities. As far as I'm aware, there has been very little written about models of evangelisation. Fr Timothy Byerley, an American diocesan priest, has published an interesting book entitled *The Great Commission: Models of Evangelisation in American Catholicism*, which was influenced by Avery Dulles's work. In fact the Cardinal wrote a foreword to the book.[10] It proposes six scripture-based models of evangelisation:

9. *The Faith that Does Justice*, 13
10. (New York: Paulist, 2008).

- The St Stephen model (witness)
- The Jerusalem model (liturgy)
- The Proclamation model (preaching)
- The Fraternity model (small faith-based communities)
- The Areopagus model (enculturation)
- The Loaves and Fishes model (charitable works).

This chapter will propose an alternative classification comprised of three models of evangelisation which correlate quite well with Haughey's and Dulles's work.

Didactic/sacramental Evangelisation

Traditional spirituality is informed by faith as assent to objective truths taught by the church (i.e. *orthodoxy*), as firm conviction about doctrine and its practical ethical implications. Adherents of this model tend to presuppose that Catholics are evangelised in a basic sense as a result of receiving the sacraments of initiation and living in the Christian community. Consequently, they see evangelisation in mainly didactic or catechetical terms. The role of pastors, teachers, and those who conduct parish missions is to build upon the foundations already laid in the sacraments of initiation. This is done directly by preaching and teaching the doctrinal and moral truths of faith in order to ensure right belief and right action. Instruction of this type is usually objective and lacking in an experiential or personal dimension. For example, preachers and teachers who espouse this model, rarely witness in a personal way about how the truths of faith have impinged upon their own lives. To do so would be considered a form of subjectivism and self-promotion. Of course, faith as trust is included in this form of evangelisation by means of traditional forms of popular piety, such as devotion to the Sacred Heart and The Divine Mercy, both of which stress the importance of trusting in Jesus. Faith as committed performance is also accommodated (e.g. by groups such as The Legion of Mary and Opus Dei). John Wimber described this approach to evangelisation in his book *Power Evangelism*, where he observed, 'Programmatic evangelism is usually characterised by message-centred communicators who present the gospel primarily through rational arguments. In some cases an appeal to the emotions is also employed. Usually it is one-way communication, a prepared message given by a speaker to passive listeners. There is also an emphasis on organisation and technique, a search for the most effective presentation of the gospel, with a tacit assumption that if people understand the propositions of the gospel they will decide to become Christians.'[11]

In this chapter we will look at an historical example of how an evangelist can adopt a particular model of evangelisation while augmenting it with elements of the other models. Vincent de Paul was the founder of the Congregation of the Mission in the seventeenth century. His approach to evangelisation was typical of the didactic/sacramental approach which was common at that time. He firmly believed that people could not be saved unless they were taught the central truths of faith and were reconciled to God and one another by means of a good general confession and mutual reconciliation. For example, in a letter to a fellow priest Francois du Coudray, he wrote: 'An eminent person, both in doctrine and piety told me the other day that he is of St Thomas' opinion that he who is ignorant of the Trinity and the incarnation, and dies in that state, dies in a state of damnation. Now that touched me very much, and still touches me, so great is my fear of being damned myself for not having incessantly occupied myself with the instruction of the poor people.'[12] In 1631 Vincent wrote again to du Coudray who was negotiating with the authorities in Rome on his Congregation's behalf: 'You must make them understand that the poor people are being damned because they do not *know* [my italics] those things necessary for salvation and because they are not going to confession.'[13] Although the didactic/sacramental model predominated in Vincent's approach to evangelisation, he sometimes augmented it with elements from the two other approaches which will be described presently.

It is probably true to say that this model of evangelisation still predominates in the church of today. Popes John Paul II and

11. (London: Hodder & Stoughton, 1985), 56.
12. Quoted by Jacques Delarue in *The Missionary Ideal of the Priest According to St Vincent de Paul* (Chicago: Vincentians, 1993), 85.
13. Luigi Mezzadri, *A Short Life of St Vincent de Paul*, (Dublin: Columba, 1992/2010), 31.

Benedict XVI have put a lot of emphasis on the need for instruction in objective truth. This is clear in the systematic and objective approach of the *Catechism of the Catholic Church* and the equally objective approach to truth in the Encyclicals *Veritatis splendor* (hereafter VS), and *Fides et Ratio*. The Pontiffs obviously feel that the modern experiential approach to religion, with its distinctive models of evangelisation, is in danger of devolving into relativism and subjectivism, (i.e. the so called *à la carte* approach to truth). Not surprisingly many preachers and teachers endorse the point of view of the two Popes in their own attitude to evangelisation.

This didactic approach has obvious strengths. It is traditional, and has worked well in the past. The fact that it stresses the importance of objective norms gives it a clear sense of focus and purpose, one that counteracts the subjectivism and relativism prevalent in contemporary culture. It does not presuppose that people have a developed sense of self-awareness and conscience and is therefore suitable for people who might not have much intelligence or education. Mary Douglas has warned in her *Natural Symbols* that subjective types of religion, which no longer put much emphasis on objective norms, rituals and symbols, can end up catering for a fairly sophisticated middle class minority.[14] The didactic/sacramental model of evangelisation also has clear weaknesses. An approach that was developed in classical times is not well suited to the existential needs of the contemporary era in which we live. It tends to favour a sociological, conformist form of Catholicism rather than deep personal commitment to Christ. As Pope John Paul II said in EE 47: 'Many of the baptised live as if Christ did not exist: the gestures and signs of faith are repeated, especially in devotional practices, but they fail to correspond to a real acceptance of the content of the faith and fidelity to the person of Jesus.' Research has clearly shown that a growing number of people want a more experiential approach to religion. The fact that people have been sacramentalised and instructed in Christian truth does not necessarily mean that they have been evangelised in a basic, kerygmatic way. For more on this see the following two chapters.

14. *Natural Symbols: Explorations in Cosmology* (London: Pelican, 1973).

Kerygmatic/charismatic evangelisation

This model of evangelisation is informed by the belief that faith is primarily a matter of trust in God. Consequently, there is a strong appreciation of the need for primary evangelisation where the aim is more experiential than didactic, (i.e. *orthokardia*).[15] For example, Bishop Flores of New Mexico expressed this point of view in 1970 when he said that many of the church's problems will not be solved by getting people to the sacraments but by a basic evangelisation. He pointed out that many Catholics have never been effectively evangelised (i.e. brought to personal trust in Jesus as Saviour and Lord), but rather have merely been sacramentalised.[16]

As a result of falsely presuming that Catholics are evangelised in the basic sense, there can be a crisis of trusting faith in the church. The purpose of evangelisation, according to Evangelicals, Pentecostals and Charismatics, is to bring people into a heartfelt awareness of the free gift of salvation won for them by Christ on the cross. It could be the result of a religious experience.[17] John Wesley's conversion experience typifies what this model aims at. Following a moral fall, Wesley was disillusioned. In his diary he tells us that he met a Moravian pastor who said: 'Do you know Jesus Christ?' I paused and said, 'I know that he is the Saviour of the world.' 'True,' replied he, 'but do you know that he has saved you?' I answered, 'I hope he has died to save me.' He only added, 'Do you know yourself?' I said, 'I do,' but I fear they were vain words.' Wesley says that sometime later he had a conversion experience when his heart was strangely warmed as a result of hearing Luther's *Preface to Romans* being read at a

15. A word derived from Greek meaning 'right-hearted.'
16. Ralph Martin, *Unless the Lord Build the House* (Notre Dame: Ave Maria Press, 1971), 11. While the church teaches that sacraments are efficacious in themselves (*ex opere operato* i.e. the objective work of the sacrament), the person only derives benefit from them to the extent that they are received with personal faith (*ex opere operantis* i.e. the subjective disposition of the person who receives the sacrament).
17. In their book *Christian Initiation and Baptism in the Spirit*, (Collegeville: Liturgical Press, 1990), 333, Montague and O Donnell have argued from a scriptural and patristic point of view that the outpouring of the Spirit is integral to the sacraments of initiation and normative for all baptised Christians.

meeting in Aldersgate Street, London. 'I felt I did trust in Christ, Christ alone for my salvation. And an assurance was given me that he had taken away my sins, even mine and saved me from the law of sin and death.'[18]

Evangelicals and Charismatics believe that the kerygma must be proclaimed and backed up with personal testimony (i.e. how one has experienced its saving truth oneself). The Life in the Spirit Seminars, devised by the Charismatic Movement, and the Alpha course are good examples of this model of evangelisation. Evangelicals and Charismatics also believe that the truth of the kerygma should be demonstrated not only in the witness of a holy and joyful Christian life devoted to deeds of mercy and action for justice, but also by means of the charisms of healing, and miracle working.[19] For example, there are videos on the internet which show how American evangelist Todd White goes out on the streets in Las Vegas where he heals people he meets, often as a result of a word of knowledge, (i.e. an inspiration from the Holy Spirit that tells him who to pray for, and what to pray about).[20] Once, the healing has taken place and the recipient is awe struck and receptive, he tells them the basic Good News message about Jesus and his transforming power. As a result of an approach like this, those who are evangelised can come into the same experience as the evangeliser. Afterwards it is expressed in a changed way of living.

Although St Vincent de Paul espoused the didactic/sacramental model of evangelisation, he did augment it with a pneumatic emphasis. For example, on one occasion he said, 'Evangelisation is a grand work ... it is to continue the labours of Jesus Christ. And hence human industry is here of no avail unless God is intimately united with it. No, neither philosophy, nor theology, nor discourses influence souls. It is essential that Jesus Christ be intimately united with us or we with him; that we operate in him and he in us; that we speak like him and in his spirit as he himself was in his Father and preached the doctrine taught

18. cf Roy Hattersley, *John Wesley: A Brand From the Burning* (London: Abacus, 2002), 136.
19. See John Wimber, 'Power versus Programme', *Power Evangelism: Signs and Wonders Today* (London: Hodder & Stoughton, 1985), 56-60.
20. Google You Tube: Todd White; healing.

him by the Father. That is what holy scripture teaches us.'[21] This model of evangelisation maintains that, after conversion, people need good teaching which is inspirational as well as catechetical in nature, and geared to consolidate and deepen their trusting faith.

This approach has a number of strengths. It stresses the primary importance of faith as trust; as such it is a very biblical. This method of evangelisation is personal, affective and therefore experiential while being suited to the needs and expectations of the historical era in which we live. As Harvey Cox has written: 'The postmodern pilgrims are more attuned to a faith that helps them find the way through life here and now. There is something quite pragmatic about their religious search. Truths are not accepted because someone says they are true, no matter what that leader's religious authority may be, but because people find that they connect, they "click" with their own everyday existence.'[22] The kerygmatic/charismatic model stresses the importance of personal witness in two senses. Firstly, people must practise what they preach. Secondly, they need to share their own personal experience of faith by giving their testimony (i.e. telling the story of their own faith journey). This approach also inspires and encourages other people in personal rather than abstract terms. It fits in with the notion that faith is caught, not taught. This model provides a good foundation for subsequent catechesis in faith and morals. Whereas didactic/sacramental evangelisation has produced disappointing results in the contemporary church, it is also true to say that this approach has been more successful in renewing faith and commitment. But like any model, the charismatic/kerygmatic one has certain weaknesses. It can tend towards individualism, 'my salvation ... my experience', and thereby neglect the community dimension. It can underestimate the importance of the sacraments as means of grace. It can also tend toward subjectivism, where people place more confidence in their own feelings, and experiences (e.g. visions, prophecies etc.) than in the official teaching of the

21. Andre Dodin, *Vincent de Paul and Charity: A Contemporary Portrait of his Life and Apostolic Spirit*, ed Hugh O'Donnell & Marjorie Gale Hornstein (New York: New City Press, 1993), 81.
22. *Fire from Heaven*, (London: Cassell, 1996), 306.

church, which can be ignored rather than rejected. It is a narrow view of evangelisation which is in danger of overlooking the importance of the socio-cultural aspects such as action for justice, ecology, enculturation, religious dialogue etc.

Political/Developmental Evangelisation

This model of evangelisation shifts the emphasis away from faith as either assent or trust, and places it on faith as right action (i.e. *orthopraxis*).[23] It advocates gospel inspired activity that helps to liberate people and communities from all that oppress them, such as the evil of personal and structural sin which are inextricably linked. For example, Albert Nolan says in his *Jesus Before Christianity* that there is no doubt that our Lord had in mind 'a politically structured society of people on earth. A kingdom is a thoroughly political notion ... Nothing that Jesus ever said would lead one to think that he might use this term in a non-political sense.'[24] John Sobrino has written in his *Christology at the Crossroads*: 'Jesus does not advocate a love that is depoliticised, de-historicised and de-structuralised. He advocates a political love, a love that is situated in history and that has visible repercussions for human beings ... Out of love for the poor, he took his stand with them; out of love for the rich he took his stand against them. In both cases, however, he was interested in something more than retributive justice. He wanted renewal and re-creation.'[25] In a chapter entitled, 'A Spirituality of Liberation' Gustavo Gutierrez says that this type of spirituality 'will centre on a conversion to the neighbour, the oppressed person, the exploited social class, the despised race, the dominated country.'[26] Notice how he does not define conversion in terms of a changed response to a transcendent God. This model of evangelisation is pragmatic in orientation, relatively new, and owes a good deal to the liberation theology which has been influential in third world countries, especially those in South America, afflicted as they are by socio-economic injustice. It has also been

23. Derived from Greek meaning 'right practice or action'.
24. (London: DLT, 1992), 59.
25. (London: SCM Press, 1978), 379.
26. Included in *Conversion: Perspectives on Personal and Social Transformation,* ed Walter E. Conn (New York: Alba House, 1978), 309.

influenced by new insights in Catholic social teaching such as those taught by Pope Paul VI in his Encyclical Letter *Populorum progressio*.

The notion of praxis is central. Committed solidarity with the poor helps one to understand the true meaning of the Good News. In this model, while the gospel is proclaimed by means of word and action, it is assumed that Christ is already with the poor, and that evangelisation is helping people to recognise and affirm their dignity as children of God. It also helps to liberate them from the evils that would be alien to their Christian identity. This liberation can take different forms.

Firstly, it can be seen in structural terms, namely, that there are laws and institutional arrangements in society which are oppressive, evil, and alien to gospel values. These need to be identified by means of social analysis, challenged and changed. By showing compassion and love in these practical ways, not only do these evangelists witness to the Good News, they themselves are evangelised in the process. This is the indispensable hermeneutical key that enables them to unlock the spiritual riches of the scriptures.

Secondly, in Western countries where there are large middle classes, oppression is seen more in psycho-spiritual terms, such as inner hurts which may be due to physical, emotional, or sexual abuse by members of the family or the wider community. Arguably these problems are not unrelated to the breakdown in social solidarity caused by the injustices and false worldly values that inevitably lead to the split between the 'haves' and 'have nots' in society. Mother Teresa referred to the new poor who suffer from psycho-spiritual problems which need to be alleviated by means of practical and therapeutic action which is prompted by love. As a result, human development courses and counselling can also be seen as an aspect of the evangelisation. For example, if one looks at the programmes that are offered by many retreat and conference centres, it is striking that many of them are to do with such things as personality tests, nurturing the inner child, dreams, healing of memories, coming to terms with the shadow side of personality, increasing self-esteem, reducing stress, overcoming addictions, engaging in psychosynthesis etc. Subjects like these are animated by a search for meaning, inner freedom and self-fulfilment, hopefully within a Christian frame of reference.[27] They assume that wholeness is virtually synonymous with holiness. Clearly, this second understanding of developmental and largely apolitical evangelisation would not always be included in the perspective of liberation theology.

Thirdly, as Paul points out in Rom 8:19-22, the Good News is for all creation. But at the moment there is an ecological crisis as a result of the ruthless exploitation of the natural world and the consequent rise in levels of pollution and global warming. It could be argued that people who draw attention to these problems and try to alleviate them (e.g. devotees of Creation Spirituality and members of Greenpeace), are engaged in a form of evangelisation which often complements the therapeutic kind already mentioned. While these forms of evangelisation have a trusting and didactic dimension, the main emphasis is on the Good News as liberating action. However, it must be admitted that therapeutic and ecological forms of liberation don't fit too easily into this model.

Although St Vincent de Paul predominately espoused the didactic/sacramental model of evangelisation, there were political/developmental aspects to this approach. He repeatedly stated that love, whether affective or not, should find effective expression in concrete forms of action. He said on one occasion: 'If there were someone among you who thought of belonging to the Congregation of the Mission, just to evangelise the poor and not to help them, to provide for their spiritual needs but not their material ones, I answer that such a person that we have to help them and get help for them in every way ... This is to evangelise them in word and *deed* [my italics].'[28] 'Let us love God,' he said on another occasion, 'but let it be in the strength of our arm and in the sweat of our brow. Sentiments of love of God, of kindness, of good will, good as these may be, are often suspect if they do not result in good deeds ... They may be consoled by

27. It could be argued that in spite of the undoubted sincerity of those who put on the courses, some of them are tainted by Pelagianism and elements of New Age spirituality. Do those retreat centres put on courses on evangelisation which is a universal call of all the baptised? If not, why not?
28. *Collected Works* XII, 87.

their fervent imagination or content with the sweet sentiments they experience in prayer. They may speak like angels. But when it's a matter of working for God ... Their courage fails them. We must not deceive ourselves: all our work consists in action.'[29] On yet another occasion he said that if a poor person required the help of a Daughter of Charity who was attending the Eucharist, 'To leave God for God, that is, to leave one work of God to do another of greater obligation, is not to leave God ... What a great comfort for a good Daughter of Charity to be able to say to herself: "I am going to help my sick poor, but God will receive this action instead of the prayer I should be making just now." Then she goes off happily to wherever God calls her.'[30] It has to be said that although Vincent de Paul advocated works of mercy, he had little or no grasp of the importance of reforming the unjust political structures of the *Ancien Regime* that had often caused that poverty.[31]

This model of evangelisation has a number of strengths. It is relevant to the needs of our time. Not only is it experiential and practical in orientation, it is motivated by important biblical themes such as, 'blessed are the poor' (Lk 6:20), and 'as often as you do it to the least, you do it to me' (Mt 25:40). Besides alleviating poverty, it also tackles its systemic causes. It interprets the healing ministry of Christ in a contemporary and holistic way to include society, ecology, body, mind and soul. But this approach also has a number of weaknesses. It can neglect the importance of personal commitment to Christ and thereby end up being too humanistic, either politically or psychologically (e.g. substituting self-fulfilment for self-transcendence). This form of evangelisation is in danger of being Gnostic and syncretistic like

29. Louis Abelly, *The Life of the Venerable Servant of God Vincent de Paul*, Vol 1, (New York: New City Press, 1993), 106-107.

30. Pierre Coste, *Saint Vincent de Paul: Correspondence, Entretiens, Documents*, vol 9 (Paris: Gabalda, 1920-1925), 319.

31. Blessed Mother Teresa was much the same. She felt that she and her sisters had been led by God to engage in works of mercy for the poorest of the poor. She was convinced that they and their other collaborators were like fire men trying to put out the flames of extreme hunger and need. It was up to the police, (i.e. other church groups) to establish what caused the flames (i.e. by means of social injustice) and to recommend how to avoid them in the future.

New Age spirituality. It can be overly reliant on secular ways of thinking (e.g. the Marxist critique of society, or the psychologies of people like Jung, Rogers, Assagioli etc). This model is new and hasn't been well tested.

Conclusion

Which of these models of evangelisation is best suited to meet the needs of the times? We are living in a fast changing society where the centre of gravity is shifting from the experience of religious authority to the authority of religious experience. This shift has been confirmed by empirical research. For example, *The European Values Systems Reports* for Ireland in 1984 and 1994 have indicated that across the generations, regardless of class or education there has been a shift from firm, to less firm adherence to religious authority *per se*.[32] A MBRI poll in the *Irish Times*[33] indicated that when Irish respondents were asked whether they followed the teachings of the church or their own consciences when making serious moral decisions, 78% said they followed their consciences rather than the teaching of the church. As Karl Rahner accurately predicted many years ago: 'The spirituality of the future will not be supported, or at any rate will be much less supported sociologically by the Christian homogeneity of its situation; it will have to live much more clearly than hitherto out of a solitary, immediate experience of God and his Spirit in the individual.'[34]

Because the didactic/sacramental model of evangelisation is essentialist in an existentialist culture, it is not well adapted to the needs of the time. However the kerygmatic/charismatic and the developmental/political models of evangelisation are both pragmatic and experiential in orientation and therefore more attuned to the modern mind set. Which of them is to be favoured? It is arguable that there is a theological sequence in the models of evangelisation. Trust in God as a result of experiencing God's

32. *Values and Social Change in Ireland*, and Mc Greil, 'Religious Attitudes and Perceptions,' *Prejudice in Ireland Revisited* (Maynooth: St Patrick's College, 1996), 218-223.

33. Monday 16 December 1996, 5.

34. 'The Spirituality of the Future,' in *The Practice of Faith: A Handbook of Contemporary Spirituality*, (London: SCM Press, 1985), 21.

merciful love comes first. Secondly, comes faith as assent to the truths revealed by God. It should be the consequence of trust – as was the case in the New Testament church – and not a substitute for it. Finally, faith as trust and assent necessarily finds expression in action/praxis, which has a reciprocal effect on the way people trust God and give assent to his revealed truth. If this is so, the fiducial/kerygmatic model of evangelisation would be the logical one to start with. Then, as the example of St Vincent de Paul illustrated, it could be augmented with relevant aspects of the other two models. It is only fair to say that, by and large, the present author writes from the perspective of the kerygmatic/charismatic model of evangelisation.

The models proposed here are tentative. They would need to be revised and improved in the light of theological reflection on the experience of evangelisation. Once the models are fine tuned, a questionnaire could be developed which would enable respondents to establish which model of evangelisation was predominating at the operative, as opposed to the professed level of their experience. In the meantime, if a person answered the Church Models questionnaire they could infer from the model of church they favoured, what model of evangelisation they would be most likely to adopt. This information could be particularly helpful for would-be evangelisers in two senses. Firstly, it would help them to become more consciously aware of their operative as opposed to their professed theology of evangelisation. Secondly, it would help them to identify and respect the models informing other people's approach to evangelisation thereby facilitating mutual understanding, and co-operation.

Models Correlated

Concept	Model 1	Model 2	Model 3
Spirituality	*Programmatic* Follows an authoritative church programme	*Pneumatic* Relies on the direct inspiration of the Holy Spirit	*Autogenous* Originates in the self
Church	- Hierarchy - Sacrament	- Herald - Mystical communion	- Servant
Faith	Intellectualist Assent to truth	Fiducial Trust in God's promises	Performative Liberating action
Evangelism	*Didactic/ sacramental* Focuses on the head. Aims at orthodoxy. Catechetical instruction. Reception of the sacraments. Example of a holy life.	*Kerygmatic/ charismatic* Focuses on the heart. Aims at orthokardia. – Inspired preaching. – Verbal testimony / witness. Deeds of power e.g. healing.	*Developmental/ political* Focuses on the hands Aims at ortho-praxis. – Solidarity with the poor. – Human development and inner healing. - Action for justice, and ecology.

Recommended Reading

- John C. Haughey, 'Contemporary Spiritualities and the Spirit,' *The Conspiracy of God: The Holy Spirit in Us* (New York: Image, 1976), 78-93.
- Avery Dulles, 'The Meaning of Faith Considered in Relationship to Justice,' in *The Faith that Does Justice*, ed John C. Haughey (New York: Paulist Press, 1977).
- Avery Dulles, *Models of the Church* (New York: Doubleday, 1974).
- Timothy E. Byerley, *The Great Commission: Models of Evangelisation in American Catholicism* (New Jersey: Paulist Press, 2008).
- *The New Evangelisation: Overcoming the Obstacles*, eds Steven Boguslawski and Ralph Martin (New York: Paulist, 2008).

SECTION TWO

The Content of Basic Evangelisation

CHAPTER FOUR

Proclamation of the Kerygma: Foundation of all Evangelisation

In the book of Tobit 12:6 we read, 'Before all men, honour and proclaim God's deeds, and do not be slack in praising him. A king's secret it is prudent to keep, but the works of God are to be declared and made known.' In obedience to that word, I would like to begin this chapter by recounting one of the memorable occasions on which the things I already knew about the unconditional mercy and love of God penetrated deeper than ever before into my heart.

A number of years ago I spent months asking the Lord to experience his love more intensely than hitherto, but nothing seemed to happen. Then I went on an eight-day, directed retreat. When I arrived at the Jesuit retreat centre I was told that Mass was about to begin. When the gospel was read, I was a little disappointed when the priest said he wasn't going to give a homily. Instead he wanted us to engage in a prayer exercise. He asked all of us to close our eyes and to allow any scene from the passion of Christ to spontaneously come to mind. When I closed mine, I immediately imagined I was in the crowd watching Simon of Cyrene reluctantly helping Jesus to carry his cross to Calvary. Then, inexplicably, I imagined that the soldiers forced me to replace Simon and that I was the one helping Jesus to carry his cross. Then the priest said, 'Have you got an image from the passion in your mind? If you have, I want you to imagine that Jesus is looking at you and saying, "I'm glad that you are with me, accompanying me in my sufferings".' In my mind's eye I saw Jesus turn his head and look back at me and say that he was glad that I was helping him in his passion. I was strangely moved and my eyes became moist with tears. I must admit that I weep easily, but I rarely do so when I pray. So I was surprised that I was so emotional on this occasion. I thought to myself, what is it that has moved me so deeply? Immediately I realised that the words of Jesus, 'Pat, I'm glad that you are with me, accompanying me in my sufferings' were enormously reassuring. At that very moment copious tears poured from my eyes. Without thinking, I was vividly aware of a number of things.

Firstly, although I sometimes felt that I was being called to be a priest during my childhood and adolescence, I wasn't enthusiastic about the idea. I didn't find the prospect of being poor, celibate and obedient very attractive. But when I was 18 I had a religious experience which was so powerful that I felt that, just as Simon had been press-ganged by the soldiers when he was on his way to engage in his own worldly pursuits in Jerusalem, so God had hijacked me when I was intending to study medicine in the Royal College of Surgeons in Dublin. As a result, I joined the seminary three days later.

Secondly, during my years of formation I had sometimes hoped that I would get sick or would be asked to leave. In the event most of the other students left, and after eight years I was ordained. Although I tried to give my best to the priesthood over the years, I often felt guilty because I had a divided heart. Part of me wanted to serve God, while the other part still wanted, like Simon of Cyrene, to do my own worldly thing. I often recalled the words of Jesus in Rev 3:15: 'I know your deeds, that you are neither cold nor hot. I wish you were either one or the other! So, because you are lukewarm – neither hot nor cold – I am about to spit you out of my mouth.' I wondered how could the Lord love me, or act powerfully through me in view of the fact that I was often lukewarm? But when Jesus looked at me and said, 'I'm glad that you are accompanying me in my passion', I knew that he knew all about my divided heart, my many failures and equivocations and yet, in spite of everything he loved and accepted me the way I was. I felt that he was overlooking all my faults and honouring my good intentions while saying 'Well done good and faithful servant, my favour rests upon you.' This knowledge of the unmerited gift of divine mercy so filled me with joy, that copious tears poured down my cheeks on to the light grey shirt I was wearing. In the words of 1 Jn 4:16, I knew and believed in the love that God had for me in Christ. In the depths of my heart I received the grace to accept that I was accepted by God, and that Christ truly lived in me (cf Rom 8:1). In fact, every time I recalled the Lord's words over the next eight days, tears of joyful consolation flowed again. I knew from that experience what St Peter meant when he said, 'though you do not see him you believe in him and rejoice with unutterable and exalted joy' (1 Pet 1:8). During that blessed retreat I experienced, as never before, the liberating power of the kerygma. It travelled from my head to my heart in such a way that I could say with St Paul, 'I live by faith in the Son of God, who loved me and gave himself for me' (Gal 2:20).

Forms of Evangelisation

While the word evangelisation is not one that is used in everyday conversation, it is frequently referred to in official church documents.[1] It comes from Greek and means, 'preaching the Good News' (i.e. about the saving mercy of Jesus Christ).[2] In EN 18, Pope Paul VI explained the purpose of evangelisation when he said, 'the church evangelises when she seeks to convert, solely through the divine power of the message she proclaims, both the personal and collective consciences of people, the activities in which they engage, and the lives and concrete milieu which are theirs.' In the year 2000, Joseph Ratzinger told a congress for catechists that, 'Human life cannot be realised by itself. Our life is an open question, an incomplete project, still to be brought to fruition and realised. Each man's fundamental question is: how will this be realised – becoming man? How does one learn the art of living? Which is the path towards happiness? To evangelise means: to show this path – to teach the art of living.'[3] In 1992 The American Conference of Catholic Bishops published a national plan entitled, *Go and Make Disciples*. In par 26 it said, 'To evangelise is to bear witness, in a simple and direct way, to God revealed by Jesus Christ, in the Holy Spirit.'

1. Pope Paul VI Apostolic Exhortation, *Evangelisation in the Modern World* introduced the idea to the Catholic faithful in 1975. John Paul II repeatedly used the word in his Encyclical Letter *Mission of the Redeemer* and in his talks and homilies.
2. For a very full explanation of the word evangelisation in Greek, see William Barclay, 'Euaggelion: The Good News' in *New Testament Words* (London: SCM, 1964), 101-6.
3. http://www.ewtn.com/new_evangelization/Ratzinger.htm

The call to evangelise applies to all baptised Christians whether clerical or lay. In CCL 781 we read, 'Because the whole church is of its nature missionary and the work of evangelisation is to be considered a fundamental duty of the people of God, all Christ's faithful must be conscious of the responsibility to play their part in missionary activity.'[4] Canon 211 says, 'All Christ's faithful, have the obligation and the right to strive so that the divine message of salvation may more and more reach all people of all times and all places.' It is worth noting that CCC 905 adds, 'Lay people fulfil their prophetic mission by evangelisation, that is, the proclamation of Christ by word and testimony of life.' For lay people, 'this evangelisation ... acquires a specific property and peculiar efficacy because it is accomplished in the ordinary circumstances of the world.'[5] In EN 27, Pope Paul wrote about the content of evangelisation: 'Evangelisation will also always contain – as the foundation, centre, and at the same time, summit of its dynamism – a clear proclamation that, in Jesus Christ, the Son of God made man, who died and rose from the dead, salvation is offered to all men, as a gift of God's grace and mercy.'

As it is used in church teaching, the word evangelisation describes a number of important and interrelated activities. John Paul II pointed out in par 18 of his Apostolic Exhortation, *Catechesi tradendae* (hereafter CT), that evangelisation, 'is a rich, complex and dynamic reality, made up of elements or one could say moments, that are essential and different from each other, and that must be kept in view simultaneously.' It is important that Catholics appreciate the fact that there are different ways of evangelising in order to avoid having the myopic impression that the particular way an individual or group feels called to evangelise is the only way. Here are a number of the more important elements.

Pre-evangelisation refers to the presence and activities of Christians in non-Christian environments. By firstly witnessing to the Lord by means of such things as lives well lived and service to the local community (e.g. in the form of health care, education, and action for justice), these Christians are engaging in re-

4. (London: Collins, 1983), 143.
5. (Dublin: Veritas, 1994), 210.

mote preparation for the verbal proclamation of the gospel. It is a bit like a farmer ploughing the earth in preparation for planting the seed. As Pope Paul VI said in EN 21, 'Take a Christian or a handful of Christians who, in the midst of their own community, show their capacity for understanding and acceptance, their sharing of life and destiny with other people, their solidarity with the efforts of all for whatever is noble and good. Let us suppose that, in addition, they radiate in an altogether simple and unaffected way their faith in values that go beyond current values, and their hope in something that is not seen and that one would not dare to imagine. Through this wordless witness these Christians stir up irresistible questions in the hearts of those who see how they live: Why are they like this? Why do they live in this way? What or who is it that inspires them? Why are they in our midst? Such a witness is already a silent proclamation of the Good News and a very powerful and effective one. Here we have an initial act of evangelisation.'

Basic, initial, primary, kerygmatic or new evangelisation refers to preaching the core truths of faith about the saving death and resurrection of Jesus to people. There are three forms of this.

- Preaching the kerygma to non-Christian unbelievers who have never heard it before.
- Re-evangelisation, where the good news is preached to people whose ancestors were Christian although they are not. This is the case in European cities where nominally Christian people no longer baptise their children. In Italy and Ireland for example, many people officially and legally de-register as Catholics.
- New evangelisation, where the Good News is proclaimed to baptised people who for all intents and purposes know very little about it.[6] It seeks to relate the Gospel to the circumstances of their lives. As Pope Paul VI stated in EN 63: 'Evangelisation loses much of its force and effectiveness if it does not take into consideration the actual people to whom it is addressed, if it does not use their language, their signs and symbols, if it does not answer the questions they ask, and if it does not have an impact in their concrete life.' John Paul II,

6. Pat Collins, 'What is the New Evangelisation?' in *Gifts of the Spirit & the New Evangelisation*, 16-36.

the prophet of the New Evangelisation, spoke about the need for a proclamation of the gospel which would be new in ardour, method and forms of expression in such a way as to take into account the unique characteristics of contemporary culture. Raniero Cantalamessa has rightly observed: 'The basic proclamation must be presented at least once, clearly and tersely, not only to catechumens but to all Christians, given that the majority of today's faithful have never passed through the catechumenate.'[7]

The proclamation of the kerygma to any of these categories of people can evoke a response of faith. As St Paul said in Rom 10:17: 'So faith comes from what is heard, and what is heard comes from the preaching [i.e. the inspired word or kerygma] of Christ.' This form of evangelisation will be the focus not only of much of this chapter but of the entire book.

Catechetical instruction or teaching[8] which builds on the basic truths by telling people more about their faith and the way it should be lived as disciples of Christ. In CT 20 John Paul II wrote: 'The aim of catechesis is to be the teaching and maturation stage, that is to say, the period in which the Christian, having accepted by faith the person of Jesus Christ as the one Lord and having given him complete adherence by sincere conversion of heart, endeavours to know better this Jesus to whom he has entrusted himself: to know his mystery, the kingdom of God proclaimed by him, the requirements and promises contained in his gospel message, and the paths that he has laid down for any one who wishes to follow him.' As a response to the Second Vatican Council a *General Catechetical Directory* was published in 1971. Following further catechetical developments each national hierarchy was encouraged to produce a national catechetical directory. The American bishops did this is 2005. The Irish bishops have received a draft version called, *Be Good News: Draft National Directory for Catechesis* (2007, 2008) which will have to be approved by the Vatican before it can be published.

Evangelisation as apologetics refers to rational argument which

7. *The Holy Spirit in the Life of Jesus* (Collegeville: The Liturgical Press, 1994), 49.
8. CT 18.

displays the reasonableness of faith.[9] An apologist is someone who defends the legitimacy of Christian teaching from the criticisms and misrepresentations of its detractors. As 1 Pet 3:15 says, 'Always be prepared to give a reason (*apologian*) for the hope that is in you. Do it with gentleness and reverence.' The late C. S. Lewis from Belfast was a gifted apologist in this sense. His book *Mere Christianity*, which was nominated as the best Christian book of the twentieth century by *Christianity Today* magazine, was an outstanding example of this form of evangelisation. Catholic apologists, Peter Kreeft of Boston College and Scott Hahn of the Franciscan University of Steubenville are well known for their books on apologetics. Among Protestants the apologetic books of Lee Strobel are also helpful.[10]

Enculturation of the faith[11] (i.e. relating Christian truths to contemporary culture while at the same time changing the culture in the light of those truths). Pope John Paul II said in RM 52, that enculturation, 'means the intimate transformation of authentic cultural values through their integration in Christianity and the insertion of Christianity in the various human cultures.' In par 40 of the Apostolic Letter, *Tertio millennio adveniente* (hereafter TMA) he added: 'Christianity, while remaining completely true to itself, with unswerving fidelity to the proclamation of the gospel and the tradition of the church, will also reflect the different faces of cultures and peoples in which it is received and takes root.' In a way, that is really what the phrase 'New Evangelisation' means. While the content of the Christian message remains the same it needs to be new in its forms of expression. John Paul II has recommended St Paul's speech at the Areopagus in Athens as a model of evangelisation as enculturation (cf Acts 17:16-34).[12] Paul entered into 'dialogue' with the

---

9. Cardinal Avery Dulles, 'The Rebirth of Apologetics,' in *Church and Society: The Laurence J. McGinley Lectures, 1988-2007*, 430-42.

10. These are some of his publications: *The Case for Faith: A Journalist Investigates the Toughest Objections to Christianity; The Case for a Creator: A Journalist Investigates Scientific Evidence That Points Toward God; The Case for Christ: A Journalist's Personal Investigation of the Evidence for Jesus; The Case for Easter: Journalist Investigates the Evidence for the Resurrection.*

11. RM 25, 37, 52-54, 76; NMI 40.

12. *Crossing the Threshold of Hope*, 106.

cultural and religious values of the Athenians. He appealed to the Greek world's belief in divinity as responsible for the origin and existence of the universe. He quoted two Greeks: Epimenides of Knossos (sixth century BC) and Aratus of Soli (third century BC). In doing so he attempted to show his listeners that God was already present in their lives as Creator and Sustainer. But to recognise him as he really is, the Athenians would need to abandon their false gods. Nowadays, Christians need to enter into dialogue with such things as science, technology, postmodernism etc.

Interreligious dialogue[13] (i.e. talking to people of other faiths in order to discover common ground and to demonstrate how Christian truth fulfils all that is best in their religions). In par 2 of *Nostra Aetate* (hereafter AE), the Second Vatican Council said that, 'The Catholic Church rejects nothing which is true and holy in these religions ... the church therefore has this exhortation for her sons prudently and lovingly, through dialogue and collaboration with the followers of other religions, and in witness of Christian faith and life, acknowledge, preserve, and promote the spiritual and moral goods found among these men, as well as the values in their society and culture.' In 1991 The Pontifical Council on Interreligious Dialogue said in par 3 of a document entitled, *Dialogue and Proclamation*, that interreligious dialogue, 'is one of the integral elements of the church's evangelising mission.' In par 3 of a companion document *Dialogue and Mission*, we read: 'Dialogue means all positive and constructive interreligious relations with individuals and communities of other faiths and are directed at mutual understanding in obedience to truth and respect for freedom.' In RM 55, John Paul II wrote: 'Dialogue should be conducted and implemented with the conviction that the church is the ordinary means of salvation and that she alone possesses the fullness of the means of salvation.' In 2000, before he was elected Pope, Cardinal Ratzinger said that Christians had to be careful to avoid a relativist position which would see their religion as merely one of many valid ways to God. In par 5 of the Declaration, *Dominus Iesus*, he wrote, 'Only the revelation of Jesus Christ, therefore, introduces

13. RM 55-57; Avery Dulles, 'The Travails of Dialogue,' *Church and Society*, 221-33.

into our history a universal and ultimate truth ... By this revelation then, the deepest truth about God and the salvation of man shines forth in Christ, who is at the same time the mediator and the fullness of all revelation.' In 2001 Pope John Paul echoed those points in (TMA 54-56).

Action for justice and peace is also an integral aspect of evangelisation.[14] In 1971 a Synod of Bishops said in par 6 of a document entitled *Justice in the World* that the social ministries of the church are an essential part of its mission: 'Action on behalf of justice and participation in the transformation of the world fully appear to us as a constitutive dimension of the preaching of the gospel, or, in other words, of the church's mission for the redemption of the human race and its liberation from every oppressive situation.' As St James wrote: 'If one of you says to a brother or sister, "Go, I wish you well; keep warm and well fed", but does nothing about his physical needs, what good is it?' (Jas 2:16). In EN 9, Pope Paul VI said that evangelisation consists among other things of, 'liberation from everything that oppresses us.' In EN 31 the Holy Father said, it is impossible, 'that in evangelisation one could or should ignore the importance of the problems so much discussed today, concerning justice, liberation, development and peace in the world. This would be to forget the lesson which comes to us from the gospel concerning love of our neighbour who is suffering and in need.'

Who is to be evangelised?

The remainder of this chapter will focus on basic, initial or kerygmatic evangelisation because of its foundational importance. Unless people have experienced the liberating power of the kerygma the other forms of evangelisation will bear little or no fruit. As was mentioned in *Gifts of the Spirit and the New Evangelisation,*[15] the faithful who engage in kerygmatic proclamation focus on the following three categories of people. It occurred to me while reading the parable of The Sower that those who 'with a noble and good heart, who hear the word, retain it, and by persevering produce a crop' (Lk 8:15) are Christ's true

14. See Benedict XVI, (CV 15).
15. 23-5.

disciples who harvest a large crop of souls by means of effective evangelisation.

1. Churchgoers who are not yet fully evangelised in the sense that they have not fully committed themselves to Jesus as the Son of God, the One who forgives their sins and fills them with an awareness of the love of God. As Paul VI said in EN 15, 'The church is an evangeliser, but she begins by being evangelised herself ... She needs to listen unceasingly to what she must believe, to her reasons for hoping, to the new commandment of love.' In terms of the parable of The Sower, these are the people 'who hear, but as they go on their way they are choked by life's worries, riches and pleasures, and they do not mature' (Lk 8:14-15), in the sense that they fail to carry out the great commission to evangelise others.

2. The unchurched (i.e. those secularised, inactive Catholics who only attend church on rare occasions). They could also be referred to as cultural or nominal Catholics. The former nomenclature refers to the fact that they have an emotional affinity with the Catholic Church, the latter indicates that they are Catholic in name but not necessarily in either belief or practice. Raniero Cantalamessa has quite rightly suggested that many of these people are Deists rather than orthodox Christians in the sense that they tend to believe in a supreme being rather than the Trinity. Often these nominal Christians will espouse beliefs that are inimical to Christian belief such as reincarnation or that Christianity is merely one of many valid ways to God. Speaking about the unchurched, GS 8 says: 'In the past it was the exception to repudiate God and religion to the point of abandoning them, and then only in individual cases; but nowadays it seems a matter of course to reject them as incompatible with scientific progress and a new kind of humanism.' In similar vein, Paul VI said in EN 56: 'There are a great numbers of people who have been baptised and, while they have not formally renounced their membership of the church, are as it were on the fringe of it and do not live according to her teaching.' Pope John Paul said in EE 47: 'It can be said as the Synod emphasised that this challenge frequently consists not so much in baptising new converts as in enabling those already baptised to be converted to Christ and his gospel, in our communities we need to be seriously con-

cerned about bringing the gospel of hope to all those who are far from the faith or who have abandoned the practice of Christianity.' It has been suggested that there are four categories of the unchurched:

a) Always unchurched (Have never been involved)
b) De-churched (Attended church as a child)
c) Friendly unchurched (Not particularly antagonistic to the church)
d) Hostile unchurched (Angry at the church because of negative experiences)[16]

In terms of the parable of The Sower, the unchurched are those, 'who receive the word with joy when they hear it, but they have no root. They believe for a while, but in the time of testing they fall away' (Lk 8:13-14). In other words they lapse from the practice of their faith.

3. Unbelievers (i.e. atheists and agnostics, together with people who belong to non-Christian faiths who do not yet know Christ or his saving power).[17] It is worth noting that in his Encyclical Letter, *Dominum et vivificantem* (hereafter DV), John Paul II noted the fact that due to the insidious lies of the evil one, there is a growing suspicion in Western culture that instead of being the friend of man, God is our enemy. In DV 38, he wrote: 'God the Creator is placed in a state of suspicion, indeed of accusation, in the mind of the creature. For the first time in human history there appears the perverse genius of suspicion.' The Pope then went on to observe that the devil, 'seeks to falsify Good itself; the absolute Good, which in the work of creation has manifested itself as the Good which expresses itself ... as creative love.' Later on he said in DV 38: 'Man will be inclined to see in God primarily a limitation of himself, and not the source of his own freedom and the fullness of good. We see this confirmed in the modern age, when the atheistic ideologies seek to

16. Ed Stetzer, Richie Stanley, & Jason Hayes, *Lost and Found: The Younger Unchurched and the Churches that Reach Them* (Nashville: B&H Publishing, 2009), 9-10.

17. While GS 16 says without explaining how it comes about, that those who, through no fault of their own, have not heard of Christ live by their consciences and are not deceived by the devil, can be saved, but only with difficulty.

root out religion on the grounds that religion causes the radical alienation of man, as if man were dispossessed of his own humanity when, accepting the idea of God, he attributes to God what belongs to man, and exclusively to man! Hence a process of thought ... in which the rejection of God has reached the point of declaring his death.' In DV 38, John Paul said, 'Satan manages to sow in man's soul the seed of opposition ... Man is challenged to become the adversary of God!' In terms of the parable of the Sower, many atheists, agnostics and other unbelievers are 'the ones who hear, and then the devil comes and takes away the word from their hearts, so that they may not believe and be saved' (Lk 8:12).

The Kerygma in the New Testament

The Second Vatican Council introduced the notion of a hierarchy of truth when it said in par 11 of *Unitatis redintegratio* (hereafter UR): 'When comparing doctrines with one another, they [theologians] should remember that in Catholic doctrine there exists a "hierarchy" of truths, since they vary in their relation to the fundamental Christian faith.' Kerygma is a word derived from Greek meaning, 'preaching' or 'announcement' of an event by a herald. In the New Testament the kerygma usually involves three elements. Firstly, there is the content of the Christian proclamation (cf Rom 16:25; 1 Cor 1:21). Secondly, as Karl Rahner and Hebert Vorgrimler pointed out in their *Theological Dictionary*, 'the kerygma is the primary source and norm of dogma and theology and finds the most intense fulfilment of its own nature in the word of faith that is spoken to the individual.'[18] Thirdly, unless people have experienced the power of the kerygma, catechesis and reception of the sacraments are not very effective because instead of being built on the rock of intimate relationship with Jesus they are built on the sand of notional belief and external ritual.

a) Jesus and the kerygma

It would be true to say that the kerygma of the early church was rooted in Jesus' proclamation of the Good News of the coming

18. (New York: Herder & Herder, 1968), 250. See also, Alfonso M. Nebreda, *Kerygma in Crisis?* (Chicago: Loyola University Press, 1965).

of the kingdom of God, (i.e. the reign of God by means of his unconditional and unrestricted mercy and love in and through the ministry of Jesus Christ). There is an outstanding biblical example of what this means. In Jn 7:48-49 we read how the temple police had been sent to arrest Jesus who was preaching to the poor, the uneducated, illiterate peasants who neither knew or observed the minutiae of the Jewish law. They returned without their prisoner because they felt unable to arrest Jesus due to the sheer eloquence and authority of his preaching. The temple authorities said to the police, 'Has any of the rulers or of the Pharisees believed in him? No! But this mob that knows nothing of the law – *there is a curse on them* [my italics].' In Gal 3:10 St Paul explained why the Jewish authorities said what they did: 'All who rely on observing the law are under a curse, for it is written: "Cursed is everyone who does not continue to do everything written in the Book of the Law".'[19] As a result, the poor were under unending condemnation. They already endured misery in this life and could only expect to experience damnation in the next.

When Jesus enunciated his mission statement in his local synagogue in Nazareth, he said that he had been anointed to bring good news to the poor, specifically to the people who were under the curse (cf Lk 4:18). He told the congregation in his local synagogue that the just condemnation of God had been lifted at this time of jubilee when all debts were being cancelled. As he proclaimed in his beatitudes, 'Blessed are you who are poor, for yours is the kingdom of God' (Lk 6:20). This was made possible because Jesus acted as our scapegoat: 'The Lord has laid on him the iniquity of us all' (Is 53:6). It is interesting to note that St Paul appreciated the fact that Jesus not only lifted the curse from the poor, he took it upon his own sinless shoulders. As Paul declared, in 2 Cor 5:21: 'God made him who had no sin to be sin for us, so that in him we might become the righteousness of God [i.e. what we ought to be, approved and acceptable and in right relationship with him].' So Paul added: 'Christ redeemed us from the curse of the law by becoming a curse for us, for it is written: "Cursed is everyone who is hung on a tree".' He redeemed us in order that the blessing given to Abraham might

19. For example, see the twelve curses listed in Deut 27:14-26.

come to the Gentiles through Christ Jesus, so that by faith we might receive the promise of the Spirit' (Gal 3:13-14).

Jesus repeatedly proclaimed the coming of the 'kingdom of God' (cf Mt 3:2, 17; Mk 1:15) or 'the kingdom of heaven' (cf Mt 13:44-45, 18:3) in his words, relationships and deeds.[20] In 2000 Joseph Ratzinger said in a talk on the new evangelisation: 'The keyword of the proclamation of Jesus is: the kingdom of God. But the kingdom of God is not a thing, a social or political structure, a utopia. The kingdom of God is God. Kingdom of God means: God exists. God is alive. God is present and acts in the world, in our – in my life. God is not a faraway "ultimate cause", God is not the "great architect" of deism, who created the machine of the world and is no longer part of it – on the contrary: God is the most present and decisive reality in each and every act of my life, in each and every moment of history.' The parable of the prodigal son encapsulates the good news in words. The younger son represented the poor who failed to keep the law, and the elder son represented the Pharisees who did try to abide by the law. The younger son felt he was under condemnation because he had failed to observe the law. The elder son believed that he had earned his father's favour by being dutiful and observing the law at all times. However, Jesus said that both sons were mistaken. They presumed that the father's (i.e. God's) love was conditional, whereas in actual fact it was unconditional, a free, unmerited gift. Both sons were invited to the kind of conversion that leads to a change in their thinking about God and to trust in the offer of his unconditional mercy and love.[21] Whereas the younger son was able to change his image of God, the elder son

20. The proclamation of the coming of the kingdom, i.e. *basileia* in Greek, is the central theme in the preaching of Jesus. CCC 2816 says that the word 'kingdom' can be translated as 'kingship', 'kingdom' or 'reign'. See also RM 12-20.

21. Leon-Dufour's *Dictionary of the New Testament* (San Francisco: Harper & Row, 1980, 146 indicates that the Greek word for repentance is *metanoia,* which literally means 'a change of mind or mentality.' The English word *repentance* usually suggests a change in behaviour. It would probably be true to say that a person's behaviour will change after his or her thinking about God has changed e.g. from the Pharisaic notion of the God of conditional love to the Christian notion of the God of unconditional love.

was unable to do so. As a result, the prodigal son entered into a new relationship with his father who clothed him with the cloak of honour, endowed him with the ring of his authority, provided him with the shoes of a beloved member of the household, and celebrated their new found relationship by killing the fatted calf. As the scriptures tell us: 'I tell you that in the same way there will be more rejoicing in heaven over one sinner who repents than over ninety-nine righteous persons who do not need to repent' (Lk 15:7). There is a profound meditation on the evangelical meaning and relevance of the parable of the prodigal son in section four of Pope John Paul's Encyclical Letter, *Dives et misercordia* (hereafter DM), and in pars 5-6 of the Apostolic Exhortation, *Reconciliatio et paenitentia* (hereafter RP). Commenting on the parable in DM 6 he says: 'The true and proper meaning of mercy does not consist only in looking, however penetratingly and compassionately, at moral, physical or material evil: mercy is manifested in its true and proper aspect when it restores to value, promotes and draws good from all the forms of evil existing in the world and in man. Understood in this way, mercy constitutes the fundamental content of the messianic message of Christ and the constitutive power of his mission.'

The story about the woman caught in adultery in Jn 8:1-11 was an example of the Good News expressed in and through relationship. The Pharisees were out to trap Jesus. The Samaritan lady was guilty of the offence, and Deut 22:23-24 stipulated that, as a married woman, she should be stoned to death. However, Roman law did not allow the Jews to execute a person for religious reasons. So they asked Jesus what they should do. If he said, 'Stone her in accordance with the law,' he would have been disobeying civil law and denying his own teachings on divine mercy (cf Jn 3:17; 12:47). If, on the other hand, he said: 'Don't stone her,' he would have been contradicting precepts of scripture. In the event, with wisdom, characteristic of Solomon of old, Jesus changed the whole focus of the debate by saying: 'Let him who is without sin among you be the first to throw a stone at her.' In other words, if anyone present is innocent of sin, if he has never lusted after a woman in his heart (cf Mt 5:27ff) let him be the first to dispense justice. One by one, beginning with the eldest, all the men slinked away because, all of them had to acknowledge their own guilty secrets and therefore their need for mercy. Jesus and the woman were left facing one another. As St Augustine observed, she was the personification of *miseria* (i.e. misery), while he was the personification of *misercordia* (i.e. mercy). Measured against his own criterion of sinlessness, Jesus had a right to stone the woman. But he didn't exercise that right. In Jn 8:10 we are told that he asked, 'Has no one condemned you?' She said, 'No one Lord.' And Jesus said, 'Neither do I condemn you; go and do not sin again.' What wonderful, liberating words. Later on, they were to find an echo in Rom 8:1: 'There is now no condemnation for those who are in Christ Jesus,' i.e. for those who are open to God's loving self-communication in the Holy Spirit.

Echoing Augustine, St Bernard, wrote on one occasion: 'The whole of the spiritual life turns on these two things: we are troubled when we contemplate ourselves and our sorrow brings salvation; when we contemplate God we are restored, so that we receive consolation from the joy of the Holy Spirit. From the contemplation of ourselves (i.e. misery), we gain fear and humility, from the contemplation of God (i.e. mercy) hope and love.'[22] Shortly before his death, Pope Paul VI told Fr John Magee, later Bishop of Cloyne in Ireland, how he had been deeply influenced by the two words, misery and mercy in Jn 8:1-8. 'Always, in all of us,' he said, 'there is a tension between my misery and God's mercy. *The whole spiritual life of all of us lies between these two poles* [my italics]. If I open myself to the action of God and the Holy Spirit and let them do with me what they will, then my tension becomes joyous and I feel within myself a greater desire to come to him and receive his mercy; more than ever I recognise the need to be forgiven, to receive the gift of mercy. Then I feel the need to say thanks, and so my whole life becomes a thanksgiving, a Eucharist to God because he has saved me, redeemed me, drawn me to himself in love. It is not anything I have done in my life that saves me, but God's mercy.'[23] It is the graced power of the kerygma that makes God's mercy present to our misery in a transforming way.

---

22. *Sermo 5 de diversis*, 4-5: *Opera omnia*, ed Cisterc. 6, 1 (1970), 103-4.
23. Peter Hebblethwaite, *Paul VI: The First Modern Pope* (London: HarperCollins, 1993), 696.

Jesus also manifested the reality of the Good News he proclaimed by demonstrating it in his deeds; by dining with public outcasts and sinners, and by performing healings, miracles and exorcisms, especially for the poor. So when we say that Jesus proclaimed the coming of the kingdom of God,[24] we need to recall what John Paul II said in RM 18: 'The kingdom of God is not a concept, a doctrine, or a programme subject to free interpretation, but it is before all else a person with the face and name of Jesus of Nazareth.' It was Jesus who revealed the incomprehensible love of his Father by his teaching, relationships, and deeds, especially his glorious death and resurrection. To see him is to see the loving kindness of the heart of our God which has visited us like the dawn from on high (cf Lk 1:77-78).

b) St Paul and the Kergyma

We see from the New Testament writings how the early disciples preached the core teachings of salvation in Christ to both Jewish and Gentile audiences. Centuries later it was expressed in the creeds of the early church such as the Apostles Creed. The message of the apostles clearly had its roots in the proclamation of Jesus. Scholars such as C. H. Dodd,[25] Raniero Cantalamessa,[26] and others have studied the kerygma which was preached in the early church. As A. M. Hunter says in his book *Introducing New Testament Theology*, if a reporter was to summarise the typi-

24. Paul VI said in EN 9: 'As the kernel and centre of his Good News, Christ proclaims salvation, this great gift of God which is liberation from everything that oppresses man but which is above all liberation from sin and the Evil One, in the joy of knowing God and being known by him, of seeing him, and of being given over to him.'

25. *The Apostolic Preaching and Its Developments* (New York: Harper & Row, 1964). Dodd said that there are six main points. (1) The Age of Fulfillment has dawned, the 'latter days' foretold by the prophets. (2) This has taken place through the birth, life, ministry, death and resurrection of Jesus Christ. (3) By virtue of the resurrection, Jesus has been exalted at the right hand of God as Messianic head of the new Israel. (4) The Holy Spirit in the church is the sign of Christ's present power and glory. (5) The Messianic Age will reach its consummation in the return of Christ. (6) An appeal is made for repentance with the offer of forgiveness, the Holy Spirit, and salvation.

26. 'Prophetic Anointing: The Spirit urges Jesus and the Church on – to evangelise,' *The Holy Spirit in the Life of Jesus*, 38-50.

cal Christian sermon of the time it would contain the following typical elements: 'The prophesies are fulfilled, and the New Age has dawned. The Messiah, born of David's seed, has appeared. He is Jesus of Nazareth, God's Servant, who went about doing good and healing by God's power, was crucified according to God's purpose, was raised from the dead on the third day, is now exalted to God's right hand, and will come again in glory for judgement. Therefore let all repent and believe and be baptised for the forgiveness of sins and the gift of the Holy Spirit.'[27]

In his excellent book, *The Central Message of the New Testament*, Joachim Jeremias made the important observation that, 'It was Paul's greatness that he understood the message of Jesus as no other New Testament writer did. He was the faithful interpreter of Jesus. This is particularly true of his doctrine of justification. It is not of his own making but in substance conveys the central message of Jesus, as it is condensed in the first beatitude, "Blessed are you poor, for yours is the kingdom of God" (Lk 6:20).'[28] Raniero Cantalamessa makes a similar point when he says that when St Paul talks about the justice of God it is a theological equivalent of Jesus' notion of the coming of the kingdom.[29] St Paul himself acknowledged in 1 Cor 15:3-4 that his gospel was derived from that of Jesus, '*what I received* [my italics] I passed on to you as of first importance: that Christ died for our sins according to the scriptures, that he was buried, that he was raised on the third day according to the scriptures.' Paul succinctly summarised the kerygma when he talked about Jesus 'who was put to death for our trespasses and raised for our justification' (Rom 4:25). He realised from his own personal experience that we are put in right relationship with God not by good works but by the faith that trusts solely in the saving grace of Christ which is available to us as an unmerited gift because of the sacrificial love of Jesus. As Paul testified: 'I have been crucified with Christ and I no longer live, but Christ lives in me. The

---

27. (London: SCM, 1966), 66.
28. (London: SCM Press, 1965), 70. James D. G. Dunn makes a similar point in, *The Theology of Paul the Apostle* (London: T & T Clark, 2003), 174-9.
29. *Life in Christ: A Spiritual Commentary on the Letter to the Romans* (Collegeville: Liturgical Press, 1990), 37.

life I live in the body, I live by faith in the Son of God, who loved me and gave himself for me' (Gal 2:20).

In Rom 5:6-11 he explained, 'You see, at just the right time, when we were still powerless, Christ died for the ungodly. Very rarely will anyone die for a righteous man, though for a good man someone might possibly dare to die. But God demonstrates his own love for us in this: While we were still sinners, Christ died for us. Since we have now been justified by his blood, how much more shall we be saved from God's wrath through him! For if, when we were God's enemies, we were reconciled to him through the death of his Son, how much more, having been reconciled, shall we be saved through his life!' As a result, Paul was firmly convinced that, 'a man is not justified by observing the law, but by faith in Jesus Christ. So we, too, have put our faith in Christ Jesus that we may be justified by faith in Christ and not by observing the law, because by observing the law no one will be justified' (Gal 2:16). Once the words of the kerygma make their home in our hearts through faith, Paul could say, 'The word is near you, in your mouth and in your heart,' that is, the word of faith that we preach (kerygma) for, if you confess with your mouth and believe in your heart that God raised him from the dead, you will be saved' (Rom 10:8-9).

It seems to me that for Paul, the resurrection of Jesus had the greatest significance. By his death on the cross, Jesus had been reduced to radical powerlessness, devoid of breath, heartbeat, or life. His powerlessness was symbolic of the powerlessness of the sinner who desires to be put at rights with God. But just as Jesus was vindicated by the Father when he raised him from death to new life as victor over sin, Satan, death and suffering, so those who trust in Jesus are raised by God's power from the darkness of sin and the prospect of the second death, (i.e. eternal separation from God) to new life in Christ. That is why St Paul could often write in a paradoxical way. Firstly, he talked about the weakness of God in Christ, 'God's weakness is greater than human strength' (1 Cor 1:25). Secondly, Paul the sinner experienced this paradox himself. He said, 'For God has bound all men over to disobedience so that he may have mercy on them all' (Rom 11:32); and again, 'But where sin increased, grace increased all the more, so that, just as sin reigned in death, so also grace might reign through righteousness to bring eternal life through Jesus Christ our Lord' (Rom 5:20-21). Thirdly, Paul saw the implications of saving grace for his whole life. 'God's power is made perfect in weakness, therefore I will boast all the more gladly about my weaknesses, so that Christ's power may rest on me ... for when I am weak then I am strong' (2 Cor 12:9). 'I can do everything through him who gives me strength' (Phil 4:13).

It is not surprising to find that the Pauline notion of justification continued on in the post apostolic period. The letter from the Christians in Rome to their fellow believers in Corinth between AD 95 and 97 is one of the earliest documents outside the New Testament. In 1 Clement 32.4 we read: 'And so we, having been called through God's will in Christ Jesus, are not justified through ourselves or through our own wisdom or understanding or piety, or works that we have done in holiness of heart, but through faith, by which the Almighty God has justified all who have existed from the beginning; to whom be the glory for ever and ever. Amen.'[30]

Conclusion

In the light of what has been said, is it any wonder that Pope John Paul II wrote in RM 16: 'The preaching of the early church was centred on the proclamation of Jesus Christ, with whom the kingdom was identified. Now, as then, there is a need to unite the proclamation of the kingdom of God (the content of Jesus' own kerygma) and the proclamation of the Christ-event (the kerygma of the apostles). The two proclamations are complementary; each throws light on the other.' Taken together, Paul was so right when he said in Rom 10:15: 'How beautiful are the feet of those who bring good news!'

30. *The Apostolic Fathers in English*, 57.

Recommended Reading

- Pat Collins, *Gifts of the Spirit & the New Evangelisation* (Dublin: Columba, 2009).
- C. H. Dodd, *The Apostolic Preaching and its Developments* (New York: Harper & Row, 1964).
- Joachim Jeremias, *The Central Message of the New Testament* (London: SCM Press, 1965).
- Raniero Cantalamessa, *Life in Christ: A Spiritual Commentary on the Letter to the Romans* (Collegeville: The Liturgical Press, 1990); *The Holy Spirit in the Life of Jesus* (Collegeville: The Liturgical Press, 1994).
- Alfonso M. Nebreda, *Kerygma in Crisis?* (Chicago: Loyola University Press, 1965).

CHAPTER FIVE

The Kerygma Today

Some time ago Fr Raniero Cantalamessa preached about the kerygma to the Pope and a number of his cardinals.[1] It is interesting to see that he said, 'Gratuitous justification by faith in Christ is the heart of kerygmatic preaching, and it is a shame that this in turn, is practically absent from the ordinary preaching in the church.' He went on to note that at the time of the Reformation, Luther and later other Protestant reformers tended to say we are justified by faith alone. By way of reaction Catholics insisted that without works a person could not be justified. Catholics rightly believe that while one is not saved by good works, one cannot be saved without them. As Jas 2:23-24 reminds us: 'You see that a person is justified by what he does and not by faith alone.' As a result of the sixteenth century split, however, Catholics have often failed to sufficiently emphasise the vital importance of faith in salvation, while Protestants have often failed to stress the need for good works.

In 1999 this imbalance was corrected in a Joint Declaration on Justification of historic significance, which was published by the Lutheran World Federation and the Catholic Church. Par 15 says: 'Together we confess: By grace alone, in faith in Christ's saving work and not because of any merit on our part, we are accepted by God and receive the Holy Spirit, who renews our hearts while equipping and calling us to good works.'[2] It seems to me that this sentence incorporates our Lord's principle of reciprocity which is mentioned in Luke 6:38, 'Give, and it will be given to you.' Let's look at the first part, 'By grace alone, through faith in Christ's saving work and not because of any

1. 'The Righteousness That Comes From Faith in Christ,' Vatican City (16 December 2005).

2. For enlightening comments on the declaration see Avery Dulles, 'Justification Today: A New Ecumenical Breakthrough,' *Church and Society*, 306-17.

merit on our part, we are accepted by God and receive the Holy Spirit.' It asserts that although, in terms of strict justice, we deserve God's judgement and condemnation on account of our sins, when we look trustingly into Christ's merciful eyes, expecting only mercy, we receive only mercy through the cleansing power of his Holy Spirit. It is a glorious truth, the very essence of the Good News. The second half of the sentence goes on to say that the Holy Spirit 'renews our hearts while equipping and calling us to good works.' Those good works are a necessary expression of the grace of justification which has already been received, but not a means of earning it. In other words, having received gratuitously from God, we have to give in like manner to other people. That notion is implicit in Lk 6:36, 'Be merciful, just as your Father is merciful. Do not judge, and you will not be judged; do not condemn, and you will not be condemned. Forgive, and you will be forgiven.' What is implied here, is the fact that, while God's unmerited mercy is always available to us, we can only experience it's liberating power as long as we are willing to be merciful to those who have injured and wronged us. So instead of judging or condemning them, as they might deserve in terms of strict justice, we should refrain from doing so while offering the wrongdoers the unmerited gift of our mercy.

Implicit in this notion of justification by grace is a distinction which has been made by Catholic theologians since the time of St Augustine between operative and co-operative grace. In biblical terms operative grace is a replacement of the heart of stone with a heart of flesh (cf Ezch 26:26). Co-operative grace is the heart of flesh becoming effective in good works. As Bernard Lonergan has observed: 'Operative grace is religious conversion. Co-operative grace is the effectiveness of conversion, the gradual movement towards a full and complete transformation of the whole of one's living and feeling, one's thoughts, words, deeds, and omissions.'[3] Preaching the kerygma leads to the experience of operative grace, whereas catechesis facilitates growth by means of co-operative grace.

As has already been noted, par 15 of the Joint Declaration on Justification is a very good modern summary of the kerygma.

3. 'Conversion' in *Conversion: Perspectives on Personal and Social Transformation*, 18.

This kind of statement of belief lies at the heart of a number of kerygmatic courses being used to good effect in the church nowadays such as *The Rite of Christian Initiation of Adults* (RCIA), Life in the Spirit Seminars, Alpha, Café, Philip Retreats, Cursillo Weekends etc. For more on these courses see chapter ten.

There are many descriptions of the kerygma ranging from St Paul's well known acclamation 'Jesus is Lord' (1 Cor 12:3), through the Apostolic Fathers of the Church, to the Nicean Creed. For example, the *Letter to Diognetus* contains an eloquent expression of the kerygma in chapters eight and nine. In chapter eight the author describes fallen human nature as follows: 'He left us to live as we pleased, giving free reign to our unruly instincts and being at the mercy of sensuality and lust.' A little later he explained: 'His purpose was that we, who in those days had been proved by our own works unworthy to achieve life, might in these days be made worthy of it by the goodness of God.' Then in chapter nine the anonymous author added, 'How surpassing is the love and tenderness of God! In that hour, [i.e. of the incarnation] instead of hating us and rejecting us and remembering our wickedness against us, he showed how long-suffering he is. He bore with us, and in pity he took our sins upon himself. He gave his own Son as a ransom for us – the holy for the wicked, the sinless for sinners, the just for the unjust, the incorrupt for the corrupt, the immortal for the mortal. For was there, indeed, anything except his righteousness that could have availed to cover our sins? In whom could we, in our lawlessness and ungodliness, have been made holy, but in the Son of God alone? O sweet exchange! O unsearchable working! O benefits unhoped for! – that the wickedness of multitudes should thus be hidden in the One holy, and the holiness of One should sanctify the countless wicked!'[4]

Kerygmatic Crisis of Head, Heart & Hands

Sadly, there are many Christians who, in spite of having been baptised and confirmed, are unfamiliar with the kerygma and unaware of its liberating power. As a result there is what could be referred to as a kerygmatic crisis of head, heart and hands,

4. 'The Office of Readings,18 December,' *The Divine Office*, vol 1 (Talbot: Dublin, 1974), 127-8.

The kerygmatic crisis of the head has to do with knowledge. Many Catholics are neither aware that there is a hierarchy of religious truths, nor the core teachings of the Christian faith. If one reads the story of the Philippian gaoler in Acts 16:25-35, and asks average Catholics to answer his all important question, 'What must I do to be saved?' they will usually be unable to answer in a satisfactory way. They will say such things as, 'You should love God and your neighbour,' 'You should obey your conscience,' 'You should obey the commandments,' and the like. What Paul actually replied was, 'Believe in the Lord Jesus, and you will be saved – you and your household' (Acts 16:31). In other words, many Catholics are not clear about the content of the kerygma. For a good, clear, succinct summary of the core Christian message see Ralph Martin's 'What is Our Message?'[5]

The kerygmatic crisis of the heart has to do with experience. Even if some Catholics are aware of the core teachings of Christianity, that doesn't necessarily mean that they are consciously aware of their liberating power in their own lives. This could be due to a lack of personal faith, a negative image of God, an unwillingness to turn away from sin, or some other personal reason. This lack of an experiential awareness of salvation in Christ is often evident in a lack of evangelical joy, which as G. K. Chesterton once observed in *Orthodoxy*, is 'the gigantic secret of the Christian.' Sadly, there are teachers in our Catholic schools who, although they teach religion to the children, fail to be credible witness to faith in Christ because they themselves have never come to experience his salvation in a personal, transforming way, or to live accordingly.

The kerygmatic crisis of the hands has to do with Christian action. If the truth of the kerygma has not fallen from head to heart, it is not surprising that nominal Catholics often fail act in a way that would be consistent with the teachings of Christ and his church. A few years ago an American booklet entitled *Fanning the Flame* spoke about, 'The disintegration of family life, the decrease in priestly and religious vocations, wasteful consumption, forgetfulness of the poor – these and many other factors are symptoms of the Catholic community's weakened state. It has left the com-

5. *John Paul II and the New Evangelisation*, 17-28.

munity prey to the pressures of a secular world where the media repeatedly mock the gospel and cheapen the centrality of a person's worth as a child of God. Increasingly many Catholics find it difficult to live according to our tradition and the teachings of our church.'[6] Are things any different here in contemporary Ireland?

Pope John Paul II observed in EE 47: 'Everywhere, then, a renewed proclamation is needed even for those already baptised. Many Europeans today think they know what Christianity is, yet they do not really know it at all. Often they are lacking in knowledge of the most basic elements and notions of the faith. Many of the baptised live as if Christ did not exist.' Is it any wonder that in NMI 40, John Paul wrote: 'Over the years, I have often repeated the summons to the new evangelisation. I do so again now, especially in order to insist that we must rekindle in ourselves the impetus of the beginnings and allow ourselves to be filled with the ardour of the apostolic preaching which followed Pentecost. We must revive in ourselves the burning conviction of Paul, who cried out: "Woe to me if I do not preach the gospel" (1 Cor 9:16).' Arguably, when it is examined in a more analytical way it could be said that the essential or core gospel message contains the following six points.[7]

The Kerygma in six points

1] *God's love.* This is where the Good News proclamation necessarily begins. In scripture we are told that 'God is love' (1 Jn 4:16). Then in Jn 3:16 we are told, in possibly the most important line in scripture, 'God so loved the world that he gave his one and only Son, that whoever believes in him shall not perish but have eternal life.' Speaking about God's love Jesus said, on one occasion to the apostles and through them to us, 'As the Father has loved me, so have I loved you. Now remain in my love' (Jn 15:9). Unlike human love which tends to be restricted and conditional, the love of Christ is unrestricted and unconditional. In Rom 5:7-8 St Paul explained: 'Very rarely will anyone die for a righteous man, though for a good man someone might possibly

6. Eds Kilian McDonnell, George T. Montague (Collegeville, The Liturgical Press, 1991), 10-11.

7. I am indebted to the John the Baptist Kononia Community in Belfast for the six headings but not the content of each point.

dare to die. But God demonstrates his own love for us in this: While we were still sinners, Christ died for us.' It is not surprising, therefore, that in Eph 3:17-19 Paul prayed that believers would have a mildly mystical experience of the incomprehensible love of Christ, and in Rom 5:5 he says the prayer has been answered because, 'God has poured out his love into our hearts by the Holy Spirit, whom he has given us.'

2] *All have sinned and are in need of salvation.* One of the reasons we do not experience the love of God is the fact that our sins act as a barrier. The word for sin in Greek, *hamartia,* literally means, 'to miss the mark,' or 'fall short'. Sin is like an arrow that fails to hit the target. In the New Testament the word refers to the fact that as a power, sin is universal.[8] God expects us to keep the commandments and to lead holy and loving lives in communion with the divine will. Judged by that criterion we all fail to measure up. St Paul spoke for all of us when he admitted, 'For what I do is not the good I want to do; no, the evil I do not want to do – this I keep on doing' (Rom 7:19). That is why the apostle to the gentiles could say in Rom 3:23-24, 'for all have sinned and fall short of the glory of God,' and St John could add, 'If we claim we have not sinned, we make God out to be a liar and his word has no place in our lives' (1 Jn 1:10). The Bible acknowledges that we humans tend to be in denial as far as our failings are concerned. In Jer 17:9-10 the Lord says, 'The heart is deceitful above all things and beyond cure. Who can understand it? I the Lord search the heart and examine the mind.' Just as bright sunlight streaming through the window reveals hidden dust on tabletops, so the light of God's love reveals our shortcomings. That is why the psalmist prayed, 'Test me and know my anxious thoughts. See if there is any offensive way in me, and lead me in the way everlasting.' Wis 12:2 explains how God answers this prayer: 'Gradually, you correct those who offend; you admonish and remind them of how they have sinned, so that they may abstain from evil and trust in you, Lord.'

In my experience, even when we sense the unconditional love and acceptance of the Lord, a lack of humility can lead some of us to be reluctant to truly admit our sins without excus-

8. See, Barclay, '*Hamaratia, Hamartanein*: The Failure Which is Sin,' in *New Testament Words*, 118-25.

ing or minimising them. Often we seek to attribute them to impersonal factors such as inherited tendencies, pathologies that are rooted in our childhood, environmental pressures, unconscious influences, genetic programming, hormonal imbalances, addictive tendencies, defects in education, the strength of temptation, etc. While we do not exactly deny that we have done wrong, we seem to lessen our responsibility for what we have freely chosen to do, or not to do. This is hardly walking honestly in the gentle light of truth. To confess one's sins in this self-serving, superficial way means that at best one will only feel superficially forgiven. To experience the depth and power of the kerygma we need to say without reserve, 'For I know my transgressions, and my sin is always before me. Against you, you only, have I sinned and done what is evil in your sight' (Ps 51:3-4).

3] *Jesus died to forgive our sins.* Every time I celebrate Mass I'm struck by the prayer the priest says over the chalice at the time of consecration: 'This is the new covenant in my blood which will be shed for you and for all, so that sins may be forgiven.' It reminds us that on the cross Jesus was our scapegoat. He took our sins upon himself so that we might be forgiven. As St Paul said, 'For our sake he made him to be sin who knew no sin, so that in him we might become the righteousness of God' (2 Cor 5:21). Knowing this to be true St Paul proclaimed: 'Therefore, my brothers and sisters, I want you to know that through Jesus the forgiveness of sins is proclaimed to you. Through him everyone who believes is justified from everything you could not be justified from by the law of Moses' (Acts 13:38-39). Paul also says in Rom 6:8-12: 'Now if we died with Christ, we believe that we will also live with him. For we know that since Christ was raised from the dead, he cannot die again; death no longer has mastery over him. The death he died, he died to sin once for all; but the life he lives, he lives to God. In the same way, count yourselves dead to sin but alive to God in Christ Jesus.'

4] *Believe and repent.* When the Good News message is proclaimed it invites the hearer to conversion, not firstly by turning from sin or changing his or her behaviour. If it did, it would make a human work (i.e. repentance), a condition for meriting God's forgiveness. As a result, a person would be put at rights with God as a result of personal merit. The basic form of conversion is to believe the Good News, to trust wholeheartedly that if you expect only mercy from God, you will receive only mercy. As St Thomas Aquinas wrote, 'The first conversion to God consists in *believing* [my italics].'[9] The late Anthony de Mello proposed a kerygmatic type meditation in his book *Sadhana: A Way to God*,[10] in which he focused on this kind of conversion process. Imagine, he says, that an angel appears to you and says, 'Listen carefully to what I have to say now: Jesus Christ, the Risen Lord, is present here and now with you. Do you believe this? Now I am going to get you to consider something that is even more difficult to believe. Jesus Christ, the Risen Lord who is present with you, loves and accepts you just as you are ... You do not have to change to get his love. You do not have to become better ... to get out of your sinful ways ... He obviously wants you to become better. He obviously wants you to give up your sin. But you do not have to do this to receive his love and acceptance. That you have already, right now, just as you are, even before you decide to change, and whether you decide to change or not ... Do you believe this? ... Take your time over it ... Then decide whether you believe it or not.' Speaking for myself, I have to admit that this meditation exercise moves me every time I use it because it helps me to relive the experience I described at the beginning of this chapter. And so once again, I become consciously aware of the amazing grace of Christ that saved a wretch like me from my sins.[11] When a person is aware of that grace, it gives him or her both the desire and the supernatural power to turn away from any sin that would grieve the Holy Spirit of God within them. So repentance as the second phase of conversion

9. *ST* I-II, q. 113, a. 4.

10. (Gujarat: Anand Press, 1978), 115.

11. Anyone who wishes to experience the power of the kerygma for him or herself could also say the following prayer. 'Jesus I open my heart to you. I believe you died and rose again, for me and for the forgiveness of my sins. I want to belong fully to you. I ask you to forgive all my sins, the ones I am aware of, the ones I am not consciously aware of, and the ones I have forgotten. I thank you that I am receiving the free gift of your unconditional forgiveness and acceptance. I offer my life to you and I promise to obey you as the number one Person in my life by turning away from anything that is contrary to your holy will. Amen.'

follows from the first, namely, complete trust in the God of mercy, and the mercy of God.

Although the saving grace of Christ is always available to those who believe in him, we can only receive and appropriate that grace when we are willing to offer the same mercy – with no strings attached – to those, living or dead, who have hurt or injured us in any way. I say this because it is the clear, consistent, and unambiguous teaching of the scriptures. Let us look at the evidence in the New Testament where a principle of reciprocity is clearly evident. In the Lord's Prayer, having said, 'Forgive us our debts, as we also have forgiven our debtors,' Jesus went on to add, 'For if you forgive others their trespasses, your heavenly Father will also forgive you; but if you do not forgive others, neither will your Father forgive your trespasses' (Mt 6:14). On another occasion, Jesus said in similar vein, 'Do not judge and you will not be judged; do not condemn, and you will not be condemned. Forgive and you will be forgiven ... for the measure you give [to others] will be the measure you will get back [from God]' (Lk 6:36-39). At the end of the parable of the Unforgiving Servant, the man who failed to show mercy was severely punished, and Jesus commented, 'This is how my heavenly Father will treat each of you unless you forgive your brother or sister from your heart' (Mt 18:35).

The later New Testament writings echo these sentiments. For example, in Col 3:13 we read: 'Bear with one another, forgive each other if one has a complaint against another. The Lord has forgiven you, you must do the same.' In Eph 3:32 the inspired author says: 'Be generous to one another, sympathetic, forgiving each other as readily as God forgave you in Christ.' Finally, St James warned: 'For judgement will be without mercy to anyone who has shown no mercy; mercy triumphs over judgement' (Jas 2:13). In view of these verses, it seems evident that to forgive those who have hurt or injured us is integral to the kerygma.

5] *Receive the Holy Spirit and his gifts.* In Eph 5:18 we read, 'Be filled with the Spirit.' Notice that it is not advice or an encouragement, rather it is a command of the Lord. Without the Spirit we can do nothing, but when the Lord and Giver of Life is active within us, we can do all things. That is why those who preach the kerygma urge those who listen to ask for the Spirit and to do so with expectant faith because, as Jesus promised, 'If you then, though you are evil, know how to give good gifts to your children, how much more will your Father in heaven give the Holy Spirit to those who ask him!' (Lk 11:13). Those who ask for the Holy Spirit should also be open to receiving the gifts of the Spirit, the traditional seven mentioned in Is 11:2, and the nine more charismatic ones mentioned in 1 Cor 12:8-10. Is it any wonder that St Paul says in 1 Cor 14:1: 'Follow the way of love and eagerly desire spiritual gifts, especially the gift of prophecy.' These special gifts are rooted in love, express love, and help to build up a loving Christian community. As LG 12 says: 'These charismatic gifts, whether they be the most outstanding or the more simple and widely diffused, are to be received with thanksgiving and consolation, for they are exceedingly suitable and useful for the needs of the church.'

6] *Enter into Christian community.* To be united to Christ is to enter a spiritual community made up of all those who have received the grace of salvation as a result of baptism and personal faith in the message of the kerygma. As Acts 2:47 tell us, 'The Lord added to their community daily those who were being saved.' We know that 'They devoted themselves to the apostles' teaching and to the fellowship, to the breaking of bread and to prayer.' This community is referred to by Paul as the Body of Christ, we are the members, and Jesus is our head. As Eph 4:11-13 puts it: 'It was he [Christ] who gave some to be apostles, some to be prophets, some to be evangelists, and some to be pastors and teachers, to prepare God's people for works of service, so that the body of Christ may be built up until we all reach unity in the faith and in the knowledge of the Son of God and become mature, attaining to the whole measure of the fullness of Christ.' Experience indicates that it is virtually impossible to grow in the Christian life without the help and nurturance of a loving community. It helps to create a feeling of belonging and builds up faith by providing teaching and practical support. Furthermore when Christians help one another they find it easier to resist the false values of secular society and thereby grow in holiness of life (cf Rom 12:2).[12]

12. cf Pat Collins, 'Unity and Evangelisation', *Gifted and Sent*, 183-192.

In EN 23 Paul VI makes the important observation that, 'the proclamation only reaches full development when it is listened to, accepted and assimilated, and when it arouses a genuine adherence in the one who has thus received it. An adherence to the truths which the Lord in his mercy has revealed; still more, an adherence to a programme of life – a life henceforth transformed – which he proposes.' Pope John Paul said something on similar lines: 'Sometimes even Catholics have lost or never had the chance to experience Christ personally: not Christ as a mere "paradigm" or "value," but as the living Lord, "the way, and the truth and the life' (Jn 14:6).'[13]

Motives for proclaiming the Kerygma

Canon 211 of CCL makes this important point, 'All Christ's faithful have the *obligation* and the *right* [my italics] to strive so that the divine message of salvation may more and more reach all people of all times and places.' In EN 24, Pope Paul VI said: 'The person who has been evangelised goes on to evangelise others. Here lies the test of truth, the touchstone of evangelisation: it is unthinkable that a person should accept the Word and give himself to the kingdom without becoming a person who bears witness to it and proclaims it in his turn.' It seems to me that in spite of the universal call to evangelisation, which is rooted in baptism, very few Catholics seem to make a conscious effort to fulfill their prophetic calling by reaching out to either the un-churched or unbelievers. Sherry Weddell of the Catherine of Siena Institute in the USA says that of those Catholics in America who go to church on a weekly basis, only about 5% are intentional disciples of Jesus in the sense that they try to share their faith with others. This regrettable lack of effort by the majority may be due to the fact that so few Catholics are truly evangelised themselves.

The vast majority of Catholics were baptised as infants[14] and

13. 'New Catechism will Promote National Recatechising Effort,' *L'Osservatore Romano*, (March 24, 1993), 3.

14. CCC 1227 reads: 'According to the Apostle Paul, the believer enters through baptism into communion with Christ's death, is buried with him, and rises with him: Do you not know that all of us who have been baptised into Christ Jesus were baptised into his death? We were buried

confirmed[15] as children. It has to be said from a theological point of view that, in receiving these sacraments of initiation, they received the grace of justification and therefore new life in Christ. As a result, Catholics tend to believe that because of this fact, they have been evangelised and are in touch with the power of the kerygma. Of course there is some truth in thinking this, because undoubtedly the love of God has been poured into their hearts by the Holy Spirit (cf Rom 5:5). But it could be argued that while reception of baptism and confirmation were undoubtedly sacramental events, they were not necessarily experiential ones.[16] The gospels tell us that a tree is known by its fruits (cf Mt 12:33). Often the fruits of the Spirit which are listed by St Paul in Gal 5:22-23 are noticeable by their absence in their lives. This may indicate that the graces given in the sacraments of initiation remain dormant because they have not been consciously appropriated by faith.

There are at least two familiar problems associated with a lack of the experience of salvation. Firstly, in the post-Reformation period large numbers of Catholics have stressed the importance of good works. As a result, many of them have tended to rely on personal merits more than they rely on faith in Christ for their salvation. For example, the notion of merit is implicit in the words of this widow, 'It is just not fair. When I prayed for my husband when he was sick with cancer, God did

---

therefore with him by baptism into death, so that as Christ was raised from the dead by the glory of the Father, we too might walk in newness of life. The baptised have 'put on Christ'. Through the Holy Spirit, baptism is a bath that *purifies, justifies, and sanctifies* [my italics].'

15. CCC 1285 reads: For 'by the sacrament of confirmation, [the baptised] are more perfectly bound to the church and are enriched with a special strength of the Holy Spirit. Hence they are, as true witnesses of Christ, *more strictly obliged to spread and defend the faith by word and deed* [my italics].'

16. That disjunction between a sacramental and experiential event is evident in the story of the Samaritans who had heard the kerygma from Philip the evangelist, believed what he had preached, and received Christian baptism. Nevertheless when Peter and John visited them they concluded that the Spirit had 'not fallen on any of them' (Acts 8:16). They seemed to be distinguishing between baptism as a *sacramental event* that enabled them to receive the Spirit, and an *experiential one* where the Spirit is released in the person in a conscious and transforming way.

not listen even though my husband went to Mass every Sunday, was honest in all his dealings with others, and was always loyal to me, whereas there is a man down the road who never attends church, has been in prison twice, and has never been sick for a day in his life.' As the lives of the Pharisees showed, the notion of salvation by means of good works can lead to related problems such as a tendency to hypocrisy, scrupulosity, an unhealthy sense of guilt, and a propensity to be moralistic, holier than thou and judgemental in attitude. Secondly, there are Catholics who for all intents and purposes live like baptised pagans in so far as their behaviour is not much different from that of unbelievers. When the Ryan Report on institutional abuse of children was published in Ireland in mid 2009, it was a striking fact that the terrible misdeeds it uncovered were committed by religious priests, nuns and brothers. How could they have done such unloving things if they had been truly evangelised?

In the past, bishops and priests tended to presume that all those who had received the sacraments of initiation were therefore evangelised. As a result they focused on catechesis, (i.e. Christian teaching about the faith and discipleship). However, if people suffer from a kerygmatic crisis of head, heart and hands, catechesis is like a house built on sand. As Jesus warned: 'The rain came down, the streams rose, and the winds blew and beat against that house, and it fell with a great crash' (Mt 7:26-27). There is considerable evidence to show that when the winds of hedonistic, and materialistic values blew in the Celtic Tiger years, many Catholics failed to stand firm as far as their Christian convictions and actions were concerned. It was precisely because they were aware of this point that members of Alpha Ireland wrote a submission to a committee who were drawing up the *Catechetical Directory for Ireland*. In it they suggested that it would be important for the directory to point out that effective catechesis has to be rooted in a conscious experience of the power of the kerygma. Because the church authorities sometimes mistakenly believe that sacramentalised Christians are also fully evangelised, they expect them to carry the yoke of Christian ethics, (e.g. to do with such things as avoiding divorce and abortion). While many un-evangelised or partly evangelised Christians may have a dutiful desire to carry that yoke, often they do not have the power to do so, because it only comes when the kerygma is experienced in a personal way. As a result, many Christians live lives of ethical defeat, disillusionment and condemnation. Consequently they associate Christianity with bad rather than good news. Is it any wonder that so many of them, especially in poorer urban areas, lapse as a result of disillusionment?

The Sacraments and the Kerygma

As has been mentioned a number of times already, it is often said that many Catholics are sacramentalised but not fully evangelised. While there is some truth in that saying, it can be misleading insofar as it implies that the sacraments are not a means of justification. It was probably because he had this idea in mind that Pope Paul VI said in EN 47: 'In a certain sense it is a mistake to make a contrast between evangelisation and sacramentalisation, as is sometimes done. It is indeed true that a certain way of administering the sacraments, without the solid support of catechesis regarding these same sacraments ... could end up by depriving them of their effectiveness to a great extent. The role of evangelisation is precisely to educate people in the faith in such a way as to lead each individual Christian to live the sacraments as true sacraments of faith – and not to receive them passively or reluctantly.' In EE 47, Pope John Paul stated that the challenge facing evangelisers 'frequently consists not so much in baptising new converts as in enabling those already baptised to be converted to Christ and his gospel.' The following points are meant to be indicative rather than comprehensive. A lot more could be said about this important topic.

a) Baptism

It has often occurred to me that by and large there is a kerygmatic dimension to many of the sacraments. For instance, in RM 47 Pope John Paul II said, 'the apostles, prompted by the Spirit, invited all to change their lives, to be converted and to be baptised ... Peter said to them, "Repent and be baptised every one of you in the name of Jesus Christ for the forgiveness of your sins; and you shall receive the gift of the Holy Spirit" (Acts 2:37-38).' It is obvious from the scriptures, (e.g. Rom 6:4; Col 2:12), and the

Fathers of the church that it is through the sacrament of baptism that a person experiences justification. In a treatise entitled, *On Baptism*, Tertullian (160-225) wrote: 'Granted that in former days, before the Lord's passion and resurrection, there was salvation through bare faith; still, now that faith has been enlarged to include belief in the birth, passion and resurrection, there is an enlargement added to the mystery, namely the sealing of baptism.'[17]

b) Sacrament of reconciliation

Much the same is true in the sacrament of reconciliation. Speaking on the Lord's behalf, St James urged: 'Confess your sins to one another, and pray for one another, that you may be healed. The fervent prayer of a righteous person is very powerful' (Jas 5:16). This practice was given a sacramental focus when Jesus appeared to Peter and the apostles after his resurrection. Having greeted them, 'He breathed on them and said to them, "Receive the Holy Spirit. If you forgive the sins of any, they are forgiven them; if you retain the sins of any, they are retained" (Jn 20:22-23).' In the sacrament of reconciliation we receive forgiveness as a free, unmerited gift and not as a matter of good works. I sometimes say something like this before giving people absolution: 'At this moment you are approaching the crucified One on Calvary. There is nothing you can do to merit, earn or deserve the forgiveness you need. But the Good News is the fact that as you trust wholeheartedly in Jesus crucified, he pours out his unconditional mercy and love upon you free, *gratis* and for nothing. He forgives and forgets your sins forever. As Heb 8:12 assures us: "I will forgive their wickedness and will remember their sins no more".'

c) The Eucharist

The Eucharist especially has a profoundly kerygmatic focus. Scripture scholar C. H. Dodd has described how the kerygma exerted a significant influence on the shaping of the liturgy. As theology developed the form and language of the church's wor-

17. *The Early Christian Fathers*, ed Henry Bettenson (London: Oxford University Press, 1974), 144.

ship adhered more closely to the forms of the kerygma. 'It is perhaps in some parts of the great liturgies of the church that we are still in most direct contact with the original apostolic preaching.'[18] For example, in the fourth Eucharistic Prayer we read: 'In fulfilment of your will he gave himself up to death, and by rising from the dead, he destroyed death and restored life. And that we might live no longer for ourselves but for him, he sent the Holy Spirit from you, Father, as his first gift to those who believe, to complete his work on earth and bring us the fullness of grace.' The acclamations after the consecration are also kerygmatic in nature. One of them reads: 'Dying you destroyed our death, rising you restored our life. Lord Jesus, come in glory.' Is it any wonder that Pope Paul VI said in EN 28: 'In its totality, evangelisation – over and above the preaching of the message – consists in the implantation of the church, which does not exist without the driving force which is the sacramental life culminating in the Eucharist.' It is a striking fact that at the end of the Eucharist, the priest says to the people, 'The Mass is ended, go in peace.' Our English word *mission* comes from the Latin *missio* meaning 'sending.' In other words, the congregation are sent into the world to love and serve the Lord in many ways, one of which is the evangelisation of others. When he spoke in Dublin and Limerick in 1979, Pope John Paul II adverted to the necessary connection between the saving faith experienced during celebration of the Eucharist and everyday life. He said: 'You cannot be a genuine Christian on Sunday, unless you try to be true to Christ's spirit also in your work, your commercial dealings, at your trade union or your employer's or professional meetings. How can you be a true community in Christ at Mass unless you try to think of the welfare of the whole national community.'[19]

Speaking of the role of priests in the administration of the sacraments, the Congregation for the Clergy said in a letter to the ordained ministers of the world: 'Priests in celebrating the sacraments, act as ministers of Christ and, through the Holy

18. 'John and Paul,' *The Apostolic Preaching and Its Developments* (San Francisco: Harper and Row, 1964).

19. *The Pope in Ireland: Addresses and Homilies* (Dublin: Veritas, 1979), 78. See also John Paul II, Encyclical Letter, *Redemptoris Hominis* par. 7.

Spirit, participate in his priesthood in a special way. Hence the sacraments are moments of worship of singular importance for the new evangelisation. It must be recalled that they have become the only effective moments for transmitting the contents of the faith. While this is true for all faithful, it is even more true for those who, having lost the practice of the faith, occasionally participate in the liturgy for family or social reasons such as baptisms, confirmations, marriages, ordinations funerals etc.'[20] While there is a lot of truth in what Cardinal Castrillon Hoyos says in the letter, surely it is a mistake to claim that a priest can evangelise only on sacramental occasions. He can also do so in the course of his pastoral work by means of such things as one-to-one contact with the people he meets and through the exercise of the charisms of power.

Popular Devotion and the Kerygma

While the liturgy is 'the summit toward which the activity of the church is directed' and 'the font from which all her power flows,'[21] popular devotion plays a complementary but subordinate role if it avoids sentimental excess, superstition, and is genuinely Christ centred. To a certain extent people's adherence to popular piety can represent an implicit protest against an overly dogmatic, ritualistic approach to God. What the supporters of popular piety are looking for are doctrines that come alive with experiential meaning. At their best, popular devotions focus on the kerygma and derive their spiritual energy from it. As Pope Pius XII stated in 1947, the purpose of popular devotion is 'to attract and direct our souls to God, purifying them from their sins, encouraging them to practice virtue and, finally, stimulating them to advance along the path of sincere piety by accustoming them to meditate on the eternal truths and disposing them better to contemplate the mysteries of the human and divine natures of Christ.'[22]

It would be hard to find an explicitly kerygmatic emphasis in many forms of popular devotion but it is evident in others, such

20. *The Priest and the Third Christian Millennium*, (Dublin: Irish School of Evangelisation, 1999), 17-18.
21. *Constitution on the Sacred Liturgy*, par 10.
22. Pope Pius XII, Encyclical letter *On the Sacred Liturgy*, par 175.

as devotion to the Sacred Heart and the Divine Mercy. The former was promoted by St Margaret Alacoque (1647-1690) as a result of revelations from the Lord. Commenting on it, a church document on popular devotion states: 'It can be said that, in a certain sense, devotion to the Sacred Heart of Jesus is a cultic form of the prophetic and evangelic gaze of all Christians on him who was pierced (cf Jn 19, 37; Zac 12, 10), the gaze of all Christians on the side of Christ, transfixed by a lance, and from which flowed blood and water (cf Jn 19, 34), symbols of the "wondrous sacrament of the Church".'[23] 'Devotion to the Sacred Heart is a wonderful historical expression of the church's piety for Christ, her Spouse and Lord: it calls for a fundamental attitude of conversion and reparation, of love and gratitude, apostolic commitment and dedication to Christ and his saving work.'[24] Devotion to the Divine Mercy was promoted by St Faustina Kowalska (1905-1938). On 22 February 1931 she saw a vision of Jesus with rays of red and white light streaming from his heart. She was told to have a painting made which would represent the image with the words, 'Jesus I trust in you' written at the bottom. The Lord explained: 'The two rays denote Blood and Water. The pale ray stands for the Water, which makes souls righteous. The red ray stands for the Blood which is the life of souls. These two rays issued forth from the very depths of my tender mercy when my agonised heart was opened by a lance on the cross. These rays shield from the wrath of my Father. Happy is the one who will dwell in their shelter, for the just hand of God shall not lay hold of him or her.'[25] On another occasion the Lord said to St Faustina, 'I desire that priests proclaim this great mercy of Mine towards souls and sinners. Let the sinner not be afraid to approach me. The flames of mercy are burning me – clamouring to be spent; I want to pour them out upon these souls.'[26] Thanks to the support of the late John Paul II, devotion to the Divine Mercy has spread throughout the

23. *Directory on Popular Piety and the Liturgy* (2001), par 167.
24. Ibid., par 172.
25. St Faustina Kaolwska, *Revelations of Divine Mercy: Daily Readings from the Diary of Faustina Kowalska*, ed George W. Kosicki (Ann Arbor: Servant Publications, 1996), 38.
26. Ibid., 30.

Catholic world and has brought countless numbers of people into a experiential awareness of the unconditional forgiveness they received in baptism. Those engaged in basic evangelisation would do well, not only to study the kerygmatic content of devotion to the Sacred Heart and the Divine Mercy, but also to actively promote it.

Conclusion

Having looked at the nature of the kerygma, and the reasons we have for proclaiming it, the remainder of this book will focus on practical ways of doing so. As Pope John Paul II so rightly observed in par 57 of *Tertio millennio adveniente*: 'Today there are many "*areopagi*", and very different ones: these are the vast sectors of contemporary civilisation and culture, of politics and economics. The more the West is becoming estranged from its Christian roots, the more it is becoming missionary territory, taking the form of many different "*areopagi*".'[27] The word '*areopagi*' is derived from an incident in Acts 17:19- 34 when St Paul preached at the Areopagus, a hill northwest of the Acropolis in Athens where intellectuals used to meet. Pope John Paul employs the Areopagus as a symbol of the new 'places' in which the Good News must be proclaimed, and to which the mission of Christ is to be directed. He said on one occasion: 'Today these *areopagi* are the worlds of science, culture, and the media; these are the worlds of writers and artists, the worlds where the intellectual elites are formed.'[28] This book will restrict itself to answering the question, how do Catholics engage in basic evangelisation in some of these *areopagi*?

27. For more, see RM 37.
28. *Crossing the Threshold of Hope*, 112.

Recommended Reading

- Ralph Martin and Peter Williamson, *John Paul II and the New Evangelization* (Cincinnati : Servant Books, 2006).
- John Paul II, 'What is the New Evangelisation?' *Crossing the Threshold of Hope* (London: Jonathan Cape, 1994), 105-17.
- Raniero Cantalamessa, *The Holy Spirit in the Life of Jesus* (Collegeville: The Liturgical Press, 1994).
- Michael Green, *Evangelism in the Early Church* (Grand Rapids: Eerdmans, 2004).
- *The New Life in the Spirit Seminars Team Manual: Catholic Edition 2000,* revised and annotated by Therese Boucher (Locust Grove: National Service Committee, 2003).

CHAPTER SIX

Good News to the Poor

A mission statement is a brief written description of the purpose of a company or organisation which guides its actions, spells out its overall goal, provides a sense of direction, and informs decision making. St Luke tells us that early in his public ministry Jesus came to Nazareth shortly after his baptism in the Jordan. On the Sabbath he took part in the weekly liturgy. The service followed a familiar pattern. An attendant, who acted as caretaker and master of ceremonies, introduced each segment. First, there was a recitation of the *Shema*. This prayer from Deut 6:4-9 was augmented by others. They were followed by a fixed reading from the law. Then, as there were no priests, Jesus as a lay man noted for learning and piety, was invited to choose a reading from the prophets and to comment on it. He solemnly and deliberately chose to read from Is 61:1-2 which begins with these momentous words: 'The Spirit of the Lord is upon me, because he has anointed me to preach good news to the poor. He has sent me to proclaim release to the captives and recovery of sight to the blind, to set at liberty those who are oppressed, to proclaim the acceptable year of the Lord' (Lk 4:18-19). Then we are told, 'he rolled up the scroll, gave it back to the attendant and sat down. The eyes of everyone in the synagogue were fastened on him, and he began by saying to them: "Today this scripture is fulfilled in your hearing" (Lk 4:20-21).' This was Jesus' mission statement, his solemn declaration of purpose. Because it is so important we need to look more closely at its meaning and implications for Christian evangelisation.

Good News for the Poor

Jesus tells us that he received the outpouring of the Holy Spirit during his baptism in order to evangelise by bringing Good News to the poor. Who exactly were the poor? The word used in the Greek text of Luke's gospel is *ptochos*. William Barclay says that it has three interrelated meanings.[1] Firstly, it refers to those who have very few worldly possessions. Secondly, it refers to the down trodden and oppressed. Thirdly, it refers to those who have little or no worldly power or prestige. As a number of Old Testament texts make clear (cf Amos 5:12; Ps 10:2, 12, 17; 12:5; 14:6; 68:10) the poor are those who recognise that they have to trust in the Lord for help. As Pope Benedict XVI has pointed out, as a result of their experiences of suffering and deprivation, 'Israel recognises that its poverty is exactly what brings it close to God; it recognises that the poor, in their humility, are the ones closest to God's heart, whereas the opposite is true of the arrogant pride of the rich, who rely only on themselves.'[2]

In Lk 18:16-17 Jesus said: 'Let the little children come to me, and do not hinder them, for the kingdom of God belongs to such as these. I tell you the truth, anyone who will not receive the kingdom of God like a little child will never enter it.' St Thérèse of Lisieux intuitively knew that this verse referred to the poor, those that are aware of their creaturely powerlessness and utter dependence on God. She said: 'To be a child is to recognise our nothingness, to expect everything from God as a little child expects everything from its father; it is to be disquieted about nothing ... To be little is not attributing to oneself the virtues that one practises, believing oneself capable of anything, but to recognise that God places this treasure in the hands of his little child to be used when necessary; but it always remains God's treasure. Finally, it is not to become discouraged over one's faults, for children fall often, but they are too little to hurt themselves very much'[3] Thérèse would have identified with the following words: 'This poor man cried, and the Lord heard him, and saved him out of all his troubles ... The Lord is close to the broken hearted; he rescues those who are crushed in spirit' (Ps 34:6,18).

The majority of people were materially and spiritually poor in our Lord's day. He knew from personal experience what they

1. *New Testament Words*, 247-9. See also, Joachim Jeremias, 'Good News for the Poor,' *New Testament Theology* (London: SCM Press, 1981), 108-21.
2.Pope Benedict XVI, *Jesus of Nazareth*, 75.
3. *St Thérèse of Lisieux: Her Last Conversations* (Washington: Institute for Carmelite Studies, 1977), 138-9.

had to endure. Taxes were heavy. Famines were frequent. Emigration was high. Roman rule was cruel. Physical and mental diseases were many and incurable. But the principal suffering of the poor was their sense of alienation from God. The religious authorities of the day had told them they were sinners without hope because they were engaged in unclean professions such as prostitution, tax collecting, thieving, shepherding, money lending, gambling, and because they failed to observe many of the requirements of the law. As was mentioned in the fourth chapter, the poor were given to believe that instead of enjoying God's favour, they were under a curse because they neither knew or kept the minutiae of the Jewish law. As a result there was a yoke of spiritual condemnation on their shoulders, a feeling that not only were they unfortunate in this life, they would be damned in the next. No wonder they were 'harassed and helpless like sheep without a shepherd' (Mt 9:36). Jesus came to bring Good News to these afflicted people. He wanted to tell them that, whereas the Scribes and Pharisees said that they were accursed (cf Jn 7:49), he was declaring a jubilee of the Lord (cf Lk 4:19). In the Old Testament a jubilee was celebrated every fifty years. At that time individuals who had incurred debts and had sold themselves as slaves or servants to others were released from their debts and were set at liberty. So Jesus was telling the poor that he had been anointed by God to proclaim to them that, through no merit of their own, all their spiritual debts were being cancelled, and that their sins were being forgiven through the outpouring of God's unconditional mercy and love. He had been sent by God the Father to open the eyes of their hearts to this great truth and so to set them free from captivity to condemnation.

Blessed are the Poor

This message was reiterated and confirmed in the beatitudes. In Luke 6:20, Jesus spoke to those who lacked material possessions, 'Blessed are you who are poor,' he declared, 'for yours is the kingdom of God.' In Mt 5:3 the words of Jesus were addressed to those who were suffering from an inward sense of deprivation, 'Blessed are the poor in spirit,' he announced, 'for theirs is the kingdom of heaven.' Those who are spiritually poor, are the ones who are painfully aware of their need for such things as the free gift of God's unconditional mercy, love, healing, peace, and joy. When these verses are separated, distortions are possible. For example, those who stress the Lucan emphasis on material poverty sometimes give the impression that unless people give away all their wealth, as the rich young man was invited to do in Mk 10:17-23, they will not have much chance of being saved. As Pope Benedict XVI observes, some people like the rich young man and St Francis of Assisi do receive a special call from God to do just this. But by and large this call is not addressed to all believers. Those who highlight the Matthean emphasis on spiritual poverty can over spiritualise our Lord's teaching by overlooking the evangelical call to live a simple, unpretentious lifestyle while being generous to the poor and working to alleviate their sufferings, (e.g. by giving them material help and changing the unjust structures of society). St Paul was to say some years later in 1 Tim 6:17-18: 'Command those who are rich in this present world not to be arrogant nor to put their hope in wealth, which is so uncertain, but to put their hope in God, who richly provides us with everything for our enjoyment. Command them to do good, to be rich in good deeds, and to be generous and willing to share.'

Surely these two versions of the same beatitude should be read in conjunction with each other. As Pope Benedict has pointed out, instead of being in opposition, they complement one another. He comments in an insightful way: 'The poverty of which this tradition speaks is never a purely material phenomenon. Purely material poverty does not bring salvation, though of course those who are disadvantaged in this world may count on God's goodness in a particular way. But the heart of those who have nothing can be hardened, poisoned, evil – interiorly full of greed for material things, forgetful of God, covetous of external possessions. On the other hand, the poverty spoken of here is not a purely spiritual attitude, either.'[4]

Christ's Identification with the Poor

Jesus went a step further by declaring that he identified completely with the poor. As his great parable about judgement day

4. Ibid., 76-7.

in Mt 25:31-46 indicates: 'I was hungry and you gave me something to eat, I was thirsty and you gave me something to drink, I was a stranger and you invited me in, I needed clothes and you clothed me, I was sick and you looked after me, I was in prison and you came to visit me … I tell you the truth, whatever you did for one of the least of these brothers of mine, *you did for me* [my italics].' Back in the 1960s Pope Benedict XVI, then a young theologian, wrote a book entitled *Christian Brotherhood* in which he commented on the parable about the last judgement in Mathew. He said: 'Nothing suggests that only the faithful, only believers in the gospel of Christ, are meant here [i.e. as brothers and sisters of the Lord], as in the case in a similar text in Mk 9:41, but rather all people in need, without differentiation.'[5] He went on to add: 'Christ sees himself generally represented in the poor and lowly especially, people who – quite apart from their ethical quality, but simply through their being lowly, and the appeal to the love of others that lies in that – make present the master. Instead of calling them the least of his brothers, it would be more correct to translate: 'my brothers (i.e. the least.).'[6] This theological point implies that instead of bringing Christ to the poor, Christian evangelists need to be aware that Christ has already embraced their condition in every way but sin. One could say that Christ's compassionate identification with the poor reached its point of greatest intensity when he cried out in anguish in the garden of Gethsemane, 'Take this chalice from me' (Mk 14:36), and in desolation of spirit on the cross, 'My God, my God, why have you forsaken me?' (Mt 7:46). His identification with human poverty was radicalised even further when he descended into the powerlessness of *Hades*,[7] the place of the dead, where lonely souls are absent from God.

When we say that Christ has completely identified with human poverty, it does not mean that Christ is therefore neces-

5. Joseph Ratzinger, *Christian Brotherhood* (London: Sheed and Ward, 1966), 27-8.
6. Ibid., 28.
7. In the Bible, the word for *Hades* is *Sheol*. The Jews believed that after death souls went into a grey, shadowy land, in which people moved like ghosts. See William Barclay, *The Plain Man Looks at the Apostle's Creed* (London: Fontana Books, 1975), 119-33.

sarily within the poor. As Joseph Ratzinger has pointed out, there is an ambiguity in human poverty which is the result of the mystery of human freedom. Will poverty lead to a humble and trusting openness to God or a proud and resentful resistance to him? That ambiguity was epitomised by the two thieves who were crucified with Jesus. Although Jesus shared their poverty, sad to say, the impenitent thief 'hurled insults at him' (Lk 23:39), whereas the good thief prayed, 'Jesus, remember me when you come into your kingdom' (Lk 23:42). Jesus loved both men. But he would have been saddened to see that one of the thieves was not open to receive the saving gift of his love. However, he knew that the good thief desired salvation. Jesus responded to his companion's prayer by giving him the good news that he was receiving the unmerited gift of eternal life: 'I tell you the truth, today you will be with me in paradise' (Lk 23:43).

Demonstrating the Good News to the Poor
Not content with declaring the Good News in words, Jesus demonstrated its truth, as CCC 547-550 points out, in deeds.

Firstly, as St Paul noted: 'For you know the grace of our Lord Jesus Christ, that though he was rich, yet for your sakes he became poor, so that you through his poverty might become rich' (2 Cor 8:9). In the incarnation the Word divested himself of his divine glory to be born as a vulnerable baby in the poverty of the stable of Bethlehem. Scripture scholars tell us that it was significant that the first people who come to show him honour were the shepherds, poor people whom the Scribes and Pharisees would have thought of as accursed. So, already implicit in this story is an intimation that Jesus had come to bring Good News to the poor. As his mother said in a prophetic way, 'He has lifted up the humble. He has filled the hungry with good things but has sent the rich away empty' (Lk 1:52-53). Apparently, by the standards of the day, Jesus was not one of the really poor or oppressed.[8] However, when he embarked on his public ministry he seemed to freely choose to live as a poor man. As he himself testified: 'Foxes have holes and birds of the air have nests, but the Son of Man has no place to lay his head' (Mt 8:20). If we want

8. Albert Nolan, *Jesus Before Christianity* (London: Darton, Longman & Todd, 1992), 34.

to evangelise the poor of our day, we need to be in solidarity with them.

Secondly, Jesus expressed Good News to the poor by relating to them in an accepting and loving way. Although the Pharisees intended to criticise him when they said, 'Here is a glutton and a drunkard, a friend of tax collectors and sinners' (Mt 11:19), unknown to them, they were highlighting a glorious truth. By enjoying table fellowship with the 'accursed poor' Jesus was declaring that all their sins were being forgiven by God because the time of God's free gift of grace had come. Many years ago Franco Zepharelli made an impressive television series called *Jesus of Nazareth*. There was one memorable scene which showed Jesus attending a party with disreputable tax collectors, prostitutes and sinners. When Peter asked a passerby where Jesus was, he was told about the party. Immediately his body language conveyed a strong sense of disapproval. When he approached the door, and discreetly looked in, he heard Jesus telling the parable of the Prodigal Son. When got to the part about the elder bother, the penny dropped, and Peter realised with dismay that he had been motivated by the overbearing and judgemental attitudes characteristic of the Scribes and Pharisees. He acknowledged that Jesus had come to bring liberating Good News to the poor, including himself. As Albert Nolan has observed, 'Because Jesus was looked upon as a man of God and a prophet, they [the outcasts and sinners] would have interpreted his gesture of friendship as God's approval of them. They were now acceptable to God. Their sinfulness, ignorance, and uncleaness had been overlooked and were no longer being held against them.'[9] As the St Vincent de Paul Society of Ireland says in its Mission Statement: 'Through person to person contact, we are committed to respecting the dignity of those we assist and thus to fostering their self-respect. In the provision of material and other support, we assure confidentiality at all times and endeavour to establish relationships based on trust and friendship.'[10]

Thirdly, as was pointed out in *Gifts of the Spirit and the New Evangelisation*, Jesus not only proclaimed the Good News, he

9. Ibid., 48.

10. Michael Casey, *A River of Love: Frederick Ozanam and the Society of St Vincent de Paul* (Dublin: Columba, 1997), 70.

demonstrated the advent of God's kingdom of merciful love by performing deeds of power such as healing and miracle working. By ridding people of the penalty of original, if not their own personal sin,[11] he was indicating to the poor that their sins too were forgiven. As Pope John Paul II said in RM 14: 'Jesus' many healings clearly show his great compassion in the face of human distress, but they also signify that in the kingdom there will no longer be sickness or suffering, and that his mission, from the very beginning, is meant to free people from these evils. In Jesus' eyes, healings are also a sign of spiritual salvation, namely liberation from sin.' It is worth noting that when John the Baptist sent messengers to ask if Jesus was truly the promised messiah, he replied: 'Go back and report to John what you have seen and heard: The blind receive sight, the lame walk, those who have leprosy are cured, the deaf hear, the dead are raised, *and the good news is preached to the poor* [my italics]' (Lk 7:22-23). Arguably, the fact that Jesus preached the Good News to the poor was *the* evangelical sign that Jesus was the Messiah, the one who was ushering in the kingdom of God.

All these points came together in the radical poverty of Christ's saving death on the cross. In 1 Cor 1:23-25 St Paul testified: 'We preach Christ crucified: a stumbling block to Jews and foolishness to Gentiles, but to those whom God has called, both Jews and Greeks, Christ the power of God and the wisdom of God. For the foolishness of God is wiser than man's wisdom, and the weakness of God is stronger than man's strength.' Is it any wonder that St Vincent de Paul said on one occasion: 'In his passion, Jesus had scarcely the appearance of being human. In the eyes of the gentiles he passed for a fool. To the Jew he was a stumbling block. But with all that, he described himself as the *Evangeliser of the Poor* [my italics].'[12]

Evangelised by the Poor

The fact that Christ identifies with the poor has important

11. As Jesus explained in the story of the man born blind in Jn 9:1-17, his blindness was neither due to his personal sins or those of his parents.

12. From the collected works of St Vincent de Paul, vol 11, 32, quoted by Robert P. Maloney, *Go! On The Missionary Spirituality of St Vincent de Paul* (Salamanca: Editorial Ceme, Sanca Marta de Tormes, 2000), 129.

implications for those who evangelise. Firstly, only people who have experienced the unconditional mercy and love of God in their own poverty, whether material and/or spiritual, can truly evangelise the poor. I learned the truth of this shortly after my ordination in 1971. My heart was full of good intentions. As a follower of St Vincent DePaul I desired to be a latter day Good Samaritan by offering my help to the poor. When I met poor people I actually came to dislike them because I found that they were well aware that, instead of being able to offer them Good News, all I could give them was good advice. I began to resent them, because, unconsciously, I saw my own emotional and spiritual poverty mirrored in theirs. I finally acknowledged this state of affairs as a result of reading a verse in Rev 3:17: 'You say, "I am rich; I have acquired wealth and do not need a thing." But you do not realise that you are wretched, pitiful, poor, blind and naked?' I reluctantly had to acknowledge to myself that although I grew up in a stable, middle class family, got a good education and never knew the pinch of material need, I suffered from irrational anxiety, loneliness and neurotic problems. From that moment onwards, instead of identifying with the Good Samaritan, as I had done heretofore, I now identified with the man on the roadside. Like him I felt wounded, weak and in need of help. That awareness of my spiritual poverty became the birthplace of a heartfelt desire for something. If I had been asked what it was I wouldn't have been able to give a clear answer. In the words of a U2 song, I could have said, 'I still haven't found what I'm looking for.' Those words would have expressed an inchoate longing for some indefinable reality over and above my everyday self. Desire gave way to fulfilment in February 1974 when I experienced a powerful and transforming infilling of the Holy Spirit. I knew with great conviction that Jesus loved me and accepted me as I was. I knew what St Peter meant when he wrote: 'Though you have not seen him, you love him and even though you do not see him now, you believe in him and are filled with an inexpressible and glorious joy' (1 Pet 1:8). I will say more about that personal pentecost in chapter nine.

That religious experience taught me the paradoxical truth that, as well as being called to evangelise the poor, we are also evangelised by them. It is by meeting them and empathising with them in their sufferings and vulnerabilities that we begin to consciously acknowledge the gift of our own personal poverty. I began to realise that I needed Jesus. He was the Good Samaritan who was willing to leave heaven to travel the roads to our troubled world to assist wounded and needy people like me by pouring in the oil of his love, and the wine of his mercy into our hurting lives. He bandages our wounds, and carries us along when we have no power to carry ourselves (cf Lk 10:34).[13] A few years ago the Lord seemed to enlighten me further about this important point when he spoke a prophetic word to my heart: 'I do not despise your imperfection. I live in it. When you see the flaws in your brothers and sisters, and the wounds in your own heart, do not feel that they will separate you from me. I live in those wounds. I reveal myself through your brokenness. When you look at the cross you do not see a perfect Lord, but a broken one. You do not see light but darkness. You do not see joy, but anguish and pain. My child, I have descended into the depths of your imperfection, there to reveal the glory of my Father. For I love you in your brokenness, and you run away from it, as if it were not acceptable to me, as if I would despise it. It is your treasure. My light shines forth in all that you fear. So look to it. Accept it, in the knowledge that I am within it, and then you will learn to see me in places you have never seen me before and in a world that frightens you today. You will see my face shining through, for you will have changed, you will see as I see, my glory is everywhere.'

I may say in passing that the extent to which we fail to acknowledge and embrace the gift of our poverty, as the birthplace of saving grace, is the extent to which our evangelisation of others will be inhibited. For example, some evangelists who have failed to acknowledge their own spiritual poverty may have a condescending attitude to the poor as somehow lesser and inferior to themselves. Others may so identify with the materially poor, that may come to resent and despise those who are well-off and influential.[14] Needless to say, both attitudes are

---

13. This notion is an adaptation of a point made by St Augustine in *De verbis Domini* sermons, 37, where he says that Jesus is the Good Samaritan, and the man on the roadside is Adam after the fall.

14. In *Ressentiment* (New York: Schocken, 1972), Max Scheler described

defective. In truth, 'evangelisation is one beggar telling another where he or she has found the bread of life.'

Is the Good News only addressed to the Poor?

When one reads the gospels and what they say about the poor, the question arises, is the gospel addressed exclusively to them? If you believe that the poor are those who know their need for God, then I think that the answer is yes. It is not that the Lord doesn't want the rich (i.e. those who are too proud, self-sufficient and preoccupied with worldly things) to hear the Good News. Of course he does. As Paul assures us in 1 Tim 2:4, 'God wants all men to be saved and to come to a knowledge of the truth.' But because they have made idols of created things Jesus said, 'You will be ever hearing but never understanding; you will be ever seeing but never perceiving. For this people's heart has become calloused; they hardly hear with their ears, and they have closed their eyes. Otherwise they might see with their eyes, hear with their ears, understand with their hearts and turn, and I would heal them' (Mt 13:14-1).

Bishop Bossuet was one of the greatest preachers France has ever produced. St Vincent de Paul invited him to preach a sermon in a Parisian church in 1659. His topic was, 'On the Eminent Dignity of the Poor in the Church.' In the course of his address he said: 'The church of Jesus Christ is truly the city of the poor. The rich, and I do not fear to say this because the truth must be told, the rich being of the world are marked as belonging to the world, and therefore their presence is only tolerated in the church. It is the poor and the indigent who since they resemble the Son of God belong to the church and are received there. This is the reason that the inspired psalmist calls them, "the poor of God" ... God has established his church where the rich are received, but only on the condition that they serve the poor.'[15]

---

how *ressentiment* (a French word) is a form of unacknowledged envy which resents those who are stronger, more gifted and successful than oneself. It might explain why some Christians have an antipathy against the rich.

15. 'On the Eminent Dignity of the Poor in the Church: A Sermon by Jacques Benigne Bossuet,' trs Edward R. Udovic, *Vincentian Heritage* 13, No 1 (1992): 37-58. Available at: http://works.bepress.com/ edward_udovic/3 (accessed 1st Sept 2009)

Clearly, Bossuet believed the Good News was addressed to the poor. Not only did materially rich people need to be poor in spirit in order to hear the kerygmatic word of God, they had to express their gratitude for salvation by being of service to the poor in whatever way they could. One author has written, 'Nobody gets into heaven without a letter of reference from the poor.'[16] So I firmly believe that it is only the poor, those who acknowledge their radical need for God, who can be truly evangelised.

How do the People of Today Experience Poverty?

In spite of the relative wealth of a developed country like Ireland there are lots of poor people. The Irish government defines poverty as follows: 'People are living in poverty if their income and resources (material, cultural and social) are so inadequate as to preclude them from having a standard of living which is regarded as acceptable by Irish society generally. As a result of inadequate income and other resources people may be excluded, and marginalised from participating in activities which are considered the norm for other people in society.'[17] In this country a person is considered to be poor if he or she has an income which is below 60% of the median national income. In 2007 that was estimated to be below 228.65 euro a week for an adult. In 2007 Combat Poverty estimated that 5.1% of Irish people experience consistent poverty and that 16.5% were at risk of poverty. At the time of writing in 2009 it can be presumed that due to the economic downturn, a rise in unemployment, and government cut backs in social welfare, the ranks of the poor have swollen in number. As a result of my contact with the poor in Ireland, especially the Travelling People, it has become apparent to me that poverty is often associated with such things as marriage breakdown, violence, addictions, depression physical ill-health, stress, neuroses, imprisonment, depression and suicide.

In recent years two things have saddened me about poverty in Ireland. Firstly, in urban areas many well-off people, who live in middle class suburbs, have little or no contact with the poor

16. Jim Wallis, *God's Politics: Why the Right Gets It Wrong and the Left Doesn't Get It* (San Francisco: Harper, 2005), 16.

17. *National Plan for Social Inclusion 2007-2116* (Dublin: Government of Ireland, 2007).

due to the fact that they rarely if ever visit the less well off areas of our cities and towns. As a result, they have not much of an idea of what daily indignities and worries the poor have to endure. While thousands of well healed Irish men and women do their Christmas shopping in cities like London and New York, and go on holidays to exotic places like Australia, Dubai or Florida, there are poor people who can hardly afford to do any shopping or ever go on a holiday. The fact that rich people rarely encounter the poverty of their suffering brothers and sisters means that many of them lose touch with their own inner poverty and their radical need for God. As Prov 21:13 warns, 'He who shuts his ears to the cries of the poor will be ignored in his own time of need.' Speaking about evangelisers in RM 88, Pope John Paul wrote that they are 'required to renounce themselves ... this they do by a poverty which sets them free for the gospel, overcoming attachment to the people and things about them, so they may become brothers or sisters to those to whom they are sent and thus bring them Christ the Saviour. This is the goal of missionary spirituality: "To the weak I become weak ... I have become all things to all people, that I might by all means save some. I do it all for the sake of the gospel" (1Cor 9:22-23).' Secondly, as was noted in an earlier chapter, while Jesus came to bring Good News to the poor, it is a sad and ironic fact that the poor are the ones who are most likely to feel alienated from the church in Ireland. Is it any wonder, when so many of their fellow Christian brothers and sisters seem to be deaf and blind to their needs?

There is also a great deal of spiritual poverty in Ireland. It is psycho-spiritual in nature and is experienced by many well-off people. In a book with the catchy title, *Affluenza*, Oliver James talks about the downside of what he refers to as 'selfish capitalism.'[18] He says that the available statistical data, (e.g. The World Health Organisation's study of rates of emotional distress in fifteen countries), indicates that in developed nations such as Ireland, rates of emotional ill health (i.e. disturbances like depression, anxiety and substance abuse) increases in direct proportion to the degree of inequality in income. The rates of such distress are at least twice as high in English-speaking countries

18. (London: Vermilion, 2007), xviii.

as they are in Western Europe. Although, not all emotional distress and unhappiness is caused by the acquisitive nature of selfish capitalism, much of it is.

Blessed Teresa of Calcutta used to refer to the troubled people in developed countries as 'the new poor'. I first heard her talk about this subject in Digby Stuart College in London in 1973. What she said that day made an indelible impression upon my mind. Mother's talk began with a vivid description of the hardships of the poor and destitute of Calcutta. I can remember her saying that many homeless people lived in concrete pipes that had been left by the roadside. Nearing the end of her address she said to all of us: 'I suppose some of you, who desire to serve the poor, think that you should buy a plane ticket and fly to Calcutta. There is no need,' she added rather dramatically, 'the poor are right here in your midst. In fact if you look to your right and your left you will see them. They are the people sitting next to you!' Then she went on to explain that while people in developing nations like India were often materially poor, they were usually spiritually rich in love. To illustrate her point she told us that on one occasion she brought enough rice to a feed a Christian woman and her family for the day. Immediately the woman divided the rice into two portions and brought one half to a Muslim lady who lived nearby. When Mother Teresa asked why she had done this, the Christian woman responded, 'because that woman's family is hungry also.' Then Mother Teresa went on to say: 'While there is sometimes a famine of the belly in developing countries such as India, many people like that Christian woman are rich in love. In developed countries like yours, however, there is often a famine of the heart due to a lack of understanding love.' Then speaking about the new poor she said that they often felt, 'unwanted, unloved, uncared for and forgotten. I think such a feeling is a much greater poverty than the person who has nothing to eat.' Finally, she added: 'I find the rich much poorer. Sometimes they are more lonely inside. They are never satisfied. They always need something more. I don't say all of them are like that. Everybody is not the same. I find that poverty hard to remove. The hunger for love is much more difficult to alleviate than the hunger for bread.'

Mother Teresa believed that a lot of the unhappiness of people in developed countries, such as drug addiction, neuroses, depression and loneliness, was due to the fact that there was an emptiness, a lack of meaning at the core of their lives. It is worth noting that in NMI 50, Pope John Paul II seemed to endorse Mother Teresa's views: 'The scenario of poverty can extend indefinitely, if in addition to its traditional forms we think of its newer patterns. These latter often affect financially affluent sectors and groups which are nevertheless threatened by despair at the lack of meaning in their lives, by drug addiction, by fear of abandonment in old age or sickness, by marginalisation or social discrimination. In this context Christians must learn to make their act of faith in Christ by discerning his voice in the cry for help that rises from this world of poverty.' Before he became Pope, Joseph Ratzinger said: 'The deepest poverty is the inability of joy, the tediousness of a life considered absurd and contradictory. This poverty is widespread today, in very different forms in the materially rich as well as the poor countries. The inability of joy presupposes and produces the inability to love, produces jealousy, avarice – all defects that devastate the life of individuals and of the world. That is why we need a new evangelisation.'[19]

Philosophy of Religion on Poverty

The philosophy of religion would maintain that the experiences of material and spiritual poverty, such as those mentioned above, are ultimately rooted in a sense of contingency, or what Rudolf Otto referred to as 'creature feeling.'[20] It is the heartfelt awareness, that although I exist, I am not the adequate explanation of my own existence. The wonder is that something rather than nothing exists and I am part of that something. In other words, our existence as creatures ultimately depends upon the Creator. Is it any wonder that Protestant theologian, Friedrich Schleiermacher said in his influential book, *The Christian Faith,*

19. 'New Evangelisation: Building the Civilization of Love,' Address to Catechists and Religion Teachers Jubilee of Catechists, 12 December 2000. http://popebenedictxvi.blogspot.com/ (accessed 8 Dec. 2009).
20. *The Idea of the Holy* (London: Oxford University Press, 1970), 9. Otto saw creature feeling as a key characteristic of the sense of the numinous, or the divine.

that religion is the 'feeling of absolute dependence,'[21] namely, on God.

That fundamental awareness of poverty can come to people in different ways. For example, Leo Tolstoy was one of the greatest novelists of the nineteenth century. At the age of fifty he went through a crisis. In spite of the fact that he owned 1,350 acres of land, had 300 horses, many serfs, a large family and enjoyed celebrity as a writer, he felt nevertheless that there was no ultimate meaning in his life. In fact he was so dejected that he was tempted to commit suicide. At that time he was fond of quoting an oriental fable which expressed his sense of contingency and need. A man pursued by a tiger climbs down a well. At the bottom he sees the gaping jaws of a dragon. Unable to go up or down, the poor man climbs to a bush growing between the loosened stones. As his strength begins to fail he spies two mice, one white, one black, gnawing at the branch he is hanging from. A few seconds more and he will fall. Knowing himself about to die, the man makes a supreme effort, and licks drops of honey he notices glistening on the leaves.[22] Tolstoy would have been glad to do the same; but the two drops of honey in his life, love of his family and love of literature, which formerly sustained him, had lost all their savour. For Tolstoy, the danger from above and below represented the fact that we have emerged from the darkness of uncreated night and will re-enter it following our death. Being is constantly under threat from non-being. As an Irish proverb puts it, 'Life is a sigh between two mysteries.' Tolstoy tells us that this sense of emptiness led him to thirst for an experience of unconditional meaning. His crisis came to an end as a result of a religious experience while walking in a forest. He tells us in his *Confessions*: 'At the thought of God, happy waves of life welled up inside me everything came alive, took on meaning. The moment I thought I knew God, I lived. But the moment I forgot him, the moment I

21. 'The Christian Faith,' in *Phenomenology of Religion: Eight Modern Descriptions of the Essence of Religion*, ed Joseph D. Bettis (London: SCM, 1969), 163. In his book *On Religion: Speeches to its Cultural Despisers*, Schleiermacher says that 'religion is the sensibility and taste for the infinite' (Cambridge: CUP, 1991), 103. Presumably, the thirst for the infinite is rooted in the feeling of absolute dependence.

22.Henri Troyat, *Tolstoy* (London: Penguin Books, 1970), 519-21.

stopped believing, I also stopped living ... To know God and to live are the same thing. God is life.'[23]

Psychology of Religion on Poverty

The psychology of religion would lend support to the previous point. Carl Jung, for instance, believed that unless people had genuine religious experience, they would be unable to integrate from a psychological point of view and that neurosis would be the inevitable outcome. He once famously said: 'In thirty years I have treated many patients in the second half of life. Every one of them became ill because he or she had lost that which the living religions in every age have given their followers, (i.e. religious experience) and none of them was fully healed who did not regain his religious outlook.'[24]

Erik Erickson suggested that our lives are made of a succession of times of relative stability and security, (they usually last up to ten years), and times of transitional crisis, (usually lasting up to three years). There are two main types of crisis, predictable and unpredictable. Predictable crises occur regularly throughout our lives. They precede the main developmental phases, e.g. before the onset of early, middle and late adulthood. The purpose of these crises is to urge us to tackle some specific developmental task. By doing so we grow into a new depth of maturity. Unpredictable crises occur when 'the slings and arrows of outrageous fortune' come our way. People can be pitched into a period of turmoil and soul-searching by the death of a close relative, the news that they have cancer or the loss of their job. Often a predictable crisis, e.g. at mid-life, will occur at the same time as one or two unpredictable ones. Transitional crises of either kind have a threefold structure. (1) There is the onset and restlessness. (2) It is followed by a longer time of darkness and exploration, often accompanied by feelings of anxiety, stress, depression and spiritual desolation. (3) They come to an end with a sense of resolution and restabilisation. When people are going through life crises, they are more aware of their vulnerability and are more likely to seek values and meanings, in-

23. Ibid., 524.
24. 'Psychotherapists or The Clergy?' *Psychology and Western Religion* (London: Ark, 1988), 202.

cluding those of a religious kind, to replace the ones they have found to be inadequate. This sense of existential seeking and longing, predisposes many people to be open to the kerygma and either a gradual or sudden conversion to Christ.[25] This happens when they turn away from their former notion of God and behaviour, in order to turn toward a new relationship with Christ and his way of living.[26]

Viktor Frankl was also persuaded by clinical evidence that the most basic drive in human beings was not the will to power as Adler had said, or the will to pleasure as Freud had suggested, or the will to self-actualisation as Maslow had maintained, but rather a will to meaning of an ultimate and unconditional kind. In postmodern, society many people have lost touch with unconditional meaning because they are victims of 'the dictatorship of relativism' referred to by Benedict XVI.[27] Postmodernism believes that the human mind cannot come to know either absolute truth or meaning. As a result, it maintains that we are adrift in a fractured world of partial and provisional truths. Friedrich Nietzsche encapsulated this point of view when he said, 'There are no facts, only interpretations.'[28] Pope John Paul II observed in FR 90: 'Many philosophies have rejected the meaningfulness of

---

25. A good deal of writing has been done by people like William James and James Pratt on the psychology of conversion. What the empirical evidence indicates is that for most people conversion is the result of gradual incremental steps, whereas only a minority experience a sudden Pauline type of conversion to the Lord. By and large, evangelical Protestants tend to focus on sudden 'born again' types of conversions, while Catholics tend to focus on more gradual forms. The outcome, i.e. firm faith in the saving merits of Christ's death and resurrection, rather than the process by which it comes about, is what is really important. See 'Conversion,' *The Psychology of Religion: An Empirical Approach*, 273-99.
26. Evelyn & James Whitehead, *Christian Life Patterns: The Psychological Challenges and Religious Invitations of Adult Life* (New York: Doubleday, 1979); Pat Collins, 'The pain of self-discovery,' *Intimacy And The Hungers of the Heart* (Dublin: Columba, 1991), 58-73.
27. Homily Tuesday 19 April 2005. Joseph Ratzinger said: 'We are moving towards a dictatorship of relativism which does not recognise anything as for certain and which has as its highest goal one's own ego and one's own desires.' See also Joseph Ratzinger, *Truth and Tolerance: Christian Belief and World Religions*, 117-21.
28. *Notebooks*, (Summer 1886-Fall 1887).

being. I am referring to the nihilist interpretation, which is at once the denial of all foundations and the negation of all objective truth … and therefore with the very ground of human dignity. This in turn makes it possible to erase from the countenance of man and woman the marks of their likeness to God and thus leads them little by little either to a destructive will to power or to a solitude without hope.' Frankl would have endorsed those observations. He believed that relativism would inevitably have negative psycho-spiritual effects. Speaking about them, he wrote: 'Sometimes the frustrated will to meaning is vicariously compensated for by a will to power, including the most primitive form of the will to power, the will to money. In other cases, the place of a frustrated will to meaning is taken by the will to pleasure. That is why existential frustration often eventuates in sexual compensation. We can observe, in such cases, that the sexual libido becomes rampant in the existential vacuum.'[29]

During the years of excess here in Ireland, especially from about 1995 to 2007, religious practice fell dramatically while financial greed, sexual promiscuity and suicides increased at an alarming rate. For example, in 2009 there was, on average, a murder every week and a rape every day in Ireland. Paul II seemed to echo and expand on Frankl's evaluation when he wrote in EE 8: 'Among the troubling indications of the loss of a Christian memory are the inner emptiness that grips many people and the loss of meaning in life. The signs and fruits of this existential anguish include, in particular, the diminishing number of births, the decline in the number of vocations to the priesthood and religious life, and the difficulty, if not the outright refusal, to make lifelong commitments, including marriage. We find ourselves before a widespread existential fragmentation. A feeling of loneliness is prevalent; divisions and conflicts are on the rise.' Implicit in the forms of inner poverty I have described is either a conscious or an unconscious desire for ultimate meaning, love and wholeness. Is it any wonder that the Alpha course is described as 'an opportunity to explore the meaning of life.'[30]

---

29. Viktor Frankl, *Man's Search For Meaning* (New York: Pocket Books, 1963), 170.

30. Nicky Gumbel, *Alpha: Questions of Life. An Opportunity to Explore the Meaning of Life*, (Eastbourne: Kingsway, 2004).

Desire for God

In John's gospel we read, 'The next day John was there again with two of his disciples. When he saw Jesus passing by, he said, "Look, the Lamb of God!" When the two disciples heard him say this, they followed Jesus. Turning around, Jesus saw them following and asked, "What do you want?" (Jn 1:35-39).' From a theological point of view the question, 'What do you want?' is important because as Jesus said in Jn 6:44: 'No one can come to me unless the Father who sent me draws him.' In other words, Jesus is implying that when we are in touch with our deepest desires we are in touch with the drawing of God, by his Spirit, within our poverty. They move us toward intimate relationship with God through Christ. It is clear from the gospel of John that the two young men were already looking for God. Firstly, we are told that they were disciples of the prophet John the Baptist. Secondly, as soon as John bore witness to Jesus as the Lamb of God, they were fascinated and began to follow him along the road.

As was noted in chapter one, the saints were agreed that our deeper desires are very important. Sometimes they are referred to as holy, religious, spiritual or transcendental desires. There are a number of things that block our awareness of them. Firstly, there are worldly attachments to things such as power, possessions, pleasure, and popularity. The English word 'attachment' comes from French, and means to pin down or to nail. In other words, the dynamism of transcendental desire which should find its satisfaction through relationship with the Creator gets pinned down to created things in an idolatrous way. Secondly, many people are so dutiful that when they are asked what they want, they can only tell you what they 'ought' or 'should' want rather than what they really desire at a gut level. It is rightly said that words of obligation belong to others and come from outside of us, whereas words of desire belong to ourselves and come from within. Thirdly, there is the problem of excessive extroversion. As a result, people lack self-knowledge and have only a superficial awareness of the deeper things of their own hearts. Pope Paul VI said many years ago: 'Today our psychology is turned outward too much. The exterior world is so absorbing that our attention is mainly directed outside; we are nearly always absent from our inner selves … we cannot silence the hubbub inside due to outside interests, images and passions.' Protestant authors Mark Mittleberg, Lee Stroblel and Bill Hybels have suggested that in contrast with those who are aware of religious desire, there are three other types of people, cynics, sceptics and spectators who are not.[31] Cynics are hostile to the kerygma and show no interest in it. Sceptics are unbelieving. They may be a little open but are plagued by intellectual doubts. Spectators are indifferent. They may be intellectually curious about Christian beliefs but do not get personally involved with them.

The emphasis on holy desires as the expression of people's sense of poverty, whether material or spiritual, is a crucial one for those who wish to engage in basic evangelisation. The God of the word and the word of God can only be received by those who, in their vulnerability and need, are open to receive them. Like our Lord, we need to have a metaphorical towel of service wrapped around our waists. We need to tune in to people's deepest needs, those that are rooted in their sense of creaturely contingency, by paying empathic attention to their verbal and non-verbal communication. It has to be said that often people will begin by telling us about their immediate problems such as concern for a sick child, coping with bereavement, overcoming depression, etc. These presenting needs are often the expressions of a deeper, but usually less articulate sense of contingency and spiritual poverty. The Spirit will help evangelists to discern what those deeper needs might be. It will also help evangelists, not only to assist people to name and express their deeper needs, but also to respond to those needs in a sensitive and understanding manner. Needless to say, evangelists have to be careful not to impose their own agenda on others, no matter how worthy it may be in itself. Rather they need to respond in a humble and docile manner to the action of the Spirit within the experience of those they seek to evangelise.

There is a striking example of that principle at work in the account of how Philip evangelised the Ethiopian eunuch he met on a desert road (cf Acts 8:26-40).[32] Just as Jesus paid undivided

31. *Becoming a Contagious Christian: Participant's Guide* (Grand Rapids: Zondervan, 1995), 128.

32. cf Pat Collins, 'Reading the Scriptures and Religious Experience,' *He Has Anointed Me*, 160-7; 'Person to Person Evangelisation,' *Gifted and Sent*, 200-8.

attention to the woman at the well of Samaria, Philip paid empathic attention to the distinguished stranger he met in the barren wilderness. Straight away he noticed that he had servants and fine clothes which indicated that he was a person of power, influence, and wealth. But it was also fairly obvious from his hairless face and high pitched voice that he had been cruelly castrated, probably in his youth. So despite all indications to the contrary, not only was this court official a lonely man who was unable to marry, he was also an outsider, who was familiar with injustice and humiliation. In a word, he was poor in spirit with a great longing for an encounter with the living God. Presumably that was why he had made such a long pilgrimage to Jerusalem. This impressive pilgrim was reading Is 53:7-8 when Philip ran alongside and asked whether he understood the passage. He replied, 'How can I unless someone guides me?' (Acts 8:31). Implicit in that statement was not only a passionate longing for a sense of ultimate belonging, it was a clear invitation to Philip to explain the word of God to him.

There is reason to suspect that the eunuch was deeply moved when Philip told him about the suffering servant; how Jesus had endured great injustice at the hands of the Jewish and Roman authorities, had been ostracised, humiliated in public, and died without heirs. He could identify with the Lord. He had suffered the childhood injustice of involuntary castration. As a result of his effeminate appearance and high pitched voice he had often endured ridicule, and because of his violently enforced infertility he could have neither wife nor children. He could see from Philip's testimony that, as God's Son, Jesus had completely identified with his suffering and shame. This was his moment of revelation, of spiritual awakening. Inwardly, he felt accepted and loved by Jesus. His response was instantaneous and wholehearted. Not only did he believe in the Good News, he immediately asked to be baptised. 'Then both Philip and the eunuch went down into the water and Philip baptised him.' At last, his search was over. Finally, he felt the joy of ultimate belonging.

When evangelists proclaim the Good News, some of those listening may fail to respond because they refuse, for one reason or another, to acknowledge their poverty. I think that Jesus may have had this in mind when he said in Mt 10:14-15, 'If anyone will not welcome you or listen to your words, shake the dust off your feet when you leave that home or town.' In other words, if people are unaware of their need for salvation, (e.g. because of a pride that represses that awareness), there is no point in trying to evangelise them. Instead, concentrate your efforts on those who acknowledge their need for God and who are ready to listen to the word of God with receptive and trusting hearts.

Conclusion

Speaking in the Vatican during the 1984 *ad limina* visit of the Columbian bishops, John Paul II said to them: 'The greatest service that we can render to others is evangelisation, which prepares them to fulfil themselves as children of God, liberates them from injustice, and leads them to fuller life[33] ... For the truly poor are those who lack material necessities, but even poorer are those who are ignorant of the path that God points out to them.'[34] Those insights are equally relevant in the Ireland of the twenty-first century. Evangelisers need to make a preferential option for the poor by firstly concentrating on less fortunate brothers and sisters who live mainly in deprived urban areas. As St James wrote: 'Listen, my dear brothers: Has not God chosen those who are poor in the eyes of the world to be rich in faith and to inherit the kingdom he promised those who love him?' (Jas 2:5). That said, evangelists must also be mindful of the new poor spoken about by Blessed Teresa of Calcutta. Not only do they need to hear the Good News of the kerygma, they also need to be encouraged to express their gratitude to God by befriending the materially poor, helping them in their needs, and seeking justice for them.[35] They do this in the knowledge that they are serving Christ in the least of the brothers and the sisters, who St Vincent de Paul referred to as, 'our lords and masters.'[36]

33. *Insegnamenti* II (1984), at 999.
34. John Paul II, Homily in Santo Domingo (12 October 1984).
35. The Irish Mission Statement of the St Vincent de Paul Society says: 'We are committed to identifying the root causes of poverty and social injustice in Ireland and, in solidarity with the poor and disadvantaged, to advocate and work for the changes required to create a more just and caring society,' *River of Love*, 70.
36. Louis Abelly, *The Life of the Venerable Servant of God Vincent de Paul*, vol 3, (New York: New City Press, 1993), 117.

By doing this, not only will the poor be blessed, as we have already seen, so will those who help them. As Jesus promised: 'It is in giving that we receive ... For the measure you give will be the measure you get back' (Lk 6:38).

Recommended Reading

- Joachim Jeremias, 'Good News for the Poor,' *New Testament Theology* (London: SCM Press, 1981), 108-121.
- Albert Nolan, 'The Poor and Oppressed,' *Jesus Before Christianity* (London: DLT, 1992), 27-36.
- David Williams, *The Mind & Heart of a Vincentian* (London: St Vincent de Paul Society England & Wales, 2001).
- Viktor E. Frankl, *Man's Search for Meaning* (New York: Pocket Books, 1963).
- Malcom Muggeridge, *Something Beautiful for God: Mother Teresa of Calcutta* (London: Collins / Fontana, 1971).

SECTION THREE

Means of Basic Evangelisation

CHAPTER SEVEN

An Evangelising Diocese and Parish

In RM 3 the late John Paul II wrote: 'I sense that the moment has come to commit all of the church's energies to a new evangelisation and to the mission *ad gentes*. No believer in Christ, no institution of the church can avoid this supreme duty: to proclaim Christ to all peoples.' When the Holy Father said that no institution of the church can avoid the call to a new evangelisation, he clearly referred to the dioceses and parishes and their structures. What is a diocese? In CCL 369 we read: 'A diocese is a portion of the people of God which is entrusted to a bishop for him to shepherd with the co-operation of the *presbyterium*, so that, adhering to its pastor and gathered by him in the Holy Spirit through the gospel and the Eucharist, it constitutes a particular church in which the one, holy, catholic, and apostolic church of Christ is truly present and operative.' What exactly is a parish? Is it a community of worshippers or a geographical area? The CCL 515, 517, 518 gives a clear answer when it says: 'A parish is a certain community of Christ's faithful stably established within a particular church, whose pastoral care, under the authority of the diocesan bishop, is entrusted to a parish priest as its proper pastor ... Where circumstances so require, the pastoral care of a parish, or a number of parishes together, can be entrusted to several priests jointly, but with the stipulation that one of the priests is to be the moderator of the pastoral care to be exercised[1] ... As a general rule, a parish is to be territorial.'

There is a problem with many contemporary parishes, especially in urban areas. They are so big that they tend to be a bit anonymous. For instance, if someone stops attending church no

1. It would seem that this canon is referring to what we call a clustered parish.

one is likely to notice, and if a latter day prodigal son or daughter comes back to the worshipping community after a long absence, they may not receive a joyful welcome because no one is aware of his or her return. There is an increasing recognition therefore, that ideally a parish should be a community of communities, a federation of smaller groups whose members have a sense of belonging and mutual nurturance. Pope John Paul II said in par 26 of *Christifideles laici* (hereafter CL): 'So that all parishes may be truly communities of Christians, local ecclesial authorities ought to foster ... small basic or so-called 'living' communities, where the faithful can communicate the word of God and express it in service and love to one another; these communities are true expressions of ecclesial communion and centres of evangelisation, in communion with their pastors.'

A number of bishops have acknowledged this point. Cardinal Cormac Murphy O Connor, the former Archbishop of Westminster, said, 'We must go and build evangelising communities.'[2] That sentiment was echoed by Archbishop Diarmuid Martin of Dublin in an address entitled, 'The Priest Evangeliser and Witness.' 'I believe,' he said, 'that the transmission of the faith in the years to come will have to be more and more linked with the creation of faith communities, like the basic ecclesial communities that we speak about in the context of Africa or Latin America. These communities will help people, young and old, to be formed in their faith and to live out their faith concretely in a cultural context which is less and less supportive of faith. These communities must then, however, find their nourishment through their insertion into the broader communion of the church in the common celebration of the Eucharist. Our *parishes must become communions of communities* [my italics], finding their unity again in the liturgy.'[3] I witnessed what Archbishop Martin might have had in mind when I visited St Estorgio, a large parish in central Milan. Fr Pigi Perini, the parish priest, has fostered the growth of as many as 125 parish groups, each of which has about eight to ten members.[4]

2. *The Tablet* (26 January 2002)
3. The National Council of Priests of Ireland, 28 September 2004
4. Pat Collins, *The Gifts of the Spirit and the New Evangelisation*137-8.

Canon Law on Evangelisation in the Parish

Following the description of what a parish is, we are told what the clergy and their people are called to do as evangelisers. It seems that CCL 762 refers to the lay people in the parish when it says that, 'The people of God are first united through the word of the living God ... For this reason sacred ministers are to consider the office of preaching as of great importance, since proclaiming the Gospel of God to *all* [my italics] is among their principal duties.' The word *all* is confusing. Does it refer to all the practising Catholics, all the baptised Catholics, or all the people in the parish? It probably means all the people who live in the parish because CCL 771 goes on to talk about two other constituencies. In part one is says: 'Pastors of souls, especially bishops and parish priests, are to be solicitous that the word of God is preached to those also of the faithful who, because of the circumstances of their lives, cannot sufficiently avail themselves of the ordinary pastoral care or are even totally deprived of it.' In the second part, the canon adds: 'They are also to take care that the Good News of the gospel reaches those living in their territory who are non-believers, since these too, no less than the faithful, must be included in the care of souls.'

Although I am aware that the following ruminations are a bit technical and dry, I'd like to reflect a little on the meaning and implications of canon 771, parts one and two. From reading the footnotes which are only printed in the scholarly edition of *The Code of Canon Law*, there is good reason to believe that the first part of the canon has two groups in mind. The first are referred to in par 18 of the Conciliar Decree *Christus dominus* (hereafter CD) which reads: 'Special concern should be shown for those among the faithful who, on account of their way of life, cannot sufficiently make use of the common and ordinary pastoral care of parish priests or are quite cut off from it. Among this group are the majority of migrants, exiles and refugees, seafarers, air-travellers, gypsies, and others of this kind.' Another group is referred to in CCL 52: 'As a result of the frequent situations of de-Christianisation in our day, it also proves equally necessary for innumerable people who have been baptised but who live quite outside Christian life, for simple people who have a certain faith but an imperfect knowledge of the foundations of that faith, for intellectuals who feel the need to know Jesus Christ in a light different from the instruction they received as children, and for many others.' It would seem therefore, that the first part of canon 771 refers to marginalised and neglected Catholics within the parish and also the un-churched.

To understand what part two of canon 771 might mean, other parts of the CCL can be consulted. Canon 748, part one, points out, '*all are bound to seek the truth* [my italics] in the matters that concern God and his church.' The word *all* here refers to all human beings. Canon 747 adds: 'It is the obligation and inherent right of the church, independently of any human authority, to preach the gospel *to all peoples* [my italics].' The footnotes to the canon then refer to par 9 of the Conciliar Constitution, *Sacrosanctum concilium* (hereafter SC). Because this document of Vatican II taught that the Eucharist was the source and summit of all grace, and that people's greatest vocation is to worship God, it is not surprising that it related the need for evangelisation to this central theological reality. 'Before men can come to the liturgy they must be called to faith and to conversion: "How then are they to call upon him in whom they have not yet believed? But how are they to believe him whom they have not heard? And how are they to hear if no one preaches? And how are men to preach unless they be sent?" (Rom 10:14-15). Therefore the church announces the good tidings of salvation to those who do not believe, so that all men may know the true God and Jesus Christ whom he has sent, and may be converted from their ways, doing penance.' Speaking of unbelievers, par 10 of the Decree, *Ad gentes* (hereafter AG), says that some un-believers are followers of one of the great religions, others remain strangers to the very knowledge of God, while still others expressly deny God's existence, and sometimes even attack it. If the church wants to evangelise these people it must live among them, 'for the same motive which led Christ to bind himself, in virtue of his incarnation, to certain social and cultural conditions of those human beings among whom he dwelt.' So part two of canon 771 asserts that parish priests and deacons together with lay people have a duty to evangelise non Christian believers, and unbelievers of different kinds, who live within the boundaries of the parish.

The Diocese assists Parish Evangelisation

Properly understood, these rather dry sounding canons have revolutionary implications for our dioceses and parishes. As Pope John Paul II said in RM 2: 'There is a new awareness that missionary activity is for all Christians, for all dioceses and parishes.' Would it not be true to say that, as they are currently constituted, our dioceses and parishes are not yet sufficiently outward looking and missionary? As Cardinal Daly observed a few weeks before his death, 'It is not enough to be stuck at a maintenance model of church, the church must be missionary at home as well as abroad.'[5] With regard to missionary zeal one could ask, how much energy do the clergy and parishioners devote to evangelising marginalised groups in their area including those who no longer come to church? How much effort is devoted to bringing the Good News of the gospel to people of other religions or no religion at all?

Where dioceses are concerned, three things could usefully be done. Firstly, every one of them should have a mission statement that mentions evangelisation. Secondly, each one of them needs to have an office of evangelisation. For instance, speaking of its office, the Diocese of Allentown in the US states that it, 'Assists parishes in implementing programs for evangelisation through various approved ecclesial movements; includes ongoing faith development for Catholics; outreach to inactive and alienated Catholics, and those with no church affiliation.' Depending on the size and resources of the diocese the office might employ one or more paid staff. Thirdly, the office of evangelisation needs to set up an evangelisation team which agrees on a plan of action. It should take note of what John Paul II said in NMI 29: 'It is in the local churches that the specific features of a detailed pastoral plan can be identified, goals and methods, formation and enrichment of the people involved, the search for the necessary resources, which will enable the proclamation of Christ to reach people, mould communities, and have a deep

5. *The Irish Catholic*, (Thurs, 1 October 2009), 1. In years gone by Catholics associated the word mission exclusively with foreign missions. However, it can also refer to the home mission, by means of the new evangelisation which focuses primarily on the unchurched and unbelievers in one's own country (cf RM 33-34).

and incisive influence in bringing gospel values to bear in society and culture.'

For example, the diocese of Northampton in England has such a group. It is a network of people who are committed to evangelisation and are conscious of their own need to be constantly evangelised. They, in collaboration with others, offer opportunities for evangelisation, training and support to parishes, groups and individuals in order to encourage evangelisation in their areas. The Northampton team serves the cause of evangelisation in parishes in the following ways:

- Organising an annual Diocesan Evangelisation Day on different aspects of evangelisation.
- Offering advice and support in order to help parishes and groups develop a strategy for evangelisation.
- Putting on training courses in evangelisation.
- Encouraging the formation and resourcing of parish or area evangelisation teams and local, practical initiatives for evangelisation.
- Partnering and networking with groups directly involved in mission.
- Raising the profile and developing the understanding of evangelisation as well as publicising evangelisation initiatives by diocesan means of communication.
- Supporting and encouraging those already involved in evangelisation in the diocese by developing a supportive network and publicising the good work that is already going on.
- Exploring with others, the role and benefits of small communities in the life of the church as a means of evangelisation.
- Providing a forum for ongoing reflection on evangelisation in the Diocese and in the culture. In particular, it would explore the ongoing implications for evangelisation of the church's preferential option for the poor.
- Drawing up a diocesan directory which mentions all the groups involved in various kinds of evangelisation, together with addresses, phone numbers, resources etc.

Here is a short checklist of questions which could be made available to parishes by the diocesan office for evangelisation. It could be used as a rough guide to assess how missionary a parish actually is.

1. Has the parish a mission statement, one that includes an explicit commitment to evangelisation?
2. Does the parish have a yearly plan that states what individuals and groups will evangelise the un-churched in the area, and how they will do it?
3. Does the parish have any form of outreach to the unbelievers in the parish?
4. What does the parish do to evangelise young adults between the ages of 18 and 35?
5. Does the parish council have an evangelisation committee that plans evangelistic activities?
6. Does the parish provide any training for parishioners who want to learn how to evangelise effectively alone and in groups?
7. Is there an evangelisation team in the parish that does house-to-house visitation?
8. If there is an occasional parish mission, is it mainly focused on those who practise or is there a conscious, organised effort to reach out to the un-churched?
9. Does the parish newsletter contain regular pieces to do with the nature of evangelisation, the motives parishioners have of engaging in it, and practical means of doing so?
10. Are there any groups in the parish, such as the housebound or an intercessory prayer group, who are praying in an intentional way for parish renewal and evangelisation in the area?

If a parish cannot answer yes to at least six of these questions, it probably means that it is too inward looking. There would be nothing unusual in that. As Cardinal Avery Dulles pointed out in a chapter entitled, 'John Paul II and the New Evangelisation,' the majority of Catholics are not strongly inclined toward evangelisation. Many of them don't understand the word, and if they do, they may think it is Protestant! As priests know only too well, the church's activities are primarily directed toward the instruction and pastoral care of its own members, whose needs and demands tax the institution and its resources to the limit. 'Absorbed in the inner problems of the church, and occasionally in issues of peace and justice,' observed the Cardinal, 'contemporary Catholics feel relatively little responsibility for spreading the faith.'[6] A wise parish

6. *Church and Society: The Laurence J McGinley Lectures, 1988-2007*, 87.

priest described the situation in more graphic terms when he observed that far from being centres of evangelisation, many parishes resemble nursing homes! Parishes need to look outward by means of evangelisation, in the belief that not only are they fulfilling the great command and the requirements of canon law, it is in giving the faith to others, principally by the witness of lives well lived, and by preaching the kerygma, that the faith of the parishioners will be affirmed and deepened. As John Paul II said in RM 2: 'I wish to invite the church to renew her missionary commitment ... Faith is strengthened when it is given to others.' In RM 11, the Holy Father added, 'Mission is an issue of faith, an accurate indicator of our faith in Christ and his love for us.'

Compared to diocesan clergy, I have spent relatively little time working in a parish. My lack of hands-on experience is a mixed blessing as far as this chapter is concerned. It is a disadvantage in so far as I am not intimately acquainted with all the complexities and difficulties of diocesan and parish life. However, I have found that my very lack of experience has enabled me to look at parishes in a more objective manner which, hopefully, enables me to be more aware of possibilities than problems. Over the years, I have noticed three interrelated difficulties. Firstly, many dioceses do not have structures in place which could promote mission by helping parishes to respond to the great commission of Jesus to evangelise. Secondly, dioceses and parishes often fail to distinguish between the satisfaction of pastoral needs and the pursuit of evangelical priorities. While there is undoubtedly overlap between the two, they are not synonymous. Those dioceses and parishes who have neither a mission statement or a yearly plan, with stated evangelising goals that can be evaluated on a regular basis, resemble rudderless ships adrift on stormy seas. Instead of being proactive in the pursuit of stated priorities, they tend to react to an endless succession of needs. As one prominent layman from the United States observed at a conference in Dublin, 'The bishop, priest or lay person who focuses on the satisfaction of urgent pastoral needs to the exclusion of evangelical priorities contributes by default to the decline of the church.'[7] Thirdly, it would probably be

7. Ralph Martin speaking at the International Charismatic Conference in the RDS in 1978.

true to say that many dioceses and parishes seem to be administered rather than governed. Administration is oriented toward the maintenance of traditions, structures and practices, whereas governance is motivated by the mission of the diocese and the parish and their duty to evangelise. To move from administration to governance requires clarity of vision and realistic goal setting. That participation in the kingly rule of Jesus (i.e. *munus regendi*) is the focus of the remainder of this chapter.

Creating a More Missionary Parish

1) The Parish Pastoral Council

According to *The Priest, Pastor and Leader of the Parish Community*, the 2002 Instruction of the Congregation for the Clergy, 'The basic task of such a parish council is to serve, at institutional level, the orderly collaboration of the faithful in the development of pastoral activity which is proper to priests. The pastoral council is thus a consultative organ in which the faithful, expressing their baptismal responsibility, can assist the parish priest, who presides at the council, by offering their advice on pastoral matters.'[8] An Irish pamphlet, *Parish Pastoral Councils: A Framework for Developing Diocesan Norms and Parish Guidelines*, asks what do parish councils do?[9] The document says that processes in which the parish pastoral council would normally be involved, include:

- Reflection and planning: in collaboration with the members of the parish community, identifying their needs and the challenges they face, and reflecting in dialogue with them on what needs to be done.

8. CCL 536 says: 'In every parish in the diocese, a Pastoral Council shall be established, if the diocesan Bishop, after consulting with the Council of Presbyters, so decides.' The Parish Pastoral Council is a structure concerned with the pastoral activities of the parish. It is made up of a representative body of the faithful and must include the parish priest. The Parish Pastoral Council shares the responsibility for building the parish into a vibrant Christian community that promotes gospel values such as love, justice, peace and evangelisation. It is a consultative body of leaders who actively seek the inspiration of the Holy Spirit and are guided by the teachings, laws and recommendations of the universal church and the local diocesan church.

9. Published in 2005 by the Irish Bishop's Commission for Pastoral Renewal and Adult Faith Development.

- Animation: enabling the baptised to discover their gifts in response to the needs and challenges of the parish, and developing these gifts through the provision of training and ongoing formation.
- Providing structures: that will make connection between the needs and the challenges of the parish with the gifts and resources in the parish and the diocese.
- Communication: ensuring that effective dialogue takes place within the parish, the diocese and the wider community.
- Evaluation: reviewing the life and activities of the parish so that parishioners might have a sense of a developing, dynamic Christian community.

Ideally the members of a parish council would be people with a mix of skills which would enable each one to contribute in a constructive way to the work of the council. It seems to me that every council should devise a consultative process which would enable it to write or revise a mission statement which contains a section on evangelisation. Furthermore, parish councils should devise parish plans which include a section on evangelisation, which states the goals to be attained during the coming year, and resources that would be provided to attain them. There is also need for accountability by assessing how the goals stated in the plan have been carried out. If they were not carried out, why so? Was it due to the fact that the goals were unrealistic? or that people failed to accomplish what they said they would do, due to lack of effort?

2) Prayer and Prophetic Vision

There is a verse in the *Amplified Bible* which reads, 'Where there is no vision [no redemptive revelation of God], the people perish' (Prov 29:18). That being true, the first thing that the priests and people need in the parish is a God inspired vision for the future of the community. When St Peter preached to the people on Pentecost Sunday he quoted Joel 2:28 and told them that the Spirit would enable the old people to dream dreams and the young people to see visions (cf Acts 2:17). This is an example of how this can happen:

When I was living in Detroit I heard Fr Mark Montminy of St Marie's in Manchester, New Hampshire, tell the story of how his struggling inner-city parish had been transformed from a dispirited, introspective community to a more extroverted, and evangelising one. Mark himself had undergone a spiritual awakening when he experienced the power of the kerygma as a result of attending a Cursillo weekend and some time later by being baptised in the Spirit as a result of attending a Life in the Spirit Seminar. He said that when he arrived in St Marie's, the parish pastoral council, like so many others, was concerned with administrative issues such as the purchase of new boilers, reducing the parish debt, fixing a leak in the church roof and the like, more than pastoral or evangelistic ones. Fr Mark met with the parish pastoral council and invited them to pray for an outpouring of the Spirit and to dream with him about the future.

For the next five months each meeting began with an hour of prayer and afterwards by sharing dreams of what the parish could look like in five and ten years' time. In his Papal Message for the Word Youth Day on 24 July 2007, Pope Benedict XVI endorsed this kind of approach when he said: 'Apostolic and missionary fruitfulness is not principally due to programmes and pastoral methods that are cleverly drawn up and efficient, but is the result of the community's constant prayer.' Realising this was so, Fr Montminy put the primary emphasis on the need for prayer in St Marie's. Too often in church circles when people decide to plan for the future, a quick prayer is said at the beginning of the meeting and then the participants get down to the serious work of discussing possibilities and setting goals. The danger is that, instead of being guided by the Spirit, as Paul advocates in Gal 5:25, they are guided by their own natural thinking and knowledge. However, as scripture warns us in Ps 127:1, 'Unless the Lord builds the house, those who build it labour in vain.' St Marie's parish council also organised a meeting where any and every parishioner, who so wished, could speak about their hopes for the future. Following this process the pastoral council wrote a mission statement, in collaboration with every existing committee, society and organisation in the parish. One section stated: 'God's call to our community today remains the same: to proclaim Jesus Christ in word and deed! This is a call to renew our baptismal commitment where we pledge to live for God and be his light in the world. We feel a particular urgency to live this call today in the midst of a disintegrating society marked by such manifestations of darkness as alienation, loneliness, and despair. Only the light of Christ can overcome this darkness; only his love can bring life out of death.'[10]

One would suspect that although the members of any parish or its parish council might be full of good will, it would not necessarily mean that they had been fully evangelised. As a result, the parish priest could perhaps suggest that, as well as praying and seeking vision, the members of the council should attend a basic evangelisation course such as a Life in the Spirit Seminar, a Cursillo Weekend, a Philip Retreat or an Alpha course. As Paul VI reminded us in EN 15, evangelisation begins at home in the local faith community: 'The church is evangelised by constant conversion and renewal, in order to evangelise the world with credibility.' Only those who have been truly evangelised themselves are able to evangelise effectively and form true Christian disciples. As St Vincent de Paul said to a young priest: 'It is essential that our Lord himself impress his mark and character upon you. Just as a wild plant on which a graft has been inserted brings forth fruits of the same sort as the graft, so too with us poor creatures. When our Lord imprints his mark on us and gives us, so to say, the sap of his Spirit and grace, we being united to him as the branches are united to the vine, will do what he did when he was on earth. I mean to say, we will perform divine actions and bring to birth, like St Paul, people filled with this Spirit, children of our Lord.'[11]

3) An Evangelising Committee[12]

As a result of living many years in religious life, I'm fully persuaded that there can be no real change in any community, in-

---

10. Mark Montminy, 'The Story of an Evangelising Parish,' *John Paul II and the New Evangelisation*, ed Ralph Martin & Peter Williamson (Cincinnati: Servant Books, 2006), 236.
11. Andre Dodin, *Vincent de Paul and Charity: A Contemporary Portrait of his Life and Apostolic Spirit*, eds Hugh O'Donnell & Marjorie Gale Hornstein (New York: New City Press, 1993), 82.
12. In some parishes the pastoral council will form a number of committees dealing with such things as finance, worship, and social justice. The evangelisation committee is another of these. Its purpose is to

cluding diocesan and parish communities, without structural change; the kind that accommodates the aspirations, values and priorities of the group. In other words, if a parish has a vision of its desired future, it needs to accommodate that vision in some organisational way. Presuming that the parish mission statement includes a commitment to evangelise, the parish priest together with his parish pastoral council could consider creating an evangelising committee as a matter of urgency. It could be charged with the responsibility of implementing the evangelisation section of the mission statement and would be accountable to the parish priest and the pastoral council for its implementation. I would suggest that such a committee should think about two things. Firstly, how will it help all the committees and groups in the parish to become more aware of their potential for evangelisation? As the American bishops said in par 85 of *Go and Make Disciples*, 'Every element of the parish must respond to the evangelical imperative – priests, religious, lay persons, parish staff, ministers, organisations, social clubs, local schools and parish religious education programmes. Otherwise evangelisation will be something a few people in the parish see as their ministry – rather than the reason for the parish's existence and *the objective of every ministry in the parish* [my italics].' To this end the evangelisation committee could arrange to bring as many members as possible of these groups and organisations together in order to explore why and how they might evangelise in their respective spheres of influence. Secondly, the evangelisation committee needs to work out how it might facilitate evangelisation of the three constituencies which were mentioned earlier in this chapter together with the following groups:

1) Young people, e.g. senior pupils in secondary schools, university students, and adults under the age of thirty five.

2) Families of different kinds. Not only are families a domestic church where primary evangelisation of children takes place, single parents and couples often need outside support to carry out their all important role.

3) Marginalised groups such as immigrants and Travelling People, who are living in the parish.

The evangelisation committee could meet at least once a

month. Having devoted a good deal of time to prayer it would try to come up with a one year plan for evangelisation both within and without the worshipping community, consistent with the stated aim expressed in the parish mission statement. For example, I came across one very succinct parish mission statement, the last third of which was devoted to evangelisation. It read: 'Our mission is to know Christ better, live as he calls us to live, *and make him better known* [my italics].' An Irish parish in County Kildare rightly mentions evangelisation in part one of its statement: 'We the Catholic family of Our Lady's Nativity parish in Leixlip, believing in and being inspired by Jesus Christ, together continue our life of worship, mission and evangelisation.' The plan of the evangelising committee could contain such things as, who will do what? and, when they will do it? For example, one thing the committee could organise would be an Alpha day. It could do this by firstly inviting personnel from the Alpha Ireland Office to come on a specified day to speak about the principles and practicalities of the well known evangelisation course. Incidentally, as chapter ten will indicate, there are different forms of the Alpha course which cater for different needs. Afterwards small group leaders could be trained before the Alpha course would be put on in the parish.[13] Experience indicates that churched people tend to come to the first two or three courses, while the un-churched and unbelievers begin to come to subsequent ones. For more on this see chapter ten. If the evangelising committee is blessed with creative imagination it will be able to come up with other evangelising initiatives. Here are a number of possibilities:

a) To create a welcoming community

When I lived in a parish in Michigan for two years I was impressed by the fact that there was a team of male and female ushers who wore a distinctive blazer. Each Sunday a number of them would be on duty. Their main job was to welcome people when they arrived at church, especially visitors. They also helped to find seats for people in the church. That sense of wel-

13. There are written and electronic resources available which explain how to run an Alpha course.

come is a form of Good News in itself. As scripture says, 'Offer hospitality to one another without grumbling' (1 Pet 4:9). Another thing that impressed me in Detroit was the fact that each Lent most Catholic parishes had suppers on Friday evenings in the parish hall. Fish and chips were cooked by parishioners and served by teenagers. Hundreds of people came, the old and the young, professional people and factory workers. I also found that folk would attend who wouldn't usually go to Mass. These suppers were joyful, noisy affairs that created a sense of belonging where people could talk in an informal way about all kinds of topics, including some to do with faith. An evangelisation committee in an Irish parish might use ideas like these in a modified way.

b) To arrange for a parish mission and follow on
A team would be invited to conduct the mission whether mainly clerical, like the Redemptorists and Vincentians, or mainly lay, like the Céilí community in Kilbeggan in County Westmeath. I found that normally traditional parish missions were attended by about a third of the people who came to Sunday Mass. Usually the mission was more like a retreat than an evangelising event which sought to convert people to the Lord and to deepen their faith. If a contemporary mission was arranged, the evangelising committee would need to consider a number of points:

- How will the parish prepare for the mission event? Here is an attractive mission prayer that was issued by one parish in the North of Ireland: 'God our Father, pour out your Spirit upon us. Free us from sin, awaken us to the sacred. Grant us a new knowledge of your love; a new experience of your power; a new faithfulness to your Word; a new commitment to Christ. Fill us with joy to celebrate the fullness of life. Mary, pray for us to your Son that we may be renewed, and that we may help to renew the face of the earth. Amen.'
- What kind of subjects will be dealt with during the mission? Will they be catechetical ones such as prayer, marriage, suffering, and the Eucharist, or more kerygmatic ones such as the unconditional mercy and love of God, healing, and being filled with the Spirit?

- How will the parish reach out to the un-churched during the mission?
- Will volunteers visit all the homes in twos to tell people about the mission; to give them a printed programme of events; and to invite them to come to all or some of the sessions?

It might be a good idea to have some events during the mission that go easy on religion. They could be held outside the church building or parish hall, for example in a golf club, pub or community centre. As part of its week long mission in a Dublin parish during the economic downturn, a priest of my acquaintance gave a talk in a hotel on the topic of reducing stress and finding peace. A local paper printed a short article he had written on the subject and it was mentioned on a local radio station before the mission. Parishioners also have to ask, what kind of follow up will there be when the mission is over? Could a Bible or an Alpha course be organised?

I have often been asked what to do with the people who have had a conversion experience during a parish mission, or as a result of attending an evangelising course. What many of us realise is that renewed Christians need to belong to smaller groups which can nurture their faith on behalf of the parish. In sociological terms, we are moving from *gemeinschaft* (i.e. communitarian), tightly-knit societies, to *gesellschaft* (i.e. individualistic), loosely-knit ones. Parishes need to be counter-cultural by creating as many special purpose groups as possible, many of which will be led by 'religious virtuosi', to use a sociological phrase. These are people of religious conviction and enthusiasm who animate their groups. So an evangelisation committee that desires to nurture people once the mission is over might think of producing a detailed list of groups in the parish, which would describe what they do, and include information about when and where they meet, together with contact names, phone numbers, and email addresses. If they are not already present, the pastoral council might think of setting up parish cell groups as one way of satisfying this need.[14] I conducted a mission in a Dublin parish

14. Rev Robert L Buschmiller, 'How To Renew Your Parish In Just Twelve Years,' and 'Building Small Christian Communities by Presentation Ministries (Manual for training home cell leaders, guide-

which included prayerful reflection and group sharing on a Bible passage each day. I was gratified to find that when the mission was over a number of parishioners kept it going once a week. They seemed to be aware that in postmodern society unconditional *belonging* is necessary for openness to right *belief* which eventually leads to right *behaviour* (cf Acts 4:32-36). Special purpose groups such as the *Lectio Divina*, Legion of Mary, St Vincent de Paul Society, and Charismatic prayer group, help in different ways to foster that sense of belonging and nurturance.

Another method of engaging in on-going evangelisation in a parish is to show movies which have a good spiritual or moral point to make. This approach is particularly appropriate for young adults. When the movie is shown it can be followed by a discussion, prayer and then by some refreshments. Movies that could be shown would be *Tender Mercies* (1983), *Amazing Grace* (2006), *Bella* (2006), *Resurrection* (1980), *Babette's Feast* (1987), *The Matrix* (1999) etc. Films like these would be very good springboards leading to the discussion of issues related to the kerygma.

c) To organise talks and courses on evangelisation in the parish

In EN 73, Pope Paul VI said: 'A serious preparation is needed for all workers for evangelisation.' Pope John Paul II said in EE 46: 'Evangelisers must be properly trained ... All the baptised, since they are witnesses of Christ, should receive a training appropriate to their circumstances, not only so that their faith does not wither for lack of care in a hostile environment such as the secularist world, but also so that their witness to the gospel will receive strength and inspiration.' The evangelisation committee needs to prepare willing parishioners to tackle the problem of evangelising in modern, secular society. They might consider topics such as evangelisation in scripture and in contemporary papal teaching, how to engage in one-to-one evangelisation with a view to sharing one's faith convictions with relatives,

---

lines for home cells, and implementing home cells in your community.) http://www.catholic-jhb.org.za/articles/hcell_renew.htm (accessed 19 October 2009). cf Michael Hurley, *Transforming Your Parish: Building a Faith Community* (Dublin: Columba, 1998).

friends, work colleagues, and strangers?[15] Happily there are Irish School of Evangelisation courses available in Dublin. The school not only trains people to spread the Good News, it conducts Phillip and Emmaus retreats.[16] There is also Our Lady's School of Evangelisation in Knock which trains lay evangelists from many countries,[17] as does Youth With A Mission (YWAM) in Belfast and Dublin.[18] The John the Baptist Koinonia community conducts evangelisation training courses in Belfast.[19] That said, it seems clear that training is required in the dioceses of Ireland where parishioners can be prepared to evangelise in parishes. Arguably, we also need a national school of evangelisation which would be sponsored by the Irish hierarchy. In the absence of these facilities, the parish evangelisation committee could make arrangements for training to be provided locally.

d) Prayer support

The evangelisation committee could also try to recruit a number of volunteers who would be willing to go on prayer walks around the parish. I arranged for this to be done in Detroit when I was an acting pastor. Some men walked in twos on different roads within the parish boundaries. As they walked they prayed the rosary and also said spontaneous prayers of intercession for all the people living in the vicinity. They asked the Lord to bless all the homes, the people who lived in them and to deliver them from any evil which would try to prevent them from responding to the gospel message. In this regard it is worth recalling what Jesus said about the role of the devil in the parable of the sower in Lk 8:11-13. Our Lord warned that Satan will do all in his power to prevent people from accepting the kerygma in faith. It is reassuring to read in 2 Cor 10:3-5: 'For though we live in the world, we do not wage war as the world does. The weapons we fight with are not the weapons of the world. On the contrary,

15. On the subject of one-to-one evangelisation see Martin Pable's *Reclaim the Fire: A Parish Guide to Evangelisation* (Notre Dame: Ave Maria Press, 2002), 92-7.
16. http://www.esatclear.ie/~isoe/
17, http://www.olseireland.org/olseaboutus.html
18. http://www.ywamireland.org/
19. http://www.koinoniajtbireland.org/

they have divine power to demolish strongholds. We demolish arguments and every pretension that sets itself up against the knowledge of God, and we take captive every thought to make it obedient to Christ.' This kind of intercession would be particularly appropriate in the period before a parish mission. It is worth mentioning that in every parish there are sick and housebound people of faith. They could be asked not only to offer their sufferings and diminishments for the sake of effective evangelisation, but also to offer prayers of intercession for renewal in the parish, deliverance from evil influences, and for those who are committed to evangelisation.

On the same lines, the evangelisation committee could arrange for one or two groups of people in the parish to commit time to periods of intercessory prayer and moderate fasting for two main intentions. Firstly, that the Lord would empower all those who are engaged in evangelisation with the Holy Spirit and his gifts.[20] Secondly, that the Lord would protect the evangelisers from the illusions, false inspirations and temptations of the devil, who inevitably opposes anyone that tries to bring people closer to Christ. As St Paul says in Eph 6:18-20: 'Pray in the Spirit on all occasions with all kinds of prayers and requests. With this in mind, be alert and always keep on praying for all the saints. Pray also for me, that whenever I open my mouth, words may be given me so that I will fearlessly make known the mystery of the gospel.'

In this context, the New Springtime Community, to which I belong, was led in prayer of an inspired kind to read Nehemiah chapters two and four. They describe how the prophet and his Jewish volunteers tried to rebuild the breached walls of

20. cf Letter of Benedict XVI Proclaiming a Year for Priests: 'While testing the spirits to discover if they be from God, priests must discover with faith, recognise with joy, and foster diligently the many and varied charismatic gifts of the laity, whether they be of a humble or more exalted kind ... the communion between ordained and charismatic ministries can provide a helpful impulse to a renewed commitment by the church in proclaiming and bearing witness to the gospel of hope and charity in every corner of the world ... Only thus will priests be able to live fully the gift of celibacy and build thriving Christian communities in which the miracles which accompanied the first preaching of the gospel can be repeated.'

Jerusalem (symbolic of evangelisation and revival). Nehemiah was so conscious of the danger of attack by enemies, (symbolic of the opposition of the evil one) that he arranged for half of the people to stand guard to detect and ward-off the insidious attacks (symbolic of intercessors who engage in spiritual warfare), while the other volunteers rebuilt the walls and replaced the gates (symbolic of the new evangelisation by renewing the faith of the un-churched).[21]

e) Mission Spirituality

The evangelising committee is also responsible for encouraging a mission spirituality in the parish. Pope John Paul II wrote in a particularly perceptive way about the main contours of such a spirituality in RM 87-91. The committee could organise weekend retreats which would give parishioners an opportunity to focus on particular aspects of mission spirituality such as the universal call to holiness (RM 90), the importance of being guided by the Spirit (RM 87), how to read and pray the scriptures in a contemplative way (RM 91) and how to pray with people for whatever they need.

I am also a great believer in pilgrimages because they help Catholics to relate to the riches of their Christian past and to look to the Christian future with hope. The evangelisation committee could organise a walk to a local holy place such as an old monastery or holy well where there would be a short talk, lots of prayer, and Christian 'craic'. I know that some Catholics in Wales have been led by the Spirit to do this. In the Summer of 2009 a number of them spent three days walking to St David's in the south of the country. By all accounts the experience strengthened the faith of those who participated, afforded them opportunities to evangelise when they met curious people on the way, and aroused a good deal of public interest. Now that they have come to terms with such things as places to eat and sleep, insurance cover, and the like, they are planning to have similar pilgrimages in the future. Much the same could be done in Ireland.

21.Pat Collins, 'Spiritual Warfare,' *Spirituality for the 21st Century: Christian Living in a Secular Age*, 170-9; 'Prayer as Intercession,' *Prayer in Practice* (Dublin: Columba, 2000), 133-47.

4) Evangelising Teams

One thing the evangelisation committee could usefully do is either to become an evangelising team itself or to create one in the parish. There are many such teams in American parishes because the national plan *Go and Make Disciples* urged them to set them up. Par 136 said: 'Every parish should have an evangelising team trained and prepared to help the whole parish implement the goals and objectives of this plan. These teams could help to train Catholics in evangelisation and provide resources to individuals, families and parish groups. Parishes might even consider designating a trained person as a full-time co-ordinator of evangelisation.' The notion of an evangelising team is one that is new in Ireland. These teams, which are answerable to the evangelising committee, are made up of volunteers who have been evangelised themselves and want to respond to both the Lord's call, and the insistent call of the contemporary church, to bring the Good News of God's unconditional love to everyone. Ideally, if there was an office of evangelisation in the diocese, it would be able to send people who would help to train the members of the evangelisation team.

Like the evangelising committee, the evangelising team meets once a month. In his useful book *The Evangelising Catholic: A Practical Handbook for Reaching Out,* Passionist priest Frank DeSiano says that evangelising teams should keep points like the following in mind when they have their meetings:

- Begin on time.
- Start with a period of prayer and faith sharing on a relevant scripture text.
- Have an agenda which has been circulated a day or two before and stick to it.
- Stress the importance of unity of mind and heart as the key to successful collaboration.
- Ensure that everyone gets an opportunity to contribute. Do not let one person monopolise the conversation.
- Be clear about the tasks that the meeting agrees to undertake and make sure that they are realistic, precise and attainable given the constraints of time and limited resources.
- Decide who will inform the parish priest and the parish

pastoral committee about the decisions. Ideally the liaison person should be a member of that committee.

- Set a time and a place for the next meeting.
- End on time.

From what I have read, it seems to me that there are two overlapping tasks that the evangelising team can accomplish.

a) Conducting a parish census or survey

Firstly, it is not easy to evangelise in a knowing and focused way unless the would-be evangelisers have accurate, up-to-date information about the needs in the area, e.g. how many people are in the family? what age group do they belong to? where do they live? and so on. The Legion of Mary have carried out such information gathering for years.[22] This being so, the evangelisation committee would do well to arrange for a parish census with the assistance of the parish priest and the parish pastoral council. Afterwards the evangelisation team could consider the following issues before drawing up a questionnaire:

- Will the team visit everyone in the area, or will it seek to revise and update data the parish already possesses? Although it is labour intensive, the advantage of visiting everyone is that it introduces representatives of the parish to non-Catholic Christians and to unbelievers. It also enables the team to get an accurate picture of how many Catholics there are in the area.
- What questions should be asked on the questionnaire form and why? They need to be respectful of people's privacy.
- Who will write down the data on the questionnaire sheet?
- What is the advantage of visiting non-parishioners and asking personal questions?

The Office of Evangelisation in the Diocese of Peoria in Illinois, USA has helpful information available on its website.[23]

22. Frank Duff, *The Official Handbook of the Legion of Mary* (Dublin: *Concilium Legionis Mariae*, 2005), 235. As the Handbook says in an awkward way: 'Included in what is learned is much that will form subject for long-continued effort on the part of priest and legionaries.'

23. http://www.cdop.org/pdfs/ParishHomeVisitation.pdf (accessed 28 August 2009)

It contains a sample census card. Irish Catholics need to be aware that in the USA where there is so much moving from one parish to another, Catholics are supposed to register in the parish when they come to live in it. Needless to say census information can be added to the parish data base.

When I was living in St Valentine's Parish in Redford, Michigan I conducted a survey with the help of a sociologist. I drew up a questionnaire which aimed to find out from those who attended the Eucharist one particular weekend why they thought other Catholics had become inactive. It contained a number of questions, some of which were to do with the inactive issue and others of a more personal nature to do with such things as the respondent's age, occupation, race etc. As a research instrument it aimed to do quantitative as opposed to qualitative, or comparative research. With the co-operation of the pastor, the questionnaires were placed on a table in the porch of the church. When the notices were being read out at the Masses on the Saturday night and the Sunday morning, as well as at a para-liturgical service on Sunday afternoon, members of the congregation were invited to answer the questionnaire. Some respondents told me they were keen to fill in the questionnaire because members of their families were no longer active Catholics, while others said that they themselves had been inactive in the past and had insight into the whys and wherefores of the phenomenon. All-in-all, 138 completed questionnaires were returned. It was estimated that between 950-1000 people attended the four services that Sunday. Statistically, the responses represented about 15% of the Sunday churchgoers. With the help of a computer programme, the sociologist helped me to analyse the responses.

While the answers were interesting and helpful, there was a clear need for another more relevant questionnaire which would be answered by inactive Catholics. It would need to be carefully constructed, with the help of a professional sociologist, and by a number of people who had an interest in the whole topic. Any data that this second survey would glean could be very useful when planning appropriate evangelistic responses. Such a questionnaire could be given to volunteers from the congregation who would then pass them on to relatives, neighbours, work colleagues, or friends who were known to be inactive

Catholics. There are also many other questionnaires that could be used by an evangelisation team in order to discover information which would be useful to evangelisers. For instance, there is a helpful book entitled *Measures of Religiosity*. It contains about 125 questionnaires which are psychological rather than sociological in nature.[24] Needless to say, only some of them would be relevant where basic evangelisation is concerned. Offices of evangelisation in the dioceses in Ireland need to commission research on topics such as people's beliefs, practices and aspirations, the incidence of religious experience and whether it correlates in a positive or negative way with church attendance, etc.

b) Home Visitation

Secondly, the evangelisation team can engage in home visits with the aim of acting as witnesses to their faith and inviting a response. In par 65 of *Familiaris consortio* (hereafter FC) Pope John Paul II said: 'The church's pastoral concern will not be limited only to the Christian families closest at hand; it will extend its horizons in harmony with the heart of Christ and will show itself to be even more lively for families in general and for those families in particular which are in difficult or irregular situations. For all of them the church will have a word of truth, goodness, understanding, hope and deep sympathy with their sometimes tragic difficulties. To all of them she will offer her disinterested help so that they can come closer to that model of a family which the creator intended from 'the beginning' and which Christ has renewed with his redeeming grace.' The idea of home visitation is not new. The Legion of Mary have been conducting such visits for many years. It has enabled Legionaries to contact practising Catholics, the un-churched, and unbelievers. Speaking about home visits the Legion Handbook says: 'The legionary visitation will be marked by humility and simplicity. People may have incorrect ideas concerning the visitation; legionaries should aim initially at listening instead of talking. Having listened patiently and respectfully, they will have won the right to be heard.'[25] Unless home visiting is carefully planned it is unlikely that

24. Eds Peter C. Hill and Ralph W. Hood Jr. (Birmingham, AL: Religious Education Press, 1999).
25. *The Official Handbook of the Legion of Mary*, 233.

Catholic lay people will volunteer to do it, or that those visited will respond in a positive way. Chapter nine of this book deals with the subject of engaging in one-to-one evangelisation. It might happen that having talked to householders about meaning of life topics, those engaged in home visitation might invite them to attend an evangelisation course that is being put on in the parish.

In Summer 2009 there was a large mission in a number of parishes in Galway City under the patronage of Bishop Martin Drennan. A few hundred lay people from Galway and other places in Ireland volunteered to evangelise there. One thing they were trained to do was to make house-to-house visitations. Many of those who participated said that when they began calling to householders they did not know, they felt nervous and apprehensive. By and large, when they introduced themselves they got a good reception. Apart from telling people about the mission, they looked out for opportunities of talking to them about faith issues. They kept in mind the six points of the kerygma, which were mentioned in chapter five, and spoke about them if it seemed appropriate. As a general guideline they aimed to talk at some point about Jesus. They were also encouraged to ask the people they were talking to whether there was anything for which they would like prayer. More often than not, they answered in the affirmative while mentioning personal needs and the needs of people they cared about. Then, relying on the inspiration and power of the Holy Spirit, one of the two evangelisers prayed out loud in a spontaneous way, sometimes with the laying on of hands while his or her companion prayed in silence. Those they prayed for were usually emotionally moved and richly blessed. Needless to say, this approach would be appropriate during parish visitation by an evangelisation team.

Conclusion

According to the teaching of the church, the parish should be the main focal point of evangelisation. The effort to change perspectives from being largely focused on those who attend church to focus on those who do not, is difficult. If priests or lay people wish to be catalysts of change they must first of all transform themselves. They must become the change they want to see in the parish, or parish cluster. Visionary leaders will normally meet with predictable resistance. Although parishioners may give notional assent to the desirability of change in accordance with the teachings of Christ and the church, at an emotional level they may be reluctant to go beyond their comfort zones while rationalising their reasons for not doing so, by saying such things as, 'Everything we do is a form of evangelisation in one way or another.' Another reason why there may be resistance is because evangelisation requires time and effort which many Catholics are not willing to spend. Others may be reluctant to join an evangelisation team because they find that the work involved, such as doing house-to-house visitation, is very intimidating.

I have found that a strong desire to do something worthwhile helps people to overcome their understandable resistance. That is why it is so necessary to motivate people to 'launch out into the deep' (Lk 5:4), by putting before them compelling reasons which may evoke in them a willingness to change. In the last analysis even a desire to change is not enough. We need to pray for the power of the Holy Spirit. As the disciples prayed in Acts 4:29: 'And now, Lord, look upon their threats, [the factors that resist evangelisation] and grant to your servants to speak your word with all boldness.'

Recommended Reading

- Robert S. Rivers, *From Maintenance to Mission: Evangelisation and the Revitalisation of the Parish* (New York: Paulist Press, 2005).
- Martin W. Pable, *Reclaim the Fire: A Parish Guide to Evangelisation* (Notre Dame: Ave Maria Press, 2002).
- Sean MacGabhann, *The New Evangelisation of Catholics: In A New Language* (Victoria, British Columbia: Trafford Publishing, 2008).
- Congregation for the Clergy, *The Priest, Pastor and Leader of the Parish Community,* http://www.vatican.va/roman_curia/congregations/clergy/documents/rc_con_cclergy_doc_20020804_istruzione-presbitero_en.html
- The Irish Bishop's Commission for Pastoral Renewal and Adult Faith Development, *Parish Pastoral Councils: A Framework for Developing Diocesan Norms and Parish Guidelines.*
- The American Bishops, *Go Make Disciples: A National Plan and Strategy for Catholic Evangelization in the United States* (Washington: USCCB, 2002).

CHAPTER EIGHT

Silent Witness to the Good News

I'd like to begin this chapter by recounting a personal experience which has influenced me ever since it occurred. On the fourth of February 1974, I underwent a spiritual awakening as a result of hearing an inspired sermon, and being prayed with afterwards. By the grace of God I was filled with the Holy Spirit and his gifts. The following morning, a Sunday, I went to the lecture room in the conference centre to join a number of people for a time of spontaneous prayer. It was a beautiful day and the sunlight was streaming in through the windows. The thought came into my mind that the light was made up of the seven hues of the rainbow. I felt that those colours were like paints made of sunlight on an artist's palette which could be mixed to create an almost infinite spectrum of different colours. Then it occurred to me that the light of the Spirit was similar. When it was poured into people's hearts it expressed itself in all kinds of gifts. I thought of each person as a small tile of colour in a large mosaic which revealed a portrait of Jesus. I thought to myself, people today ask, 'Where will we find the risen Lord?' Ever since that morning, I have believed that he is be found in the Christian community. If you are looking for Christ the prophet, the healer, the teacher, the servant, the leader, the pastor and so on, you will find him in this or that brother or sister who has been gifted with those particular abilities whether ordinary or more extraordinary. If you are looking for Christ who was loving, joyful, peaceful, patient, kind, good, faithful, gentle and self-controlled you will find him in those members of the community who are blessed with those fruits of the Spirit (cf Gal 5:22-23)

Surely, Fr Werenfried van Straaten, the founder of the charity Aid to the Church in Need, was correct when he said in a homily for Pentecost: 'The gospel has been printed millions of times on paper. It is sold in all languages. But people, nowadays do not ask for a paper gospel. They demand a living gospel. They hunger for Christ who is the living Good News. They are waiting to meet men and women in whom Christ becomes visible again, in whom they can recognise and love Christ. They demand of us that we should give Christ a living form again.'[1] Fr van Straaten's words were reminiscent of what St Paul said in 2 Cor 3:2-3: 'You yourselves are our letter, written on our hearts, known and read by everybody. You show that you are a letter from Christ, the result of our ministry, written not with ink but with the Spirit of the living God, not on tablets of stone but on tablets of human hearts.' This chapter will look at some ways in which communities and individuals can bear silent witness to the Christ of the kerygma.

Commissioned to be witnesses

Before he ascended into heaven Jesus spoke to the disciples for the last time and solemnly promised: 'You will receive power when the Holy Spirit comes on you; and you will be my witnesses in Jerusalem, and in all Judea and Samaria, and to the ends of the earth' (Acts 1:8). The witness Jesus was referring to was one which could be expressed in words and deeds. This chapter will concentrate on wordless forms of evangelisation. In Mt 5:14-16 Jesus talked about this type of witness: 'You are the light of the world,' he said, 'a city on a hill cannot be hidden. Neither do people light a lamp and put it under a bowl. Instead they put it on its stand, and it gives light to everyone in the house. In the same way, let your light shine before men, that they may see your good deeds and praise your Father in heaven.' What is significant in this statement is the fact that the witness of the disciples would be in deeds rather than words. A number of points can be made about it. Firstly, the witness that Jesus spoke about included such things as loving relationships in the Christian community, virtuous lives, charitable service of others, especially those in need, action for justice, and the exercise of deeds of power. Secondly, he stressed that this kind of witness would only be possible when the believers were filled with the power of the Holy Spirit. Thirdly, Luke's gospel depicts the ministry of Jesus as an evangelistic journey from his home in Nazareth to

1. Werenfried van Straaten, *Feasts and Seasons* (Sutton Surrey: Aid to the Church in Need, 1999), 50.

Jerusalem where he would suffer and die for the salvation of the world. In the Acts, the evangelist sees the Good News spreading out from Jerusalem to the ends of the earth, principally by means of apostolic witness. There is another interesting passage on the importance of non-verbal witness to Christ in 1 Pet 3:1-3, where the leader of the church said to Christian wives who were married to pagan husbands: 'Wives, in the same way be submissive to your husbands so that, if any of them do not believe the word, they may be won over without words by the behaviour of their wives, when they see the purity and reverence of your lives.' Is it any wonder that Pope John Paul II said in RM 26: 'Even before activity, mission means witness and a way of life that shines out to others.'

The word 'witness' in the Greek of the New Testament is *martys* (from which we get the English word *martyr*), which is derived from its cognates *martyria* and *martyrion*. It involves two interrelated elements: firstly, attesting to a fact on the basis of firsthand experience, as one would do in a court case. Secondly, it is as an attestation to a truth about a person (e.g. when Jesus died, the centurion said, 'Surely this was a righteous man'). American scripture scholar John McKenzie says, in his *Dictionary of the Bible*, witness 'is subject to examination, but the examination consists in seeing whether more than one person makes the attestation. If this is verified, it was the part of a reasonable person to accept the witness.'[2] In the early church the apostles not only witnessed to the historical fact of the crucifixion and resurrection of Jesus, they bore witness to their personal conviction that he was the divine Son of God, the One who forgives sins and pours out the Spirit on all who believe in him. It is worth noting the criterion that was used by the apostles when they were looking for a replacement for Judas: 'So now we must choose someone else to take Judas' place,' they said, 'and to join us as witnesses of Jesus' resurrection. Let us select *someone who has been with us constantly from our first association with the Lord*

2. (Milwaukee: Bruce, 1965), 935. In an influential book, *Jesus and the Eyewitnesses: The Gospels as Eyewitness Testimony*, (Grand Rapids, MI: Eerdmans, 2006) author Richard Bauckham has offered convincing arguments to show that the gospels were based on reliable eyewitness accounts of the life and the ministry of Jesus.

[my italics], from the time he was baptised by John until the day he was taken from us into heaven' (Acts 1:21).

It is interesting to see that St Paul showed his esteem for personal witness when he referred to the eye-witness reports of the apostles and the religious experience of many post-resurrection believers like himself. In 1 Cor 15:3-8 he wrote: 'For what I received I passed on to you as of first importance: that Christ died for our sins according to the scriptures, that he was buried, that he was raised on the third day according to the scriptures, and that he appeared to Peter, and then to the Twelve. After that, he appeared to more than five hundred of the brothers at the same time, most of whom are still living, though some have fallen asleep and last of all he appeared to me also, as to one abnormally born.' These verses have important implications. A credible Christian witness is only possible by those who believe the truth about the saving life, death and resurrection of Jesus as taught by the apostles, and who experience its liberating effects in their personal lives. They bear witness to what they know. In the Bible the word to know was used to describe sexual intercourse between husband and wife. In other words it is an intimate, personal, and experiential kind of knowledge. When a believer knows Jesus in this way, he or she will be able to bear convincing and enthusiastic witness to him.

In the early church, a time eventually came when there were fewer and fewer people who had actually seen and heard the earthly Jesus. For instance, St Luke the evangelist was a gentile convert to Christianity. He had never met the earthly Jesus. In his story of the disciples on the road to Emmaus in Lk 24:16-35, he answered the question, how do post-resurrection believers meet with the risen Lord? He responded in a nuanced way when he said that they meet him in the Eucharistic community where people gather together, share their concerns, hear the word being proclaimed, and listen to the homily which relates the scriptures to everyday life. Finally, they meet with the risen Jesus by sharing in holy communion following the blessing, breaking and giving of the consecrated bread and wine. Not only do their hearts often burn within them as they understand the meaning and relevance of the scriptures, they recognise the presence of the eucharistic Lord among those who have come together in his name. As Jesus promised in Mt 18:20, 'For where two or three come together in my name, there am I with them.' This Lucan notion of Christ's presence in the eucharistic community is echoed in SC 7 when it talks about the four presences of Christ in the Eucharist, in the minister who represents Christ the head, in the congregation, in the word of God, and in holy communion. Having experienced the Lord in this mystical way, the believers are sent out to witness to him in their daily lives. As Pope John Paul II said in the Phoenix Park in 1979: 'Our union with Christ in the Eucharist must be expressed in the truth of our lives today – in our actions, in our behaviour, in our lifestyle, and in our relationships with others. For each one of us the Eucharist is a call to ever greater effort, so that we may live as true followers of Jesus: truthful in our speech, generous in our deeds, concerned, respectful of the dignity and rights of all persons, whatever their rank or income, self-sacrificing, fair and just, kind, considerate, compassionate and self-controlled – looking to the well-being of our families, our young people, our country, Europe and the world.'[3]

Non-verbal Witness

Recent Popes have drawn attention to the importance of non-verbal witness to Christ. Pope Paul VI said in EN 41: 'It is appropriate first of all to emphasise the following point: for the church, the first means of evangelisation is the witness of an authentically Christian life, given over to God in a communion that nothing should destroy and at the same time given to one's neighbour with limitless zeal. As we said recently to a group of lay people, "Modern man listens more willingly to witnesses than to teachers, and if he does listen to teachers, it is because they are witnesses".' Some years later, Pope John Paul said something very similar in RM 42: 'People today put more trust in witnesses than in teachers, in experience than in teaching, and in life and action than in theories. The witness of a Christian life is the first and irreplaceable form of mission: Christ, whose mission we continue, is the "witness" *par excellence* (Rev 1:5; 3:14) and the model of all Christian witness. The Holy Spirit accompanies the church

3. *The Pope in Ireland: Addresses and Homilies*, 11.

along her way and associates her with the witness he gives to Christ (cf Jn 15:26-27).' In EE 49, John Paul II wrote: 'What is needed are forceful, personal and communal testimonies of new life in Christ. It is not enough that truth and grace are offered through the proclamation of the word and the celebration of the sacraments; they need to be accepted and experienced in every practical situation, in the way Christians and ecclesial communities lead their lives. This is one of the greatest challenges set before the church in Europe at the beginning of the new millennium.'

It is interesting to note that the earliest Irish manuscript which is still extant is the *Cambrai Homily*. It was written in old Irish around the seventh century AD. It deals with three kinds of wordless witness or martyrdom, white, green and red. People experience white martyrdom when they separate from everything that they love for God, (e.g. leaving kith and kin to go overseas on mission). People undergo green martyrdom when, as a result of fasting and penance, they control their worldly desires in order to become more Christ like. People suffer red martyrdom when they shed their blood and die for Christ's sake.[4]

Communion and mission

It is a striking fact that as soon as the early Christians were changed by their faith in the kerygma, they quickly formed communities of believers. There are two outstanding descriptions of the way they lived. In Acts 2: 42, 46-47 we read: 'They devoted themselves to the apostles' teaching and to the fellowship, to the breaking of bread and to prayer ... Every day they continued to meet together in the temple courts. They broke bread in their homes and ate together with glad and sincere hearts, praising God and enjoying the favour of all the people. And the Lord added to their number daily those who were being saved.' Then in Acts 4:32-35 we are told that: 'All the believers were one in heart and mind. No one claimed that any of his possessions was his own, but they shared everything they had. With great power the apostles continued to testify to the

4. *Celtic Spirituality*, ed Oliver Davis & Thomas O'Loughlin, (New York: Paulist Press, 1999), 370.

resurrection of the Lord Jesus, and much grace was upon them all. There were no needy persons among them. For from time to time those who owned lands or houses sold them, brought the money from the sales and put it at the apostles' feet, and it was distributed to anyone as he had need.' In other words faith in the kerygma gives birth to *koinonia* or Christian communion.[5]

A number of comments can be made about these verses in Acts. Firstly, the opening one is intended to remind the reader of Pythagoras who founded a community of friends in Greece in the fourth century BC. The first two of his community's four guidelines read as follows: 'Friends share in the perfect communion of a single spirit and friends share everything in common.'[6] Some scholars have said that in Acts 4:32 Luke is stating that the Greek ideal of friendship, which was an admirable but unattainable one, became a living reality in the Christian community. Although some members of the early church may have been intimate friends, I don't think that Luke was implying that all the members were necessarily sharing their inmost thoughts and feelings with one another. They were one in mind and heart in so far as they were conformed to the mind and heart of Christ.

Not surprisingly, therefore, St Paul repeatedly urged: 'Be of the same mind, having the same love, being in full accord and of one mind … Let the same mind be in you that was in Christ' (Phil 2:2, 5). In another place he added: 'May the God who gives endurance and encouragement give you a spirit of unity among yourselves as you follow Christ Jesus so that with one heart and mouth you may glorify the God and Father of our Lord Jesus Christ' (Rom 15:5-6). He also said: 'I appeal to you, brothers and

---

5. The Greek word *koinonia* is derived from *koinon* meaning common, and *koinoo* meaning to share, e.g. worldly goods. In RM 26, John Paul said: 'To live in "fraternal communion" (*koinonia*) means to be "of one heart and soul" (Acts 4:32), establishing fellowship from every point of view: human, spiritual and material.' The Holy Father talked about 'Ecclesial Basic Communities' in GS 51, and about four aspects of the spirituality that informs them in NMI 43. See Avery Dulles, 'The Church as Communion,' *Church and Society*, 129-41; William Barclay, 'Koinonia, Koinonein, Koinonos,' *New Testament Words*, 173-5.
6. Rosemary Radar, *Breaking Boundaries: Male/Female Friendships in Early Christian Communities* (New York: Paulist Press, 1983), 24.

sisters, in the name of our Lord Jesus Christ, that all of you agree with one another so that there may be no divisions among you and that you may be perfectly united in mind and thought' (1 Cor 1:10). Speaking about relationships in general Paul said: 'Do nothing from selfishness or conceit, but in humility count others better than yourselves. Let each of you look not only to his own interests, but also to the interests of others' (Phil 2:3-5). In Eph 4:3-6 Paul again appealed for unity: 'Make every effort to keep the unity of the Spirit through the bond of peace. There is one body and one Spirit – just as you were called to one hope when you were called – one Lord, one faith, one baptism; one God and Father of all, who is over all and through all and in all.'

Now to return to Acts 4:32-36. What is really significant is the fact that Luke inserted a verse about evangelisation into the middle of a passage on community relationships: 'With great power the apostles continued to testify to the resurrection of the Lord Jesus, and much grace was upon them' (Acts 4:33). What he seemed to be saying was that *koinonia* and *kerygma* were inextricably linked. When it was received with faith, the proclamation of the kerygma gave birth to Christian community. Then in turn, the spirit of merciful love which permeated the community energised the subsequent proclamation of the kerygma by the evangelists, while bearing concrete witness to its truth. Unbelievers who heard the kerygma for the first time could see the Good News incarnated in the Christian community which was a parable or icon of new life in Christ. However, the extent to which the community was divided and unloving was the extent to which it negated the words of the evangelists. For example, in the Second Letter of Clement (AD 100 approx) the anonymous author says that it is not too surprising that the name of the Lord was blasphemed by the pagans. 'For when the pagans hear from our mouths the words of God, they marvel at their beauty and greatness. But when they discover that our actions are not worthy of the words we speak, they turn from wonder to blasphemy, saying that it is a myth and a delusion. For when they hear from us that God says, "It is no credit to you if you love those who love you, but it is a credit to you if you love your enemies and those who hate you", when they hear these things, they marvel at such extraordinary goodness. But, when they see that we do not only not love those who hate us but do not love those who love us, they scornfully laugh at us, and the Name is blasphemed.'[7]

As in the early church, friendship and friendliness in the Christian community has been valued throughout Christian history. For instance, in his book *Friendship and Community: The Monastic Experience 350-1250*, Brian Mc Guire has shown how the ideal of friendship was cultivated in Christian communities from the Fathers of the church to the high middle ages.[8] For example, in the twelfth century, St Aelred of Rievaulx wrote his book, *Spiritual Friendship* in which he suggested that, at its best, monastic life was a matter of interlinking friendships between the members. Speaking about his own experience Aelred said: 'The day before yesterday, as I was walking the round of the cloister of the monastery, the brothers were sitting around forming as it were a most loving crown ... In that multitude of brothers I found no one whom I did not love, and no one by whom, I felt sure, I was not loved. I was filled with such joy that it surpassed all the delights of this world. I felt, indeed, my spirit transfused into all and the affection of all to have passed into me, so that I could say with the prophet: "Behold how good and how pleasant it is for brothers to dwell in unity".'[9]

In seventeenth-century France, St Vincent de Paul, founder of the Congregation of the Mission, saw a close connection between friendly relationships in community and effective evangelisation. He wrote, 'Brotherly love should always be present among us, as well as the bond of holiness, and these should be safeguarded in every possible way. For this reason there should be great mutual respect, and we should get along *as good friends* [my italics], always living in community.'[10] Speaking about the affective dimension of Christian love, he said: 'We should be

7. *The Apostolic Fathers in English*, 83.

8. *Cistercian Studies Series: Number Ninety-Five,* (Kalamazoo, MI: Cistercian Publications Inc., 1988)

9. *Spiritual Friendship* (Kalamazoo, MI.: Cistercian Publications Inc., 1974), 112; Aelred Squire, *Aelred of Rievaulx: A Study* (Kalamazoo: Cistertian Publications, 1981), 48-50.

10. John Rybolt CM ed 'Codex Sarzana,' *Vincentiana* 33 (1991): 307- 406. Pat Collins, 'Friendship and Evangelisation in the Vincentian Tradition,' *Vincentiana* (Jan/Feb 1998): 45-57; 'Friendship and Evangelisation,' in *Spirituality for the 21st Century*, 180-99.

prompt in letting others know of our affection, not at the wrong time or in the wrong way but at a suitable moment and in a suitable way, and without overdoing it.'[11] Knowing that effective preaching is rooted in unity, he said to eight priests who were being sent on mission to Ireland: 'Be united together and God will bless you. But let it be in the love of Jesus Christ, for any other union will never be cemented by the blood of this Divine Saviour, and cannot last. It is therefore in Jesus Christ, by Jesus Christ, and for Jesus Christ, that you should be united to one another. The Spirit of Jesus Christ is a spirit of union and peace.'[12]

What was true in the history of the church is equally true today. Unity can only be preserved if the members of communities, whether families, groups in a parish, religious orders of priests, sisters and brothers, or lay ecclesial communities, by refraining from condemning or criticising one another; dealing with the conflicts that inevitably arise in a constructive and charitable way; and by being willing to forgive hurts as soon as they arise. Unity can be nurtured by means of such things as communal prayer, faith sharing, having meals together, mutual empathy, selfless service, encouraging non-exclusive friendships, and enjoying leisure pursuits together. Some communities or groups arrange to have meetings which focus specifically on community relationships. A trained and trusted facilitator is invited, with the consent of the community, to spend an hour or two with the members. Each one is free to share how he or she feels about his or her participation in the group. It gives each person an opportunity to speak about any negative emotions he or she may be experiencing (e.g. as a result of being hurt, annoyed, misunderstood, etc). Meetings of this kind can be painful, but they have a great ability to clear up misunderstandings, resolve conflicts, and deepen the bonds of unity. Lived Christian experience indicates that effective evangelisers come from united, loving communities.

The Witness of Contemporary Communities

---

11. 'Charity,' 30 May 1659, trs Tom Davitt CM, *Colloque: Journal of the Irish Province of the Congregation of the Mission* (Autumn 1993, No 28): 234.
12. Louis Abelly, *The Life of the Venerable Servant of God Vincent de Paul*, vol 2, 126.

T. S. Eliot has written in *Choruses on the Rock*: 'What life have you if you have not life together? There is no life that is not in community, and no community not lived in praise of God.'[13] There are many forms of community in the contemporary church. They begin with the family, then there are the many special purpose groups in parishes such as the local prayer meeting, the St Vincent de Paul conference, and a praesidium of the Legion of Mary, the choir, and sometimes households of religious men and women. The parish itself has a number of official groups such as the parish council and its various committees, the baptism team, and the RCIA group.

In recent years new ecclesial movements have been formed.[14] In a letter to the World Congress of Ecclesial Movements in May 1998, Pope John Paul II defined a movement as 'a concrete ecclesial entity, in which primarily lay people participate, with a dynamic of faith and Christian testimony that founds its own pedagogical method on a charism given to the person of the founder in determined circumstances and modes.'[15] This definition focuses on three characteristics of the new movements: Firstly, they are primarily lay. Secondly, their work is to evangelise. Thirdly, their charism comes from their founder/s. Pope John Paul II invited members of these movements to a meeting in Rome in 1998.[16] He said on that occasion: 'In our world, often dominated by a secularised culture which encourages and promotes models of life without God, the faith of many is sorely tested, and is frequently stifled and dies. Thus we see an urgent need for powerful proclamation and solid, in-depth Christian formation. There is so much need today for mature Christian personalities, conscious of their baptismal identity, of their voc-

13. *Selected Poems* (London: Faber & Faber, 1969), 114.
14. Tony Hanna, *New Ecclesial Movements: Communion and Liberation, Neo-Catechumenal Way, Charismatic Renewal* (Olathe, KS: St Paul's Publishing, 2007). Among the new communities in Ireland would be the Céilí Community, The New Springtime Community, The John the Baptist Koinonia Community, Micah Community and Emmaus Community.
15. Pope John Paul II, 'Movements in the Church', *Laity Today* (1999), 18.
16. For an account of the gathering and the address of Pope John Paul II see, 'This is the day the Lord has made! Holy Father holds historic meeting with ecclesial movements and new communities,' *L'Osservatore Romano* in English (3 June 1998), 1-2.

ation and mission in the world! There is great need for living Christian communities! And here are the movements and the new ecclesial communities: they are the response given by the Holy Spirit.'[17] John Paul went so far as to say that the new ecclesial movements, 'represent one of the most significant fruits of that springtime in the church which was foretold by the Second Vatican Council.'[18] Pope Benedict XVI convened a similar gathering of new ecclesial movements in Rome at Pentecost in 2006. He too stressed the fact that the witness of the new ecclesial movements represented a real hope for the future of the church.

Truly united and loving Christian communities, of whatever kind, are counter-cultural in many ways. Some sociologists such as Ferdinand Tonnies, Emile Durkheim and David Putman have noted the fact that in Western capitalist democracies there has been an erosion of community bonds and an increasing emphasis on individualism, together with secular beliefs and values. For example, we have moved from large, extended families of a stable kind, to smaller, more atomic ones which are often unstable, (e.g. as a result of divorce). It is also a striking fact that an increasing number of couples do not marry at all. It is also true to say that families, of whatever kind, engage in fewer and fewer activities together, such as sharing meals. T. S. Eliot described this state of affairs when he observed: 'And now you live dispersed on ribbon roads, and no man knows or cares who is his neighbour unless his neighbour makes too much disturbance, but all dash to and fro in motor cars, familiar with the roads and settled nowhere. Nor does the family even move about together, but every son would have his motor cycle, and daughters ride away on casual pillions.'[19] Because of these trends it is also harder to run voluntary organisations because people have very little time to spare due to heavy work commitments. As a result, what is referred to as social capital is decreased.[20] This means that individuals who are troubled in one way or another have

17. Par 7, Meeting with Ecclesial Movements, 10 May 1998.
18. 'Movements, a New Springtime in the Church,' The Zenith Weekly Report, *Zenith News Agency* (May 31, 1998).
19. *Selected Poems*, 114.
20. Social capital can be described as the collective value of all social networks and the impetus that arises from these networks to do things for each other.

fewer people and resources they can rely on. So one of the most urgent needs in contemporary society is to provide for, and foster a sense of belonging. That is something that Christian groups can and do offer.

So parishes, the groups within them, and new ecclesial communities all bear silent witness to the Good News by the loving and joyful way they live. Without a word, they seem to say, 'come and see' how the Good News message of God's unconditional mercy and love, which was expressed through the saving life, death and resurrection of Jesus, is now animating our lives together. I'm reminded in this regard of a saying which is probably wrongly attributed to St Francis of Assisi: 'Preach the gospel at all times. Where necessary, use words.' In a document entitled *The Role of Women in Evangelisation,* we read something similar, 'The true witness is a life lived according to the gospel. This goes before any other consideration. "If you would preach a sermon you must yourself be a sermon".'[21]

Mother Teresa of Calcutta was a great believer in the efficacy of silent witness. She said on one occasion: 'Often we Christians constitute the worst obstacle for those who try to become closer to Christ; we often preach a gospel we do not live. This is the principle reason why the people of the world don't believe.'[22] An interviewer observed: 'You do not evangelise in the conventional sense of the term.' Mother Teresa responded: 'I'm evangelising by my works of love,' to which the interviewer responded: 'Is that the best way?' to which Mother Teresa replied: 'For us, yes. For somebody else, something else. I'm evangelising the way God wants me to. Jesus said, go and preach to the nations. We are now in so many nations preaching the gospel by our works of love. "By the love that you have for one another will they know you are my disciples." That's the preaching that we are doing, and I think that it is more real.'[23] Who could argue with what Blessed Teresa said?

If Christian people not only live in a loving, united way, but

21. *Vatican Collection vol II: Vatican Council II, More Post Conciliar Documents,* ed Austin Flannery (Dublin: Dominican Publications, 1982), 321.
22. Mother Teresa, *In My Own Words*, compiled by Jose Luis Gonzales-Bolado, http://www.stmary-church.com/mteresav2.pdf (accessed 7 September 2009)
23. Interview with Edward W. Desmond, *Time* (1989)

also welcome strangers who may be materially or spiritually poor, they are already evangelising by providing them with a sense of acceptance and belonging. I can remember a priest in an English diocese telling me that before Christmas one year he attached sheets of paper to the notice board in the church porch and left a supply of pencils beside them. He asked the parishioners to write down a list of undesirables who normally would not be welcome in a Catholic church. The parishioners mentioned people such as those in second relationships, unmarried mothers, sexually active gays, prostitutes, drug pushers, pedophiles, abortionists, murderers and the like. The following week the priest had a large poster printed and displayed outside the church. At the top it said: 'This Christmas the following people are welcome in this church.' Beneath the heading was a list of the kinds of people the parishioners had mentioned. I know that this kind of approach can create problems where holy communion is concerned. One way of getting over it is to invite everyone to come forward at communion time, and to say, 'If for one reason or another you are unable to receive the Eucharist at this time, cross your arms on your chest as an indication that you want a blessing.' I know from experience in America that it can work well.

Ecumenism and evangelisation

The scandal of the division between the Christian churches has had an adverse effect on the credibility of Christian evangelisation. Ever since the Second Vatican Council the Catholic Church has advocated the importance of fostering Christian unity. When he spoke to ecumenical leaders in Dublin in 1979, Pope John Paul II said: 'Dear brothers: with a conviction linked to our faith, we realise that the destiny of the world is at stake, because the credibility of the gospel has been challenged. Only in perfect unity can we Christians adequately give witness to the truth.' He added in practical terms: 'As we each, in our respective churches grow in our searching of the holy scriptures, in our fidelity to and continuity with the age-old tradition of the Christian Church, in our search for holiness and for authenticity of Christian living, we shall also be coming closer to Christ, and therefore closer to one another.'[24] John Paul II reiterated that point at different times.[25] For instance, in EE 54, he wrote: 'The task of evangelisation involves moving toward one another and moving forward together as Christians, and it must begin from within; evangelisation and unity, evangelisation and ecumenism are indissolubly linked.' When people who have no firm faith in Christ see his followers working closely together in a spirit of love and mutual esteem (e.g. on an outreach to the homeless in the neighbourhood), it bears silent witness to the truth of the gospel. As Pope John Paul II said in UUS 98: 'How indeed can we proclaim the gospel of reconciliation without at the same time being committed to working for reconciliation between Christians?' Over the years I have found that not only can Catholics and Protestants preach the kerygma together, their joint ministry seems to be unusually blessed, as if the Lord were expressing his approval. As Ps 133:1, 3 says: 'How good and pleasant it is when brothers live together in unity! ... For there the Lord bestows his blessing.'[26]

Personal Witness

The scriptures and the teaching of the church make it clear that the main way an individual bears silent witness to the kerygma is by means of holiness of life. That is one reason why St Paul says in 1 Thess 4:3: 'This is the will of God, your sanctification.' The Second Vatican Council included a section entitled 'The Universal Call to Holiness,' in LG ch 5. Its teachings were encapsulated in CCL 210, which says: 'All Christ's faithful, each according to his or her own condition, must make a wholehearted effort to lead a holy life, and *to promote the growth of the church* [my italics] and its continual sanctification.' It is interesting to note that this canon makes a clear connection between holiness and church growth by means of evangelisation. That point was reiterated by Pope John Paul II in NMI 30: 'I have no hesitation in saying that all pastoral initiatives must be set in relation to holiness. In RM 90 he added: 'The universal call to holiness is

---

24. *The Pope in Ireland: Addresses and Homilies*, 36, 35.
25. cf EN 77, pars 98-9 of *Ut unum sint*, and NMI 48.
26. See Peter Hocken, 'Ecumenical Issues in Evangelisation,' in *John Paul II and the New Evangelisation*, 276-87; Pat Collins, 'Friendship and Ecumenism,' *Gifted and Sent*, 62-68.

closely linked to the universal call to mission. Every member of the faithful is called to holiness and mission.' The Holy Father suggested that holiness is rooted in a contemplative attitude. It can be fostered in different ways, such as paying attention to the glories of creation as a reflection of God's glory, reading and praying the scriptures by means of *lectio divina*, or some other form of contemplative prayer. In NMI 16-28 John Paul included a long section entitled, 'A Face to Contemplate,' in which he spoke in moving terms about paying sustained attention to the face of Christ. He went on to say in EE 91 that anyone who has a contemplative life, 'is a witness to the experience of God, and must be able to say with the apostles: –that which we have looked upon … concerning the word of life … we proclaim also to you" (1 Jn 1:1-3).'

Contemporary Christians have the vocation of being Christ in the world of today. As was already noted in chapter one, CCC 521 states the important truth that, 'Christ enables us to live in him all that he himself lived, and he lives it in us.' Like their Saviour, Christians need to be filled, guided and empowered by the Spirit (cf Eph 5:18; Gal 5:18; 5:16). As St Teresa of Avila was fond of reminding her sisters: 'Christ has no body but yours, no hands, no feet on earth but yours. Yours are the eyes with which he looks with compassion of this world, yours are the feet with which he walks to do good, yours are the hands with which he blesses the world.' While it is true that we receive the Holy Spirit in a sacramental way in baptism and confirmation, we only become aware of what St Teresa talked about when the mercy and love of Jesus are manifested to us at a conscious level of awareness as a result of a religious awakening through baptism in the Holy Spirit.[27] This is not a once-off event, but the initiation of a life-long process. As St Thomas Aquinas pointed out, Christians can experience repeated in-fillings of the Spirit.[28]

As was mentioned in chapter one, Christians, like Jesus, need to be guided by the Spirit.[29] This is the key to Christian ethics and holiness. If they truly desire to discover God's will,

27. See Pat Collins, 'Baptism in the Spirit and the Universal Calls to Holiness and Evangelisation,' *The Gifts of the Spirit and the New Evangelisation*, 111-28.
28. *Summa Theologiae ST*, I, q. 43, a. 6, rep. Obj. 2.

they can only receive inspired insight if their lives are moulded by the values and beliefs of Jesus. In Eph 4:23-24 we read: 'Be made new in the attitude of your minds; and to put on the new self, created to be like God in true righteousness and holiness.' In Rom 12:2 Paul adds: 'Do not conform any longer to the pattern of this world, but be transformed by the renewing of your mind. Then you will be able to test and approve what God's will is – his good, pleasing and perfect will.' Paul would have been familiar with the Greco-Roman practice of making statues by pouring molten metal into moulds. He was saying to the people, don't let yourselves be moulded by the false values and beliefs of the pagan world, but rather let your mind and heart be moulded by the values and teachings of Jesus Christ.

Like Jesus, our activities have to be empowered by the Spirit. This means that the true witness to Christ is a humble person, one who in poverty of spirit acknowledges his or her complete dependence on the power of God. Without the help of the Holy Spirit we can do nothing (cf Jn 15:5), but with God's help all things are possible (cf Mk 9:23). This will only happen if Christians act in conformity with the will of God. As 1 John 5:14-16 assures us: 'This is the confidence which we have in him, that if we ask anything according to his will he hears us. And if we know that he hears us in whatever we ask, we know that we have obtained the requests made of him.' Once we rely on God's Spirit working in and through us, we will be able to do great things, even to the point of healings or miracles. It is worth noting that speaking of extraordinary charismatic deeds of power, St Paul described them in 1 Cor 12:7 as *phanerosis*, (i.e. a manifestation or epiphany of the presence and glory of the Lord).

Here are just a few examples of what typically happens in the more humdrum circumstances of everyday life, when Christians are being guided by the Spirit. Employees are chatting during a coffee break. Not only are they taking the Holy Name in vain and using profane language, they also begin to tell dirty jokes. However, a conscientious Christian refuses to join in. Young people go on holidays together to Spain. They arrange

29. cf Pat Collins, 'Seeking God's Will in Prayer,' *Prayer in Practice: A Biblical Approach*, 91-113.

to sleep together, but one girl declines the offer because she doesn't intend having sex until she is married. A group of friends are bad mouthing and criticising a person they know, but one of them not only says nothing negative about the person in question, she actually draws attention to good points in that person's character. A man buys a new suit in a tailor's shop. He pays by cash and finds that he has been given fifty euro too much in change. He draws the attention of the cashier to the mistake and hands it back. A family have fallen on hard times in the parish, they have a daughter who needs an expensive operation. An anonymous donor sends a thousand euro in the post with a typed note which says that he is praying to the Lord for the girl's recovery. There is an anti-abortion rally and hundreds of Catholics protest with dignity outside Government Buildings on a cold, rainy day. A widow hears about a recovering drug addict who can't find anywhere to live. She offers to take the girl into her home. She remains with the widow for four months during which time the widow feeds her and often listens to the sad story of her life. A young man knows that L'Arche are looking for volunteers who will live with mentally handicapped adults. He offers his services for six months. Surely Cardinal Suhard was correct when he said: 'The great mark of a Christian is what no other characteristic can replace, namely, the example of a life that can only be explained in terms of God (in Christ).'

Just as recent church scandals have tended to alienate people from Christ and his church, so the silent witness of holy Christians attracts people to the Lord and adds credibility to his gospel. I work for a charity called Aid to the Church in Need. I never cease to be amazed at the generosity of many Catholics who give us funds in person, or send them in by post. For example, one man I met offered to give me twenty thousand euro for the charity. When I asked if he would be leaving himself short he said: 'Not really, I got the money from an insurance company as compensation for injuries I received in a car crash a few years ago. I don't really need the money, so I want to give it to the church in need.' A donor came to our office during the year and handed in an envelope. When we opened it, we found it contained a cheque for three hundred thousand euro! The Bible says that the love of money is the root of many evils (cf 1 Tim

6:10). I have found that financial generosity to the less fortunate members of society is a powerful witness to the generosity of Jesus who did not give us silver or gold but rather the very last drops of his sacred blood, so that sins might be forgiven.

Conclusion

Speaking of Christians, Friedrich Nietzsche, one of the fathers of modern atheism, once exclaimed, 'They would have to sing me better songs to teach me to believe in their Saviour, his disciples would have to look more saved.'[30] In other words, if their verbal testimony is to be credible, Christians have to walk the walk as well as talking the talk. This chapter ends with a poem entitled, *Sermons we See*, which was written by poet Edgar Guest who was born in Birmingham, England in 1881 and died in Detroit in Michigan in 1959.[32]

> I'd rather see a sermon than hear one any day;
> I'd rather one should walk with me than merely tell the way.
> The eye's a better pupil and more willing than the ear,
> Fine counsel is confusing, but example's always clear;
> And the best of all the preachers are the men who live their creeds,
> For to see good put in action is what everybody needs.
>
> I soon can learn to do it if you'll let me see it done;
> I can watch your hands in action, but your tongue too fast may run.
> And the lecture you deliver may be very wise and true,
> But I'd rather get my lessons by observing what you do;
> For I might misunderstand you and the high advise you give,
> But there's no misunderstanding how you act and how you live.
>
> When I see a deed of kindness, I am eager to be kind.
> When a weaker brother stumbles and a strong man stays be-

31. *Thus Spoke Zarathustra* II.4, quoted by Henri de Lubac in 'Spiritual Warfare,' *Theology in History* (San Francisco: Ignatius Press, 2003).
32. *Collected Verse of Edward Guest* (New York: Buccaneer Books, 1976), 599.

hind
Just to see if he can help him, then the wish grows strong in me
To become as big and thoughtful as I know that friend to be.
And all travellers can witness that the best of guides today
Is not the one who tells them, but the one who shows the way.

One good man teaches many, men believe what they behold;
One deed of kindness noticed is worth forty that are told.
Who stands with men of honour learns to hold his honour dear,
For right living speaks a language which to every one is clear.
Though an able speaker charms me with his eloquence, I say,
I'd rather see a sermon than to hear one, any day.

Recommended Reading

- Tony Hanna, *New Ecclesial Movements: Communion and Liberation, Neo-Catechumenal Way, Charismatic Renewal* (Olathe, KS: St Paul's Publishing, 2007).
- Rosemary Radar, *Breaking Boundaries: Male/Female Friendships in Early Christian Communities* (New York: Paulist Press, 1983).
- St Aelred of Rievaulx, *Spiritual Friendship* (Kalamazoo, MI: Cistercian Publications Inc, 1974).
- Brian Mc Guire, *Friendship and Community: The Monastic Experience 350-1250* (Kalamazoo, MI: Cistercian Publications Inc, 1988).
- Pat Collins, 'Witness to Uncompromising Discipleship,' *Gifted and Sent* (Luton: New Life Publishing, 2009), 218-24.

CHAPTER NINE

Verbal Witness to the Good News

Jesus bore witness to the Good News in many ways, some of them silent. That said, it is abundantly clear that, like the prophets of old, he also proclaimed the message of salvation in words. Christians are called to do the same. As Paul VI said in EN 22: 'Even the finest witness will prove ineffective in the long run if it is not explained, justified and made explicit by a clear and unequivocal proclamation of the Lord Jesus.' This chapter will focus on basic evangelisation of a verbal kind while being aware that there are many other forms, such as doctrinal or *paraenetic* (i.e. advisory or hortatory) evangelisation. Kerygmatic type evangelisation can take many forms such as:

- Liturgical and non liturgical preaching.
- Instructing children at home or in school in the basic truths of the Christian faith.
- Giving a teaching on the basics of faith, (e.g. as part of a Life in the Spirit Seminar, prayer meeting, etc).
- Giving one's testimony, in other words, telling the story of how one came to have a firm and personal faith in Jesus Christ. In a sense this is an account of one's conversion or spiritual awakening, whether gradual or sudden.
- Witnessing to Christ by recounting some way in which you experienced his saving mercy and love in the humdrum circumstances of everyday life.
- One-to-one evangelisation by taking the opportunity to speak to a relative, neighbour, friend, colleague or stranger about the importance of personal faith in Christ.

Later in this chapter we describe these verbal methods of witnessing to Jesus. But before doing so we will look briefly at the theology of the word of God which needs to inform them all.

The Word of God

The world is awash with words, written words, spoken words, and words that are broadcast on radio and TV. But no matter how eloquent and profound they may be, they are merely human words. The Bible is unique because it is the only book that contains the inspired and inspiring word of God. However, commenting on contemporary culture, T. S. Eliot observed in *Choruses from the Rock*: 'The endless cycle of idea and action, Endless invention, endless experiment, Brings knowledge of motion, but not of stillness; Knowledge of speech, but not of silence; Knowledge of words, and ignorance of the Word.'[1] In Western society words describe pre-existing reality. In the Bible, however, God's word is constitutive of reality. It contains the unique power to effect what it says. George Montague points out: 'When the Hebrew speaks a word, he is not taking in the outside world and shaping it within himself. Rather he is thrusting something creative and powerful outward from himself into the external world and actually changing that world.'[2] Is 55:10-11 testifies: 'As the rain and the snow come down from heaven, and do not return to it without watering the earth and making it bud and flourish, so that it yields seed for the sower and bread for the eater, so is my word that goes out from my mouth: It will not return to me empty, but will accomplish what I desire and achieve the purpose for which I sent it.' For example, in Gen 1:3, 'God said, "Let there be light," and there was light.' In Jer 49:13 the Lord swore by his own divine authority and faithfulness to act in accord with the divine promises. God has both the intention and the power to carry out the divine undertakings. Knowing this to be true, outstanding people of faith used to say 'amen' to those undertakings. The word is derived from a Hebrew root *'mn* which means, 'to show oneself firm and stable.' So to say amen to God's word of promise is tantamount to saying 'So be it, it is a fact because God's word is dependable.'[3]

All the books of the Old Testament point to Christ and find their fulfilment in him. Jesus himself made this clear to the two

1. *Selected Poems*, 107.
2. *Riding the Wind* (Ann Arbor: Word of Life, 1977), 56-7.
3. cf Leon-Dufour, *Dictionary of the New Testament*, (San Francisco: Harper & Row, 1980), 91.

disciples on the road to Emmaus. Having poured out their sorrows to their companion, 'Jesus replied: "You foolish men! So slow to believe the full message of the prophets! Was it not ordained that the Christ should suffer and so enter his glory?" Then starting with Moses and going through all the prophets he explained to them the passages throughout the scriptures that were about himself' (Lk 24:25-28). The gospels record the words and actions of Jesus. They are like so many panes in the stained glass window of his humanity. When they are illuminated by the Spirit and contemplated with the eyes of faith, they can become an unequalled source of revelation. Through them we begin to see what God is like. As Jesus said: 'To have seen me is to have seen the Father' (Jn 14:9). The remaining books of the New Testament record the impact and implications of Christ for the first Christians.

The New Testament authors often speak about the importance of God's word: 'All scripture is inspired by God ... it is something alive and active .... it is the sword of the Spirit ... it can judge the secret thoughts and emotions of the heart ... and is useful for teaching truth, rebuking error, correcting faults, and giving instruction for living' (2 Tim 3:16; Heb 4:12; Eph 6:7; 2 Tim 3:16). Vatican II also stressed the fundamental importance of scripture. In par 11 of the Dogmatic Constitution *Dei verbum* (hereafter DV) we read: 'The books of scripture must be acknowledged as teaching firmly, faithfully and without error that truth which God wanted put into the sacred writings for the sake of our salvation.' Catholics believe that the Holy Spirit can lead the individual believer into the spiritual meaning of God's word. No doubt these points will be reiterated and expanded when Pope Benedict publishes his Apostolic Exhortation on the Word of God following the Synod of Bishops which explored that theme in 2008.[4]

The church highly esteems scripture reading, meditation and prayer. In SC 21 we read: 'The church has always venerated the divine scriptures just as she venerates the body of the Lord.' Not

4. The bishops of England, Wales and Scotland have published a very helpful booklet entitled, *The Gift of Scripture* (London: Catholic Truth Society, 2005). Available for download at, http://www.catholic-ew.org.uk/ccb/content/download/3999/2739

surprisingly, therefore, she encourages the faithful to develop a scripture-based spirituality. For example, in CCC 133 we read: 'The church forcefully and specifically exhorts all the Christian faithful ... to learn the surpassing knowledge of Jesus Christ, by frequent reading of the scriptures.' John Paul II reiterated that point in TMA 40 where he wrote: 'Christians ... should turn with renewed interest to the Bible, whether it be through the liturgy, rich in the divine word, or through devotional reading, or through instructions suitable for the purpose or other aids.' Again in EE 65 the Pope urged: 'Enter the new millennium with the Book of the Gospels! May every member of the faithful hear the Council's plea to learn the surpassing knowledge of Jesus Christ (cf Phil 3:8) by frequent reading of the divine scriptures. "Ignorance of the scriptures is ignorance of Christ." May the Holy Bible continue to be a treasure for the church and for every Christian: in the careful study of God's word we will daily find nourishment and strength to carry out our mission ... Let us devour the Bible (cf Rev 10:9) so that it can become our very life. Let us savour it deeply: it will make demands of us, but it will give us joy because it is sweet as honey (cf Rev 10:9-10). Filled with hope, we will be able to share it with every man and woman we encounter on our way.'

The church recommends the use of *lectio divina*.[5] It is a personal or communal reading of a scripture passage of any length, received as the Word of God, which through the impulse of the Holy Spirit leads to meditation, prayer and contemplation. Guigo the Carthusian described its overall purpose in a twelfth century treatise entitled the *Scala Claustralium*. He wrote: 'Seek in reading and you will find in meditating; knock in prayer and it will be opened to you in contemplation.'[6] The scriptures need to be pondered in a contemplative way. Speaking about this kind of contemplation, St Vincent de Paul said to Daughters of Charity: 'The other sort of prayer is contemplation. In this the soul, in the presence of God, does nothing else but receive from him what he bestows. She is without action, and God himself inspires her, without any effort on the soul's part, with all that she

5. CCC 2708; NMI 39.

6. *The Companion to the Catechism of the Catholic Church: A Compendium of Texts Referred to in the Catechism of the Catholic Church*, 921-8.

can desire, and with far more. Have you ever experienced this sort of prayer? I am sure you have and you have often been astonished that, without doing anything on your part, God himself has replenished your soul and granted you knowledge you never had before.'[7] As the Lord promises in Is 48:6-8: 'From now on I will tell you of new things, of hidden things unknown to you. They are created now, and not long ago; you have not heard of them before today. So you cannot say, "Yes, I knew of them." You have neither heard nor understood; from of old your ear has not been open.'

On one occasion St Vincent de Paul said: 'Prayer is the great book for the preacher. In this prayer you will descend into the depths of the divine truths of which the Eternal Word is the source, to give them to the people. It is greatly desirable that evangelisers deeply love this holy exercise. Without it, they will produce little or no fruit. By prayer they will make themselves fit to touch hearts and convert souls.'[8] Speaking to a young priest on another occasion, Vincent had this to say about preaching: 'Establish a close union between yourself and our Lord in prayer. That is the reservoir in which you will receive the instructions you need to fulfill your duties. When in doubt, have recourse to God and say, O Lord, your are the Father of light, teach me what I ought to say in these circumstances ... so that you may learn directly from God what you shall have to preach, following the example of Moses who proclaimed to the people of Israel only what God had inspired him to say.'[9] Clearly, St Vincent believed in prophetic preaching which is rooted in scriptural prayer of a contemplative and inspired kind.

The Primacy of Preaching the Kerygma

In the light of the preceding paragraphs, is it any wonder that Pope John Paul II could say in NMI 39: 'It is above all the work

7. St Vincent de Paul, 'Conference on Prayer, 31 May 1648,' *The Conferences of St Vincent de Paul to the Daughters of Charity* ((London: Collins Liturgical Publications, 1979), 374.
8. Louis Abelly, *The Life of the Venerable Servant of God Vincent de Paul*, vol 3, 62-3.
9. Andre Dodin, 'Texts,' *Vincent de Paul and Charity* (New York: New City Press, 1993), 82.

of evangelisation and catechesis which is drawing new life from attentiveness to the word of God.' In RM 20, John Paul added: 'Preaching constitutes the church's first and fundamental way of serving the coming of the kingdom in individuals and in human society.' The church's conciliar documents stress that preaching is crucial in the church's mission[10] and the chief means of her evangelisation.[11] It plays a central role in the ministries of bishops,[12] priests and deacons,[13] as well as some lay people.[14] Kerygmatic preaching calls people to faith and conversion.[15] As par 4 of the Decree *Presbyterorum ordinis* (hereafter PO) explains: 'Since no one can be saved who has not first believed, priests as co-workers with their bishops, have as a primary duty the proclamation of the gospel of God to all.' CCL 767 says: 'The most important form of preaching is the homily, which is part of the liturgy, and is reserved to a priest or deacon.' As Paul VI pointed out in EN 43: 'It would be a mistake not to see in the homily an important and very adaptable instrument of evangelisation. Of course it is necessary to know and put to good use the exigencies and the possibilities of the homily, so that it can acquire all its pastoral effectiveness. But above all it is necessary to be convinced of this and to devote oneself to it with love. This preaching, inserted in a unique way into the eucharistic celebration, from which it receives special force and vigour, certainly has a particular role in evangelisation, to the extent that it expresses the profound faith of the sacred minister and is impregnated with love.' The preaching of homilies can be dated back to the early church. For instance, in the *First Apology* of St Justin Martyr, which was written in the mid-second century, we read: 'And on the day called Sunday all who live in the cities or in the country gather together in one place, and the memoirs

10. LG 17; AG 3.
11. AG 6.
12. LG 25; CD 12.
13. AG 4; LG 28; CCL 757. The canon says, 'It belongs to priests, as co-operators of the bishops, to proclaim the gospel of God. For the people entrusted to their care, this task rests especially on parish priests, and on other priests entrusted with the care of souls. Deacons also are to serve the people of God in the ministry of the word, in union with the bishop and his priests.'
14. LG 12; CL 2; GS 43.
15. SC 9.

of the Apostles or the writings of the prophets are read, as long as time permits. Then when the reader has finished, the Ruler (presumably the bishop or priest) in a discourse instructs and exhorts to the imitation of these good things.'[16]

What exactly is a homily? It is an exposition of the meaning of the readings while relating them to the circumstances of everyday life. Reiterating the teaching of the Second Vatican Council,[17] CCL 769 says: 'Christian teaching is to be explained in a manner that is suited to the conditions of the hearers and adapted to the circumstances of the times.' Canon 767 adds: 'In the course of the liturgical year, the mysteries of faith and the rules of Christian living are to be expounded in the homily from the sacred text.' Speaking about the content of homilies, canon 768 says: 'Those who announce the word of God to Christ's faithful are first and foremost to set out things which it is necessary to believe and to practise for the glory of God and the salvation of all.' Principal among these, of course, is the kerygma. With regard to giving homilies, St Vincent Ferrer, one of the greatest preachers of all time, had this to say: 'Be simple, be practical; avoid all general statements and come to particular things, illustrating your teaching by examples. Do not let your language be harsh; never show anger, but act as a tender father would act towards his children who are sick; act as a mother who caresses her children and encourages them, and who rejoices at the progress they have made.'[18] St Vincent de Paul, who was an admirer of Vincent Ferrer, used to recommend the so-called, 'Little Method.'[19] It consists of three interrelated elements. Firstly, when it seems appropriate the homilist describes the nature of

16. St Justin Martyr, *The First and Second Apologies*, Ancient Christian Writers: The Works of the Fathers in Translation, no 56, ed Burghardt, Dillon & McManus (New York: Paulist Press, 1997), 71.

17. Speaking about the homily, PO 4 explains: 'Such preaching must not present God's word in a general and abstract fashion only, but it must apply the perennial truth of the gospel to the concrete circumstances of life.'

18. Vincent Ferrer, *Treatise on the Spiritual Life* (Fitzwilliam: Loreto Publications, 2006), 24. Available online at this address: http://www.archive.org/stream/saintvincentferr00hogauoft_djvu.txt (Accessed 19 Feb 2009).

19. Arnaud d'Angel, 'Some Lessons from a Reformer of the Art of preaching,' *St Vincent d Paul: A Guide for Priests* (London: Burns Oates Washbourne, 1932), 106-33.

the subject under consideration, (e.g. the kerygma). Secondly, he proposes motives for believing the kerygma. Thirdly, he suggests practical means of doing so while describing its implications for action, (e.g. forgiving others the way Christ has forgiven us).

While canon law makes it clear that lay people cannot preach a homily at Mass, they can preach in other circumstances. CCL 766 says: 'The laity may be allowed to preach in a church or oratory if in certain circumstances it is necessary, or in particular cases it would be advantageous, according to the provisions of the Episcopal Conference.' Although liturgical preaching takes pride of place, both clergy and laity alike often preach in non liturgical settings such as parish halls, retreat centres, hotels, etc. Many of us are well aware that some of the finest preachers in the English speaking world today are lay people.

When administering the sacraments, priests have an ideal opportunity to highlight the kerygma whenever possible, for example by means of a short ferverino[20] in the sacrament of reconciliation, or in a homily based on the liturgical readings of the day. When it seems appropriate, it is good to relate the theme in the readings to the Eucharist which has many kerygmatic elements. For example, the creed is a summary of the Good News, and the core teaching of Christianity is implicit in the words of consecration: 'This is the new covenant in my blood *which shall be shed for you and for all so that sins may be forgiven* [my italics].' When administering the sacrament of the anointing of the sick to a dying person, the priest could say these reassuring words: 'There is no need to worry about your past sins, if you look only into the eyes of God's mercy, expecting only mercy, you will receive only mercy, now and at the moment of your death. Jesus is waiting to welcome you with love. Just say his holy name with complete trust.' As scripture assures us in Rom 10:13 and Acts 2:21: 'Everyone who calls on the name of the Lord will be saved.' When lay people preach they should, whenever possible, ground their words in the kerygma.

Among Catholic writers, it is arguable that papal preacher Raniero Cantalamessa has the clearest grasp of the foundational importance of kerygmatic preaching in the Christian life. In his

20. An Italian word which is used in Catholic circles to refer to a brief, but inspiring word of exhortation and encouragement.

wonderful book, *Come Creator Spirit: Meditations on the Veni Creator*, there is an eloquent description of such preaching. Having heard him speak, I strongly suspect that Cantalamessa is describing not only his own experience but that of many other evangelists he knows. He says that it is chiefly in the proclamation of the kerygma that the work of the Holy Spirit continues. What is it that actually happens? At a certain point while the preacher is speaking, quite apart from any decision of his own, he becomes aware of an intervention, as though a spontaneous inspiration is expressing itself through his voice. He becomes aware of this because he begins to feel deeply stirred, invested with a strength and an extraordinary power of conviction that he clearly recognises as not being his own. His prophetic words come out with incisiveness, conviction and great assurance. In biblical terms, he speaks with authority (cf Mk 1:27; Lk 4:36; Jn 7:46).

Unlike many other forms of evangelisation, kerygmatic preaching addresses human misery, which is ultimately the result of sin, with the proclamation of the saving grace of Jesus Christ. It does not rely on subtle arguments of a rational kind for its effectiveness. As St Paul testified in 1 Cor 2:4-5: 'My message and my preaching were not with wise and persuasive words, but with a demonstration of the Spirit's power, so that your faith might not rest on men's wisdom, but on God's power.' Again in 1 Thess 1:5 he said: 'Our message of the gospel came to you not in word only, but also in power and in the Holy Spirit and with full conviction.' It is probable that at least four important points are implicit here. Firstly, if an evangelist has experienced the power of the kerygma him or herself and speaks it in an anointed way, his or her words will be like a 'sword of the spirit' (Eph 6:17) which will enter the hearer's deepest and darkest self with a Good News message of saving grace (cf Heb 4:12). Secondly, that proclamation contains the power to effect what it says because the word of God will not return to God without achieving the saving purpose for which it was sent (cf Is 55:11). Just as surely as the words of consecration at Mass lead to the transubstantiation of the bread and wine, so the words of the kerygma will have transforming power when received with faith. As St Paul said in 1 Thess 2:13: 'We also thank God continually because, when you received the word of God, which you heard from us, you accepted it not as the word of men, but as it actually is, the word of God, which is at work in you who believe.' Thirdly, the Lord may demonstrate the truth of the proclamation by performing a confirmatory charismatic deed of power such as a healing, miracle or deliverance.[21] Fourthly, Paul's mention of the Spirit reminds us of the central role of the third person of the Trinity in effective evangelisation.[22] In the light of these points, it is not difficult to see why renowned French theologian Yves Congar could say: 'If in one country Mass was celebrated for thirty years without preaching and in another there was preaching for thirty years without Mass, people would be more Christian in the country where there was preaching.'[23]

One-to-One Evangelisation

In EN 46, Pope Paul VI said: 'Side by side with the collective proclamation of the gospel, the other form of evangelisation, the person-to-person one, remains valid and important.' It can take many forms such as a parent talking to a child about Jesus; a person sharing his or her faith story with a friend or relative; engaging in house-to-house visitation, perhaps as a member of a parish evangelisation team; doing street contact work; or exploiting a providential opportunity to talk to a colleague or acquaintance about meaning of life issues. In this, as in all things, Jesus is our role model.

Although Jesus preached a lot to crowds he also engaged in one-to-one evangelisation. That is what happened when he met the Samaritan woman at Jacob's well. He noticed that she was attractive and had a certain charm about her. But her body language conveyed to him that, in spite of her apparent confidence, she was mistrustful, vulnerable, and longing to be loved. Jesus understood the reasons for the woman's feelings. He sensed that over years she had been disappointed in love. She had looked in vain for lasting affection in the arms of a number of

21. Pat Collins, *The Gifts of the Spirit and the New Evangelisation.*
22. Raniero Cantalamessa, *Come Creator Spirit* (Collegeville: The Liturgical Press, 2003), 230-1.
23. 'Sacramental Worship and Preaching,' *The Renewal of Preaching: Theory and Practice,* Concilium 33 (New York: Paulist Press, 1968), 62.

men. Instead of offering her true romance they had made her empty promises, flattered her, used her, and eventually abandoned her. Not surprisingly she felt abused and rejected. As a result of her many affairs she had been ostracised by her fellow townspeople, especially the women. That was the main reason she had gone to the well at mid day. She knew that no one else would be there. She was prepared to endure the sweltering heat rather than put up with the hurtful taunts and criticism of her neighbours.

Clearly, Jesus did not judge or condemn the Samaritan woman in any way. By means of his gestures and words he showed her great respect. Indeed, he broke a number of taboos in order to convey his unconditional acceptance. Firstly, Jewish men were not supposed to speak to women in public, especially Samaritan women, but Jesus spoke to the woman at the well. The gospel says that when the apostles returned they were surprised that Jesus was talking to a female. But they did not say anything. Secondly, as a Jew, Jesus was not supposed to ask a Samaritan for a drink because if he touched anything she had touched he would be ritually unclean. But he also broke that taboo by asking her for a drink. The woman would have got the message. This Jewish man is showing me a respect and acceptance that no Samaritan man has ever done.

As Jesus talked to the woman he reflected back his understanding of how she felt. He intuited the fact that she was looking for the kind of vitality and well-being that comes from knowing that you are truly loved. That is why he talked to her about living water that would truly satisfy. Unbeknown to her he was the wellspring of that water. Even as she sensed his understanding, and reverence, the water of life was already springing up secretly within her. It is interesting that at this stage of their conversation Jesus felt free to talk to her about her painful past. He began by asking about her husband. The woman replied, quite truthfully, that she had no husband. Then Jesus said that she was correct, because in the past she had five different partners. Suddenly, the woman realised that, from the first moment of their meeting, this extraordinary man had known all about her and her dysfunctional relationships. But nevertheless she felt completely accepted by him. This was a moment of great healing and relief for her. Already she was consciously experiencing a spring of living water welling up within her as the merciful love of God was released within her heart by the Holy Spirit. She experienced the fulfilment of something St Paul would write about some time afterwards: 'I pray that out of his glorious riches he may strengthen you with power through his Spirit in your inner being' (Eph 3:16).

Because he had been able to read the secrets of her heart, the Samaritan woman realised that Jesus was a prophet. Not surprisingly she began to discuss religious issues with him such as Jewish and Samaritan forms of worship. Then she said, 'I know that Messiah – that is Christ – is coming: and when he comes he will tell us everything.' To which Jesus replied, 'I who am speaking to you, I am he.' It is an extraordinary revelation. In great humility the Samaritan woman had opened her heart and eventually her suppressed desires to Jesus. He reciprocated by revealing his true identity to her. It was an act of remarkable love and friendship that filled the woman with joy. No wonder she forgot all about her water jar. She put it down and hurried back to the town to tell her neighbours all about Jesus. Many of them were intrigued by what she shared with them, and so they went out to see Jesus for themselves. They were so impressed that they invited him to stay with them for a couple of days. We are told that as a result of their interaction with him, they came to believe that he was the Saviour of the world.

When one reflects on this story, a number of points seem to be implicit as far as one-to-one evangelisation is concerned. Here are four of them:

1. *Listen* with what has been called a contemplative and empathic attitude by paying sustained attention to the person you are interacting with.
2. *Discern* in what way is the person experiencing his or her need for God.
3. *Affirm* the person's transcendental desire by focusing on it, thereby enabling the person to become more consciously aware of it and of any barriers that might stand in its way, such as un-repented sin and unforgiveness.

4. *Share* your emotional reaction in a spontaneous and appropriate way, while also talking about the Christian message,
   - Either in a scriptural way, by telling them about it, if it seems appropriate.
   - About any of the six aspects of the kerygma which were mentioned in chapter five.
   - Talk about the kerygma in a more personal way by telling the person something relevant and helpful about your own faith journey.[24]

In his book *Power Evangelism: Signs and Wonders Today*, John Wimber refers to the Engel Scale.[25] It is a way of representing the journey from no knowledge of God to spiritual maturity as a Christian believer. The model is used by some Christians to emphasise the process of conversion. As Wimber remarks, if an evangelist talks to a person who barely has an awareness that there is a Supreme Being in the same way as to someone who grasps the personal implications of the gospel, he or she will speak a message he cannot understand. The Engels Scale has been modified over the years and there is an updated version called The Matrix. Both are intended to help evangelisers to listen to, and discern where a would-be convert might be situated where two interrelated axes are concerned, one open, the other closed, one spiritually aware, the other spiritually unaware. Useful information about the Engel Scale and The Matrix are available for those who are interested, on the internet.[26]

An Example of a personal testimony

It is advisable that every Catholic write down a brief account of his or her conversion story. It could be structured in three sections: a) What were you like before you developed a deep personal relationship with Jesus Christ? b) How did you come to relate to Jesus in a more intimate way and to experience the free gift of his saving mercy and love? c) How did your new-found relationship with Jesus have a transforming effect upon your

24. Pat Collins, 'Spiritual Growth and the Counsellor,' *Catholic Marriage Advisory Council Bulletin*, no 104, vol 26 (October 1986): 14.
25. (London: Hodder & Stoughton, 1985), 63-7.
26. http://www.hazelden.org.uk/pt02/art_pt068_modified_engel_full.htm and http://tgm.integralgc.com/

life? Here is my own testimony which I have briefly adverted to earlier in the book. It is divided into the tree sections. For other Irish examples see *Adventures in Reconciliation: Twenty-nine Catholic Testimonies*.[27]

1) Before I had a personal relationship with the Lord

My life was made up of a combination of hope and disillusionment during my seminary years. At the end of the Second Vatican Council I had the hope that the church would experience a time of great renewal. In actual fact hope quickly gave way to disillusionment as a result of disputes, divisions and desertions. Following my ordination in 1971, hope and disillusionment characterised my life again. At that time my mind was full of theology and my heart full of good intentions. I hoped to be an effective preacher and to be helpful to the poor. Within a year or so, however, I became disillusioned. Whereas in the past I had tended to identify with the Good Samaritan in the parable, I began to identify with the man on the roadside. Like him I felt wounded and weak. This awareness became the birthplace of a heartfelt desire for some sort of spiritual awakening.

2) My spiritual awakening

Desire gave way to fulfilment in February in 1974. I was invited to attend a conference in the North of Ireland. One of the talks was given by a Protestant clergyman. He spoke about Jesus as the source of our peace. Quite frankly, his inspired words moved me to tears. I wanted to know the Lord the way this man obviously did. Afterwards a nun introduced me to him. We had a brief chat and arranged to meet privately. When we did, I told the minister that I was looking for a new awareness of God in my life. He read a memorable passage from Eph 3:16-20, which asks that the person 'may have power, together with all the saints, to grasp how wide and long and high and deep is the love of Christ, and to know this love that surpasses knowledge – that you may be filled to the measure of all the fullness of God.' Instinctively I found myself saying inwardly, 'This is exactly what I deep down desire with all my heart.' Then the

27. Preface by Cardinal Cahal Daly, eds Paddy Monaghan & Eugene Boyle (Guildford: Eagle Publishing, 1998).

Church of Ireland clergyman began to pray for me, firstly in English, then in tongues. Suddenly, and effortlessly I too began to pray fluently in tongues. I knew with great conviction that Jesus loved me and accepted me as I was. I realised what St Peter meant when he wrote: 'Though you have not seen him, you love him and even though you do not see him now, you believe in him and are filled with an inexpressible and glorious joy' (1 Pet 1:8).

3) Some transforming effects of being filled with the Spirit

During the following months and years the inner effects of that spiritual awakening became obvious from that blessed day onwards. Prayer was easier, scripture a revelation, I had fewer fears, a greater ability to love, and I was able to exercise some of the gifts of the Holy Spirit. The main effect of my conversion was that I felt that Jesus had walked though the walls of my body, so to speak, to live within me. As St Paul observed in 1 Cor 6:17: 'The one who is united with the Lord is one spirit with him.' We, as St Paul pointed out in Gal 2:20, 'no longer live, but Christ lives within.' The indwelling of Christ had a number of important implications for me. I had an experiential awareness that Jesus loves me in the way the Father loved him. It was as if I, a sinful creature, were divine and adorned with every perfection of divinity. As Jesus himself said, 'As the Father has loved me, so I love you' (Jn 15:9). The seventh Sunday preface says that the Father sent Jesus that he 'might see and love in us what he sees and loves in Christ.' That is why the Father says to those who have received justifying grace, 'You are my beloved son or daughter in whom I am well pleased' (Mt 17:5).

It has been said with good reason that St Paul's spirituality can be summed up in the words 'in Christ,' which he used at least eighty six times in the letters attributed to him. As was mentioned in chapter one, Christ enables the believer to live in him all that he himself lived by means of the Holy Spirit active within. So when I am about to embark on different tasks such as writing, preaching, teaching, praying for others, struggling to love, etc, I may run into the buffers of my own natural weakness and limitations. But then I can say to Jesus, 'Lord, the good I wish to do, I cannot do, but you are living out the mysteries of your life in me. Enable me by the Spirit that animated your life of evangelisation, to continue and fulfill that same loving evangelisation in my own life. Give me the ability to do this task (I state what it is …), and I thank you that you are achieving even more than I can ask, or imagine, through the power of your Spirit, even now, at work within me.' I have found that when I affirm the divine indwelling in this way, I have the conviction, not only that my efforts are being blessed, but that they will bear lasting fruit.

Personal Witness

I learned from the Charismatic Movement that although there are similarities, testimony and witness are different. Whereas a testimony describes how a person came to know the Lord in a deeply personal way, a witness describes the way in which God has been active in the person's everyday life. In his book, *Build With the Lord*, Bert Ghezzi says that witness is made possible as a result of answering these four questions:[28]

1) In what ways were you aware of the Lord's presence or activity in the recent past?
2) What has the Lord been teaching you in your prayer time or scripture reflection?
3) In what ways has the Lord used you recently in order to serve or help others?
4) What changes has the Lord been urging you to make in order to become holy by loving and serving him in your neighbour?

A witness is an account of the working of God's grace in a person's life. The beauty of this approach to evangelisation is that it is experiential rather than didactic or abstract. Often this kind of honest sharing prompts the hearer to say within, ' if God could do that for him or her, he could do it for me also.' Furthermore, it can lead the hearer to ask more questions, ones which can open the door to sharing the kerygma, perhaps by talking about how you came to have a deep personal awareness of the mercy and love of God.

28. (Ann Arbour: Word of Life, 1976), 102.

Spiritual conversations

We all need to think about how we might initiate spiritual conversations. There are at least three ways of doing this, direct, indirect and invitational.

1. Typically, the direct method takes the form of a question or statement such as, 'Did you ever think about what happens after we die?' or 'Did you know that people who are truly religious are happier and live, on average, seven years longer than people who are not?'
2. The indirect method latches on to some topic that has come up in conversation, and relates it to a spiritual one. For example, the person is talking about the difficulty of dieting or giving up smoking. That would leave the door open to saying something about twelve step programmes and the need for reliance on the Higher Power, namely God, which is closely related to Paul's notion that God's power is made perfect in our weakness. You could also think of relatives, colleagues and friends that you would like to evangelise. Could you prepare transition topics, going from what they are interested in to something spiritual?
3. The invitational method is used when you ask a colleague or friend to come with you to a Christian event you are hoping to attend such as a lecture, an Alpha Course, a Christian concert, a carol service etc.

Rick Warren who voiced an official prayer at the inauguration of President Barack Obama, is the author of *The Purpose Driven Life* which has sold thirty million copies. It contains two chapters on evangelisation. In one he says that God wants to redeem human beings from the powers of darkness and to reconcile them to himself, 'so we can fulfil the five purposes he created us for: to love him, to be part of his family, to become like him, to serve him, and to tell others about him.'[29] A little later he echoes this point when he says that God, 'made you to be a *member* of his family, a *model* of his character, a *magnifier* of his glory, a *minister* of his grace, and a *messenger* of his Good News to others.'[30]

29. (Grand Rapids: Zondervan, 2002), 282.
30. Ibid., 295.

Warren suggests that Christians can extract lessons from their everyday experience which later on they can share with others when the opportunity presents itself. He suggests that the following questions might serve to stimulate useful reflection:

- What has God taught me from failure?
- What has God taught me as a result of not having enough money?
- What has God taught me as a result of pain, sorrow or depression?
- What has God taught me through waiting?
- What has God taught me from disappointment?
- What have I learned from my family, my church, my relationships, my small group, my critics?[31]

Street Evangelism

A growing number of Catholics are beginning to engage in street evangelism. A couple of years ago I travelled to Galway City to give a talk in An Tobar Nua, a Christian restaurant and bookshop. When my talks came to an end, Mike Short, one of the full time workers in the restaurant, gathered the adult participants, gave them a brief pep talk, divided them into twos, prayed with them, and then went with them into the nearby streets to evangelise. I discovered that they had been trained to do this, and had been given suggestions about ways in which they could approach people with a view to engaging them in conversations about meaning of life issues and God. I seem to recall that they had imitation one million euro notes which they could offer people as a symbol of the free gift of God's grace. They aimed, when circumstances allowed, to lead the people through three interrelated steps.

1. Realise that you have messed up: that you have said, thought or done things that were wrong (what the Bible calls sin). Check out this list to help shine a light on your life: outbursts of anger, bitterness, sex outside of marriage, drunkenness, bad language, lying, stealing, violence, lust, dishonouring your parents, abortion, gossiping and being jealous of what others

31. Ibid., 292.

have (cf. Gal 5:19-21; Deut 5:6-21). These produce spiritual death in our lives both now and for eternity (cf Rom 6:23).

2. Understand that because of the death and resurrection of Jesus Christ you can be forgiven no matter what you have done. Jesus desires that you experience eternal life now, and that you go to be with him in heaven when you die (cf Rom 6:23; Jn 10:10, Jn 3:16; Rom 4:25).
3. Surrender your life to Jesus Christ and ask him to fill you with his Holy Spirit. Ask him to help you turn away from the things in your life that are wrong (cf Acts 2:38; Rom 10:9-10; Gal 5:16).

Commenting on the outcome of these steps, the An Tobar Nua website observes: 'When we make this choice to give our lives to Jesus, the power of the Holy Spirit is released in our lives and we begin to experience the love, joy and peace that God desires to give us, even in times of suffering. A wonderful way for Catholics to confirm this decision is through the Sacrament of Reconciliation and to celebrate their relationship with Jesus in Holy Communion.'[32]

I know an English Catholic called John Ghazal who, every Saturday afternoon, goes out to spread the Good News in the Lanes, a tourist area made up of narrow streets, boutiques and restaurants in Brighton, England.[33] For the last year or so, John has joined people like Tarot readers and mediums by placing his prayer chair next to them. The idea is simple. He has a board advertising his services and an empty chair for clients. He says: 'This is my idea of evangelisation, just sitting there with a latte or a coca cola and waiting for people to come by and chat.' Usually he has a backup team from his family and the local prayer group who intercede on his behalf. Many passers by sit into the chair, chat with John, and finally he offers to pray for whatever they need. True to the divine promises, God often moves in power and many blessings, such as physical healings, are received. These are palpable manifestations of the presence of the kingdom of God. I also know a woman called Jenny Baker

32. http://www.antobarnua.com/my_faith/power_for_living.php
33. John Ghazel, 'Evangelising Through the Family,' *Goodnews* (July/August 2009): 14-16.

of Café, who does much the same thing between 2 and 4 pm each Saturday, in St Albans near London. She has written about her experiences in an article entitled, 'Healing on the Streets.'[34] Interestingly, she says that the inspiration for this kind of evangelism came from the Vineyard fellowship in Coleraine, Northern Ireland. In a chapter entitled, 'Catholic Street Evangelism Today,' Leonard Sullivan describes how to bring the Good News to people by means of street meetings reminiscent of the soap box approach of The Catholic Evidence Guild of Frank Sheed's day.[35] People need to be trained in order to engage in this form of street evangelism.[36] It has to be said that this type of evangelisation is not common in Ireland.

It takes real courage and conviction to engage in street evangelism. Happily, however, a growing number of people seem prepared to overcome their fears and human respect in order to share the Good News in this unusual way. I heard one leader say that when people cross the line, so to speak, from relative passivity and privacy to publicly affirm their faith by telling others about it, they themselves begin to own their Christian beliefs with new and fresh conviction.

Conclusion

It goes without saying that this chapter has failed to do justice to the complexity and many facets of this important topic. That said, it seems fairly obvious that there is a need to train lay people in the theory and practice of the different forms of verbal evangelisation mentioned here. As was mentioned in chapter seven each diocese needs to have an evangelisation office and an evangelisation team. One of the key things that they can do is to organise diocesan training courses. Speaking of the new ecclesial communities, Pope John Paul II seemed to indicate in RM 51 that 'these communities are a sign of vitality within the church, *an instrument of formation* [my italics] and evangelisation.' In EE 49 the Holy Father wrote: 'Europe calls out for credible evangelisers ... such evangelisers *must be properly trained* [my italics].'

34. Ibid., 10-11.
35. *John Paul II and the New Evangelisation*, 150-64.
36. cf Masie Ward and Frank Sheed, *Catholic Evidence Training Outlines* (Steubenville: Franciscan University Press, 1993).

Ecclesial communities could be commissioned to run training courses on behalf of the dioceses. New ecclesial communities, such as the Sion community in England, and the John the Baptist Koinonia community in Belfast, already conduct that kind of training. Some of our theological colleges could also provide training such as that which is on offer in the Maryvale Institute, Birmingham, England. Its beginners course, which is sponsored by The Catholic Agency to Support Evangelisation (CASE) deals with the principles and practice of evangelisation. These are the topics it deals with:

1. Introduction to evangelisation.
2. The new evangelisation.
3. Evangelisation initiatives in England and Wales: a practical guide.
4. *Ecclesia in Europa:* the application of key themes from the Apostolic Exhortation.
5. Evangelisation and our relationship with other faiths.
6. Ecumenism and evangelisation: the possibilities and parameters of working with partners.
7. Evangelisation and schools.
8. Making the parish, the home and school focal points of communion, collaboration and mission.
9. Worship and evangelisation.
10. Evangelisation and the internet.

Recommended Reading

- Frank P. DeSiano, *The Evangelising Catholic: A Practical Handbook for Reaching Out* (New York: Paulist Press, 1998).
- Mary Catherine Hilkert, 'Anointed and Sent: The Charism of Preaching,' *Retrieving Charisms for the Twenty-First Century*, ed Doris Donnelly (Collegeville: The Liturgical Press, 1999), 47-64.
- Mary Ann Fatula, *Thomas Aquinas: Preacher and Friend* (Collegeville: The Liturgical Press, 1993).
- George Montague, *Riding the Wind* (Ann Arbor: Word of Life, 1977).
- *Adventures in Reconciliation: Twenty-nine Catholic Testimonies*, eds Paddy Monaghan & Eugene Boyle (Guildford: Eagle Publishing, 1998).

CHAPTER TEN

Kerygmatic Evangelisation Courses

Catholics can engage in effective basic evangelisation by running one or other of the kerygmatic evangelisation courses that are currently available. This chapter will look at a number of the better known ones, RCIA, Life in the Spirit Seminars, Alpha, Café, and the Philip retreat. It will deal with things such as the origins, aim, content, methodology, resources and training associated with each one. The beauty of these courses is that they are run by a group of people, their dynamics and content are pre-prepared, and they are aimed at different constituencies such as church goers who are not fully evangelised, the unchurched, and unbelievers of different kinds, all of whom were mentioned in previous chapters.

1) RCIA

During the Second Vatican Council there was a call for the reinstatement of the catechumenate which was a feature of life in the early church. In 1966 a provisional ritual was distributed and followed by a revised version in 1969. In 1972 Pope Paul VI promulgated the *Order of Christian Initiation of Adults*. Later on it was called the *Rite of Christian Initiation of Adults* or RCIA. It is the process by which interested adults, (e.g. men and women who intend getting married to a Catholic), are gradually introduced to the faith and way of life of Catholics. The RCIA is a communal process, and involves a number of stages punctuated by liturgical events which help potential converts toward the final rite, usually at the Easter Vigil during which they are baptised and confirmed, which enables them to become full members of the Catholic Church. The entire process takes at least a number of months, and ideally a complete liturgical year. That said, participants are generally invited to proceed at a pace which suits them individually. The church prefers to call this a process rather than a programme. The RCIA has several distinct parts which are based on a four-stage process of conversion which was outlined in a document called *The Apostolic Tradition* which was attributed to St. Hippolytus.[1]

1. *Inquiry*: the initial period before people decide to enter the Catholic Church. They are encouraged to ask questions and to check it out, but without having to commit themselves.
2. *Catechumenate*: Those who decide to enter the church and to be trained for a life in Christ are called catechumens. This is an ancient name from the early church. In this stage, candidates develop their faith and are 'catechised' – they are told basic points about the Catholic faith, including the kerygma, and the Christian way of living.
3. *Purification and preparation*: The church helps candidates to focus on and intensify their faith as they prepare to commit their lives to Christ and to be received into the church at Easter. If they are following the RCIA process, the candidates go through a series of beautiful gospel-based meditations during Lent.
4. *Initiation*: The culmination of the whole process. The candidates are received into the church during the Easter Vigil Mass, where they receive the sacraments of initiation: baptism, confirmation, and Eucharist. (If they have already been baptised, they are not baptised again.)
5. *Mystagogy*: After reception into the church at Easter, this period lets the new Catholics reflect on and learn more about the mysteries of the Mass and the Sacraments in which they now fully participate.[2]

In my limited experience, mainly in the United States, the people who attend the RCIA course are often men and women who are intending to marry a Catholic and want to join the

1. cf Alan Kreider, *The Change of Conversion and the Origin of Christendom* (Harrisburg: Trinity Press, 1999), 21-26.

2. There are many useful books available such as, Deborah M. Jones, *The RCIA Journey* (Mystic Ct: Twenty-third Publications, 2006); Nick Wagner, *The Way of Faith: A Field Guide to the RCIA Process* (Mystic Ct: Twenty-Third Publications, 2008); Lisa M. Coleman, *Basics of the Catholic Faith* (Mystic, Ct: Twenty-third Publications, 2000); Richard N. Fragomeni, 'Conversion,' in *The New Dictionary of Catholic Spirituality*, ed Michael Downey (Collegevile: The Liturgical Press, 1993), 232-4.

church. I have been told that as many as 50% of those who are baptised and confirmed into the church tend to lapse and to stop attending church. In *Gifts of the Spirit and the New Evangelisation* it was said that adults who are being prepared to receive the sacraments of initiation should be told about baptism in the Spirit and the gifts of the Holy Spirit in Is 11:2 and also in 1 Cor 12:8-10.[3] Furthermore, they should be encouraged to expect both kinds of gifts. It is the fullness of the Spirit that empowers recipients of the sacraments of initiation to live the Catholic faith in an enthusiastic and committed way.

2) Life in the Spirit Seminars

In chapter five we saw how there can be a kerygmatic crisis of head, heart and hands in the contemporary church. The Life in the Spirit Seminars, which were devised by the Word of God community in Ann Arbor in 1969, were designed to tackle that problem.[4] They were mainly intended to help Catholics who were sacramentalised but not fully evangelised by,

- Providing basic Christian teaching for the head.
- Helping people to come into a heartfelt awareness of God's unconditional mercy and love in their hearts.
- Assuring them that with new power in their hands, so to speak, their characters and lives can be transformed.

The team manual lists four aims of the seminars:[5]

1. To help those who come to them to establish, re-establish, or deepen a personal relationship with Christ.
2. To help those who come to the seminars to yield to the action of the Holy Spirit in their lives so that they can begin to experience his presence working both in them and through them.

---

3. (Dublin: Columba, 2009), 127-8.
4. Pat Collins, 'Life in the Spirit Seminars,' *Maturing in the Spirit: Guidelines for Prayer Groups* (Dublin: Columba, 1991), 83-95.
5. Over the years there have been a number of editions of the seminars. The first was entitled, *The Life in the Spirit Seminars: Team Manual* (Notre Dame, Charismatic Renewal Services, 1973), 17; *The Life in the Spirit Seminars Team Manual: Catholic Edition* (Ann Arbor: Servant Books, 1979); *The New Life in the Spirit Seminars Team Manual: Catholic Edition 2000*, revised and annotated by Therese Boucher (Locust Grove: National Service Committee, 2003).

3. To help those who come to the seminars to be joined to Christ more fully by becoming part of a community or a group of Christians with whom they can share their Christian life and from whom they can receive support in that life.
4. To help them begin to make use of effective means of growth in their relationship with Christ.

The seminars consist of seven meetings and talks. They can be divided into three groups.

Firstly, seminars one to four prepare people for baptism in the Spirit.[6] Numbers one and two deal with the nature of salvation. The first is about the way our loving Father calls us to experience his unconditional love, and calls us, in the light of that awareness, to love and serve God by loving and serving our neighbours. The second shows how salvation comes through Jesus Christ and can transform every aspect of our lives. Seminars three and four are about the how of salvation. Number three is about the nature of the new life a person receives when he or she is baptised in the Holy Spirit. Number four describes how a person can prepare to receive the new life mentioned in the preceding seminar.

Secondly, the fifth seminar stands on its own. It is brief, practical and very important because it explains how each person will be prayed with for baptism in the Spirit, and how to be receptive to the gift of tongues, or any other gift the Lord might want to bestow. The talk is followed by prayer ministry when people often come into a new experience of the Lord. As the Irish Bishops said in a joint pastoral, baptism in the Spirit is: 'The outpouring of the Holy Spirit, a conversion gift through which one receives a new and significant commitment to the Lordship of Jesus and openness to the power and gifts of the Holy Spirit.'[7]

Thirdly, seminars six and seven are about Christian growth after the infilling of the Spirit. The sixth seminar gives practical instruction about how to grow in the Spirit, for example, by

6. Pat Collins, 'Baptism in the Spirit and the Universal Call to Holiness and Evangelisation,' *The Gifts of the Spirit and the New Evangelisation*, 111-28.
7. Par 7, *Life in the Spirit: Pastoral Guidance on the Catholic Charismatic Renewal: A Statement from the Irish Bishops* (Dublin: Veritas, 1993).

means of daily prayer and scripture reading. The seventh and last seminar is about the way in which people can put off their old nature with its worldly desires to put on their new nature in Christ. It also draws attention to predictable difficulties in the aftermath of baptism in the Spirit.

As people participate in the Life in the Spirit Seminars they are strongly encouraged to buy and use a small booklet entitled *New Life in the Spirit*. It contains scripture texts and reflections for every day of the seven weeks. The people attending the Seminars are not only encouraged to use the booklet in their daily prayer time, they are also encouraged to share their insights during the weekly group sharing. This kind of prayer and trustful communication not only helps the participants to open up to one another, it also helps them to open up to the outpouring of the Holy Spirit in week five.

The Life in the Spirit Seminars are an inspired response to a pressing pastoral need, both within and beyond the Charismatic Renewal. In an age of growing indifference to the church and its teachings and disciplines, they have helped millions of people to come into a deeper personal relationship with Jesus and to experience the infilling, guidance and charismatic gifts of the Holy Spirit. The Seminars, therefore, have proved to be one of the most effective means of renewal and evangelisation in the contemporary church. That said, it has to be admitted that unlike the Alpha Course which has widespread appeal, they have been mainly effective within the Charismatic Renewal.

3) The Alpha Course

From 1984 to 1992 I conducted parish missions around Ireland as a member of the Vincentian parish mission team. By and large my colleagues and I tended to preach to the converted. While it is important to nurture the faith of the committed, we regretted the fact that we often failed to reach the growing number of people who had lapsed. We could see that there was an urgent need for a new evangelisation, one that would reach those who were alienated from God and the church. But we did not know of any practical and effective method of doing this at the local level. The Life in the Spirit Seminars were good, but they were too closely identified with the Charismatic Movement to have widespread appeal. Cursillo weekends were also effective for a number of people, especially in Northern Ireland, but we felt, rightly or wrongly, that it was unlikely that they would ever be effective on a wide scale in the South.

In 1998 a Church of Ireland clergyman told me that he was hoping to introduce the Alpha Course to Ireland. Evidently, he had been in touch with Nicky Gumbel in England who had advised him that he should get a priest to collaborate with him, because Ireland is a mainly Catholic country. He invited me to fill that role. Following some prayerful reflection I accepted for a number of reasons. Firstly, I was already fully persuaded that we needed a kerygmatic type of basic evangelisation in Ireland. Alpha seemed to meet that need. Secondly, I could see that if a mission was conducted in a parish, the local people could be encouraged to continue the mission by putting on the Alpha course afterwards. Thirdly, I had a personal conviction that, in so far as it was possible, there should be an ecumenical aspect to evangelisation. Surely the teaching of our Lord is unmistakable. The credibility of his mission in the world, and here in Ireland in particular, is dependent upon the unity and love of his disciples. As he prayed in Jn 17:21: 'May they all be one, as you Father are in me, and I in you, so also may they be one in us, that the world may believe that you sent me.' Alpha was an ecumenical course, in so far as it was being used to evangelise in all the Christian churches. Fourthly, I felt that Alpha employed a kergymatic/ and charismatic approach which was well suited to contemporary historical culture, with its emphasis on religious experience and subjectivity.

In his interesting book *God's Continent: Christianity, Islam and Europe's Religious Crisis,* Philip Jenkins says: 'The Alpha course is designed for a society in which Christians possess minority status and can assume no wider knowledge whatever of their doctrines or beliefs. With its assumptions of individualism, popular scepticism, and non-hierarchical networking and its unwillingness to invoke dogmatic authority it is intended to confront the forces driving toward secularisation and to use those forces for evangelistic ends.'[8] Alpha started off as a ten-week introduc-

8. (Oxford: Oxford University Press, 2007), 83.

tion to the Christian faith that included fifteen talks. They are available in Nicky Gumbel's *Alpha: Questions of Life*.[9] The topics covered include; 'Christianity: boring, untrue and irrelevant?' 'Who is Jesus?' 'Why did Jesus die?' 'Who is the Holy Spirit?' and 'Why and how should I read the Bible?' It is important to stress the fact that the Alpha course is designed primarily to meet the needs of unbelievers and lapsed people. While it is true that the first Alpha course or two is usually attended by people who do practise their faith, they only become truly effective from an evangelistic point of view, to the extent that those first participants invite non-practising relatives, friends and colleagues to attend subsequent courses. The kerygmatic talks presume nothing and appeal to mind and heart. They try to persuade the listeners without pressurising them in any way.

A typical session begins by welcoming the participants. Some groups start with a simple meal which is intended to build relationships and to foster a sense of belonging. Then there is a brief time of prayer and hymn singing. Sometimes the leaders look at a few of the scripture texts that will be mentioned later in the talk. Then everyone listens either to the longer 40 min or the shorter 20 min version of one of the talks by Rev Nicky Gumbel on DVD. Sometimes the talk is given live by a speaker who expresses in his or her own words the substance of what is in Gumbel's book.[10] There is a back-up booklet that reminds participants of the key points. Then there is a 20 min break for bis-

9. Eastbourne: Kingsway Communications Ltd., 2004; *The Alpha Course Manual* (London: Alpha International, 2005); *How to Run the Alpha Course* (Eastbourne: Kingsway, 2004); *The Alpha Course Leaders' Training Manual* (London: Alpha International, 2003); *Alpha: Questions of Life* (London: Hodder & Stoughton, 2003); *Challenging Lifestyle* (Eastbourne: Kingsway, 2001); *Searching Issues* (Eastbourne: Kingsway, 2001); *Why Does God Allow Suffering?* (Eastbourne: Kingsway; 1999); *Why Christmas?* (London: Alpha International, 1995); *Why Jesus?* (London: HTB, 1991).

10. The full range of topics dealt with on an Alpha course are as follows: 1) Christianity: Boring, Untrue, Irrelevant? 2) Who is Jesus? 3) Why did Jesus die? 4) How can I be sure of my Faith? 5) Why and how should I read the Bible? 6) Why and how do I pray? 7) How does God guide us? 8) Who is the Holy Spirit? 9) What does the Holy Spirit do? 10) How can I be filled with the Spirit? 11) How can I resist evil? 12) Why and how should we tell others? 13) Does God heal today? 14) What about the church? 15) How can I make the most of the rest of my life?

cuits tea and coffee, i.e. if there was no meal before the meeting. It is followed by a discussion in groups of five or six, each of which is facilitated by a member of the Alpha team. The evening ends at a predetermined time with a concluding prayer, such as the Our Father. On week seven there is either a weekend or an extended day away. This enables people to deepen friendships, to hear a number of talks on the Holy Spirit, and also to receive prayer for an infilling of the Spirit. Following the Holy Spirit weekend or day, there are five more sessions.

A slightly arbitrary acronym is sometimes used to describe Alpha:

A is for anyone. Anyone can come to the sessions. They are primarily aimed at the un-churched and non believers. (These are the two groups that are mentioned in CCL 771).

L is for laughter. Alpha courses are entertaining as well as informative. The talks contain many jokes and humorous anecdotes.

P is for pasta. Those attending Alpha courses often eat a spaghetti dish. In other words some courses centre around shared meals of a modest kind. Many of them substitute a tea and coffee break for the meal. They help to create a context of unconditional belonging, which is a prerequisite for receptivity to the beliefs which are shared in the Alpha course.

H is for helping. Alpha is a process, where people assist one another, for example believers helping those who are struggling to believe.

A is for asking anything. Participants are encouraged to ask questions within a context of acceptance and respect.

Although Alpha started within an Anglican context, it has been accepted and approved at the highest level in the Catholic Church. For example, before introducing the course to the Dublin Archdiocese, Bishop Jim Moriarty gave the Alpha materials to Cardinal Connell who found nothing in them contrary to Catholic faith. When the first Alpha conference was held in St Patrick's College, Drumcondra, Bishop Moriarty welcomed those attending on the Cardinal's behalf. Sometime later Archbishop Diarmuid Martin appointed a priest of the archdiocese to liaise between himself and the Catholics on the Alpha board. In 2006 those Catholics wrote to the hierarchy seeking official recognition and the appointment of a liaison person between Alpha Ireland and the bishops. In January 2007 the Executive Secretary of the Conference of Bishops wrote to say that it had granted our request. In his letter he said: 'I am to assure you of the bishop's ongoing interest and support for your work of evangelisation.' In saying this, the Irish bishops were echoing what their counterparts had said in a number of other countries. Cardinal Seán Brady, Catholic Archbishop of Armagh, in welcoming an Alpha Conference said that: 'Alpha has developed a reputation as an inspirational programme of Christian Education and formation, producing excellent results and having a long-lasting and positive effect for those who participate and beyond. I pray … that it may continue to grow and develop.'

In recent years a number of new Alpha courses have been developed.

1) *Student Alpha* was designed with university students in mind. If a person is attending a college or university, and is wondering about the bigger questions in life, Student Alpha can propose answers.

2) *Youth Alpha* was designed with the needs of older teenagers in mind. It provides those who attend with an opportunity to explore the Christian faith in a relaxed, non-threatening way over ten thought-provoking sessions.

3) *Alpha in the workplace* was designed for use by employees in their place of work. The talks used are the 20 minute version, so that they can be conducted during a lunch break. Some are run in the office meeting room, others in a neutral venue nearby.

4) *Senior Alpha* is designed for use by those who are over 65. It follows the same format as a standard Alpha course. There are large print manuals available with all the Bible verses printed. A large print edition of the 'Why Jesus?' booklet is also available. Courses are run in churches, people's homes, in sheltered accommodation and residential homes.

5) *Alpha for Prisons* was launched in 1995 in response to a demand from inmates.[11] Since then enthusiasm for Alpha for

11. cf http://caringforexoffenders.org/

Prisons has grown. It is now registered in 80% of the prisons in the UK as well as running in prisons in 74 countries. The course has been run in Mountjoy prison in Dublin.

6) *Deaf Alpha* may be developed in the near future accompanied by a DVD which will contain the Alpha talks in Irish sign language. Negotiations are in progress seeking permission to use a British version for translation into the Irish signs.

7) *Polish Alpha* was introduced recently in order to evangelise the large number of young immigrants that have come to Ireland from that country in recent years.

Those who run the Alpha course are constantly asked about follow-up. Involvement in small groups, such as the parish cell groups, already mentioned, is one which is recommended because they provide such things as fellowship, a sense of belonging, teaching, and training. However, adult education courses can also be recommended, ones that seek to build in a catechetical way upon the kerygmatic foundations laid by Alpha. At this point, difficult and controversial issues arise. For example, in Britain Alpha found that the following issues were the ones most frequently raised by people: 'Suffering', 'Other Religions,' 'Sex Before Marriage,' 'The New Age,' 'Homosexuality,' 'Science and Christianity' and 'The Trinity'. A certain amount of research will have to be done in Ireland to find out whether they are the most pressing issues with the Irish people. I suspect that our list would not be all that different to the British one. Alpha Ireland will also provide a certain amount of teaching material, either in printed form, on CDs and DVDs, or as podcasts. Alpha Ireland has already produced a pamphlet on the Lord's prayer, based on the *Catechism of the Catholic Church*, and a shortened version of the *Confessions of St Patrick*. Aid to the Church in Need in Ireland has produced a 32 page booklet entitled, *Rekindle the Faith through Prayer, Self-denial and Witness*.[12] It could be used in an up-building way by people who have completed an Alpha course. There is a post-Alpha Catholic course available which was produced in Canada. It is entitled, *Catholicism 201: A Catholic Follow-up to the Alpha Course*, which contains eight talks

12. Aid to the Church in Need, 151, St Mobhi Rd., Glasnevin, Dublin 9. Email: churchinneed@eircom.net

by Fr James Mallon on subjects ranging from the sacraments, Mary and the saints, to Christian morality.[13] While the content is excellent, the production values are not as high as the DVDs produced by Alpha in Britain. There is also *The Alpha Marriage Course* which was developed by Nicky and Sila Lee. It is backed up by a book, and a DVD version of the course. It is intended to be a support to married couples, especially those who have attended an Alpha Course.[14] It lasts for eight weeks and is designed to help any married couple to build a healthy marriage that lasts a lifetime. It was launched in 2000 and by 2009 over 2324 marriage courses had been run.[15] Nicky and Sila Lee have also written a helpful guide, *The Parenting Book* which will also be backed up by a course on DVD.[16] That said, the task of Alpha follow-up is largely the responsibility of parishes and dioceses and not of Alpha itself, which necessarily has limited aims.

Alpha has many merits. Firstly, we live in a culture where many people are looking for meaning, as the writings of logotherapist Viktor Frankl have suggested.[17] The Alpha course is designed to answer meaning-of-life questions. Secondly, it is a tried and tested means of basic evangelisation which is proving effective all over the world. By the year 2009, up to twelve million people had attended Alpha courses. Thirdly, it is easy to run because there are so many helpful materials available, especially the teaching DVDs. Fourthly, one reason why the Alpha course has been remarkably successful all over the world is the fact that it is so professional in its approach. Its motto could be,

---

13. Produced by John Paul II Media Institute, 1725 Oxford St, Halifax, NS, Canada B3H 3Z7. www.jp2mi.ca

14. *The Marriage Book: How to Build a Lasting Relationship* (London: Alpha International, 2000); *The Marriage Course Leader's Guide* (London: Alpha International, 2000); *The Marriage Course: How to Build a Healthy Marriage that Lasts a Lifetime* (London: Alpha International, 2000); *The Marriage Preparation Course Leaders' and Support Couples Guide* (London: Alpha International, 2004). Cf. http://themarriagecourse.org/

15. The eight sessions cover: building strong foundations; the art of communication; resolving conflict; the power of forgiveness; parents and in-laws; good sex; love in action; the marriage course party.

16. London: Alpha, 2009.

17. cf Pat Collins, 'Transpersonal Psychology and Spirituality,' *Mind and Spirit: Spirituality and Psychology in Dialogue*, 43-50.

'Only the best is good enough for God.' As a result it has well designed, attractively produced materials that cover every aspect of the Alpha courses such as training manuals, audio tapes, DVDs, posters, and books. For example, there is even a cook book with simple, cheap recipe suggestions for the Alpha meal. An Alpha newspaper is published a few times a year which keeps its readers up to date and contains inspiring stories about how people, some of them celebrities, came to faith in Christ as a result of attending an Alpha course. Fifthly, the course does not require the involvement of the local clergy who often feel overstretched and pressured. Sixthly, it trains lay people to accept positions of responsibility and leadership in their parishes. As such, it prepares them to become evangelisers. Seventhly, the fact that the same course is used in all denominations and that those who attend have a similar experience of coming to faith in Christ, means that Alpha increases a sense of ecumenical unity where the essentials of the faith are concerned (cf Eph 4:5).

4) Cursillo

The word *Cursillo* is Spanish and means 'short course.' (i.e. in Christianity). It was first developed in 1944 in Majorca by a group of Catholic laymen.[18] The cursillo method focuses on training lay people to become effective leaders over the course of a three-day, residential weekend which begins on a Thursday night and ends on Sunday afternoon. It includes a number of talks given by priests and lay people. The titles include the following: Ideal, Grace, Laity, Faith, Holiness, Formation, Evangelisation, the Sacraments, Obstacles to a Life of Grace, Life of Prayer, Study, Leaders, Christian Life, Christian Community. Each talk is followed by a small group discussion. Like the courses already described, Cursillo focuses on the basic message of Christianity with the aim of enabling the participants to develop a personal relationship with Jesus so that they can bring his message into every aspect of the world in which they live. When I was conducting parish missions around Ireland I found

18. Marcene Marcoux, *Cursillo, Anatomy of a Movement: The Experience of Spiritual Renewal* (Lambeth Pr, 1982); For good information on Cursillo see http://www.episcopalrenewalcenter.org/cursillo/Whatis.html

that this basic evangelisation course was mainly being run in Northern Ireland, especially in Derry and Belfast.[19] On 26 June 2009 Cardinal Seán Brady said in a homily given in St Nicholas's Church, Dundalk:

> Approximately 60 years ago, somewhere in Spain, probably in the diocese of Ciudad Real, the Holy Spirit inspired that first team of clergymen and laymen to give the first Cursillo – something wonderful was born. It is typical of the humble spirit of the Movement that the names of those first individual contributors remain anonymous. They had learned well from Jesus who told us to learn from him who is meek and humble of heart. What was born was a great Movement of Spiritual Renewal in the Church – a great Movement of spiritual awakening that tries to convey a new sense of the powerful and personal aspects of our faith in Jesus Christ – our one and only Saviour of the world. We need that awakening, right now, here in Ireland in a big way.
>
> I want to thank God for those in this diocese who have heard and heeded the message. The seed has fallen on good ground and has borne fruit one hundred fold. That was plainly obvious to me when some of your number came to Dromantine recently and gave a brilliant personal testimony on what the Cursillo Movement has meant in their lives. It was really powerful stuff – I am glad to have the opportunity to come here this evening and tell you that. But what is more important is that together we tell God and thank God.
>
> I also want to thank God for the deeper and richer appreciation which you have for God from Cursillo. 'In Christ' is a great phrase so beloved of St Paul. He uses it so often to convey his deep union with his beloved Saviour. He said: 'I live not now, but Christ lives in me. He wants to know nothing else but Jesus Christ and him crucified. He wants to fill up in his own life what is wanting in the sufferings of Christ. I am here to encourage you, with all the power at my disposal, to embark on a new programme of promoting Cursillo at every

19. For information see http://cursillowalktoknock.com/gallery.html

possible opportunity. We need the new evangelisation as never before.'[20]

Once the Cursillo course is over there is follow up. The Cursillo weekend is the starting point of a process that lasts the rest of life. It consists of three parts:

a) Group Reunion. The heart of Cursillo is a small group of friends, usually of the same sex, who meet weekly to hold each other accountable for their spiritual journey. They report on their piety, study and apostolic action.

b) Ultreya, which is held monthly, is a reunion of 'reunions' to provide support and build community by sharing communal experiences.

c) Spiritual Direction is a commitment to seek out skilled lay persons or clerics for spiritual direction to provide help in deepening union with Christ.

5) Café

Catholic Evangelisation Services (CES) was set up by the Crew Trust in 1996 to promote the Alpha Course in the Catholic Church. Sometime later a small group from CES developed a sequence of 8 videos called Catholic Faith Exploration (Café) which can be used for parish renewal. These DVDs include initial kerygmatic evangelisation and catechesis. They seek to enliven the faith of parishioners and to help them form vibrant small groups which can become catalysts for evangelisation. The Café DVDs can be used in RCIA classes, Lenten groups, Confirmation preparation etc. The Café process seems to have hit a chord and is being used in many areas in the UK. The first module, 'Knowing God Better,' is a kind of do-it-yourself mission. It has proved to be particularly popular in parishes. Following that, participants are encouraged firstly to attend the module on the sacraments by Professor D'Ambrosio and secondly, the module entitled, 'Catholics Making a Difference,' which features Lord David Alton, James Mawdsley and others. It encourages Catholics to witness to their faith in verbal and non verbal

20. http://www.armagharchdiocese.org/cardinal/homilies/126-2009/706-26-june-mass-of-thanksgiving-irish-cursillo-movement-st-nicholas-church-dundalk

ways. The idea is that, after these three modules, the group would do some kind of outreach themselves (e.g. by running an evangelistic course like Alpha or the Life in the Spirit Seminars). By the way, Café has a five talk series in which Michele Moran, of the Sion Community in London, talks about ways in which Catholics can share their faith with others. There is a similar DVD entitled *Catholics Making a Difference* where a number of speakers talk about evangelising by means of words, witness and works. It is part of a series entitled, *Pass it On*. There are other Café DVDs such as, *Believe: Reflections on the Creed; This is my Body: A Two part reflection on the Mass;* and *Parents: You, your Children and their Catholic Faith*, comprised of seven lively, amusing and thought-provoking talks by David Wells Director of RE, Plymouth Diocese. Café has also published, *Plugged In – Youth Café*. It is a well produced, fast moving and inspiring resource for teenagers. It is ideal for confirmation candidates and consists of six sessions, each lasting about thirty minutes.

What is good for potential parish organisers to know is that by using Café resources everything has been done for you. You just need to book the hall, set out the chairs, make the coffee and turn on the DVD. It can be said in passing that CES has also produced a series of small booklets to use alongside the Café course with titles such as *God's Love, Forgiveness, Help, Word, Spirit* and *Hope*. They also stand alone and are ideal to give away to neighbours, friends, workmates and those in need of help in the areas covered.[21]

6) Philip Retreats

Following a powerful calling from the Lord, Fr Ricardo Argañaraz founded The John the Baptist Koinonia Community in Italy, in 1979. It is made up of priests, religious and about 3,500 lay members. It has spread to a number of countries in Europe including Ireland. The lay members enjoy many of the benefits of the internal members including:

1. Monthly meetings and Masses with the consecrated members.

21. For anyone who is interested in this well thought out and well resources approach to integral evangelisation see the CaFÉ website at http://www.faithcafe.org/

2. Weekly prayer groups (called Houses of Prayer) with other lay members to keep their faith strong and to bring others into a personal relationship with our Lord
3. Intense training in evangelisation
4. Fellowship with other believers
5. Knowledge that you are serving God in a meaningful and lasting way.

The John the Baptist Koinonia Community is devoted to bringing people to have a personal relationship with Jesus. To this end it has developed the Philip Course.[22] It is a beginner's introduction to the basics of the Christian faith and follows the six-point structure of the kerygma which was described in chapter five. The 'Philip Course' is based on the biblical story told in Acts 8:26-32 about the way one man's questions about faith are answered in a single life-altering encounter with Philip the evangelist. Through a series of talks and spiritual exercises, the Koinonia community take people on a three day journey of faith discovery. This course, like Alpha, is for non-believers and believers alike. It has helped to infuse thousands of people with a new, enthusiastic sense of the Christian commitment. The John the Baptist Koinonia community also runs the Paul, Ruth, John, and other courses. Each year it puts on an International School of Kerygmatic Evangelisation which aims to offer a systematic and formative programme to help people to engage, in an effective way, in the new evangelisation.[23]

Conclusion

When I was living in Detroit I used to talk about the need for parishioners to get involved in the new evangelisation. At first they did not have any clear idea of what it involved. When I explained that, among other things, it meant reaching out to the un-churched, they would be non-plussed and ask, 'How on earth will we do that?' What this chapter has proposed is the fact that any lay people who wish to respond to the church's re-

---

22. A English manual entitled *The Philip Course* is available from the Federal Office of Koinonia John the Baptist, Dobřanská 41, 301 00 Plzeň-Valcha (CZ). Tel. +420377423585; e-mail: seg@koinoniagb.org

21. http://www.koinoniagb.org/index.html

peated call to engage in the new evangelisation can do so effectively by becoming involved in one or other of the forms of collective evangelisation listed here. It can be said in passing that besides the courses listed above, there are also many others.

Recommended Reading

- Deborah M. Jones, *The RCIA Journey* (Mystic, CT: Twenty-third Publications, 2006).
- Nicky Gumbel, *Alpha: Questions of Life* (Eastbourne: Kingsway, 2004).
- *The New Life in the Spirit Seminars Team Manual Catholic Edition 2000*, revised and annotated by Therese Boucher (Locust Grove: National Service Committee, 2003).
- David Payne, *Alive: A Café Resource* (Luton: Café Resources, 2009).
- The Federal Office of Koinonia John the Baptist, *The Philip Course.*

CHAPTER ELEVEN

Some Key Forms of Evangelisation

Although this book on basic evangelisation has dealt with many aspects of the subject, nevertheless it has said little or nothing about some important topics such as evangelisation of, and by the family; evangelisation of, and by adolescents and young adults; basic evangelisation by means of the mass media of communication; and the transformation of the culture in which we live by means of gospel values. The intention in this chapter is to make relatively brief comments about each one of these areas.

Family Evangelisation

John Paul II stated in FC 86: 'The future of humanity passes by way of the family.' The Apostolic Exhortation AA 11 had a number of interesting things to say about evangelisation of, and by the Christian family. Firstly, echoing the point already made, it states: 'The family has received from God its mission to be the first and vital cell of society.' Secondly, because this is so, married couples need to be evangelised themselves because you cannot give what you haven't got. This can happen in many ways, such as the evangelising efforts of another married couple. In a chapter entitled, 'Evangelising Married Couples,' Frank and Gerry Padilla suggest how this can be done as a result of three interrelated steps,:

a) Attracting married couples by building a personal relationship with them.

b) Converting them, (e.g. by inviting them to attend a Cursillo weekend, an Alpha Course, or a Life in the Spirit Seminar).

c) Nurturing the couple's faith by inviting them to join such things as a prayer, meditation or parish cell group.[1]

It can be said in passing that marriage relationships can be

1. *John Paul II and the New Evangelisation*, eds Ralph Martin & Peter Williamson, 188-96.

strengthened by attending Marriage Encounter, an Alpha Marriage Course, or by contacting Accord, a voluntary Catholic organisation that promotes good marriages, for counselling.[2]

Secondly, basic evangelisation of children begins at home by means of silent witness and verbal instruction in the faith. As AA 11 states: 'Christian husbands and wives are co-operators in grace and witnesses in faith for each other, their children, and all others in their household. They are the first to communicate the faith to their children and to educate them by word and example for the Christian and apostolic life.' In EN 71 Pope Paul VI said: 'In a family which is conscious of this mission, all the members evangelise and are evangelised. The parents not only communicate the gospel to their children, but from their children they can themselves receive the same gospel as deeply lived by them. And such a family becomes the evangeliser of many other families, and of the neighbourhood of which it forms part.' Similar points are expressed in FC 53 where John Paul II said: 'The ministry of evangelisation carried out by Christian parents is original and irreplaceable.'

Parents witness to the Good News by showing the example of their affection for one another, and such things as their mutual patience, empathy, respect and willingness to forgive one another whenever they feel hurt or let down. It is also important that parents refrain from talking about other people in a hostile, judgemental or prejudiced way. They also witness to the gospel by being kind and generous to the poor and the marginalised. It is also important that children not only see their parents praying together but also that they teach their children to pray by praying with them on a regular basis. It is a striking fact that shortly before his departure from Ireland in 1979, Pope John Paul spoke about the importance of family prayer. 'Your homes', he said, 'should always remain homes of prayer. As I leave today this island ... may I express a wish: that every home in Ireland may remain or may begin again to be a home of daily family prayer. That you would promise me to do this would be the greatest gift you could give me as I leave your hospitable shores.'[3] In CCC

2. http://www.accord.ie
3. *Pope John Paul II in Ireland: Addresses and Homilies*, 81.

2685 we read: 'The Christian family is the first place of education in prayer. Based on the sacrament of marriage, the family is the "domestic church" where God's children learn to pray "as the Church" and to persevere in prayer. For young children in particular, daily family prayer is the first witness of the church's living memory as awakened patiently by the Holy Spirit.' It is not surprising, therefore, that Pope Paul VI asked: 'Mothers, do you teach your children the Christian prayers? Do you prepare them, in conjunction with the priests and school teachers for the sacraments that they receive when they are young? Confession, Communion and Confirmation? Do you say the family Rosary together? And you, fathers, do you pray with your children … your example of honesty in thought and action, joined to some common prayer is a lesson for life, an act of worship of singular value. In this way you bring peace to your homes.'[4]

Thirdly, the family members can also evangelise others by the witness of their Christian lives. 'At all times and places but particularly in areas where the first seeds of the gospel are being sown, or where the church is just beginning, or is involved in some serious difficulty, Christian families can give effective testimony to Christ before the world by remaining faithful to the gospel and by providing a model of Christian marriage through their whole way of life. To facilitate the attainment of the goals of their apostolate, it can be useful for families to be brought together into groups.'[5] As a priest I meet wonderful couples who evangelise others by inviting them into their homes and by engaging in all kinds of evangelising activities. For example, many couples run prayer groups, Alpha Courses, conferences, retreats etc. I also know husbands and wives who, with permission from the speakers, record evangelistic talks and either sell them or give them to others as an effective way of sharing the word of God.

Evangelisation of Adolescents and Young Adults

Although the practice of religion has fallen by half in Ireland during the last quarter century, the decline is more pronounced among adolescents and young adults. A Red C poll conducted on behalf of the Iona Institute in November 2009 discovered that

4. 11/8/1976.
5. AA 11.

although church attendance by young people is lower than the national average it is still reasonably high. Almost a third of 18-24 year olds go weekly to Mass and another 22% go monthly or more.[6] Another all Ireland survey conduced by Lansdowne Marketing in 2007, for the Iona Institute, discovered that 15-24 year olds are almost entirely ignorant of basic Christian teachings. Only 5% of 15-21 year-old could quote the first of the Ten Commandments. Almost one-third could not say where Jesus was born, and more than one-third did not know what is celebrated at Easter. The survey found that only 52% of young people could name Matthew, Mark, Luke and John as the authors of the gospels, while only 38% knew that there were four gospels. Fewer than half of those surveyed could name 'Father, Son and Holy Spirit/Ghost' as the three persons of the Trinity, while only 48% were able to name Genesis as the first book of the Bible. Thirty-eight per cent were aware that there were seven sacraments, but just 15% knew that 'transubstantiation' was the term used to describe what takes place at Mass. Only one in 10 of the young people surveyed was able to say that the Immaculate Conception referred to Mary, the mother of Jesus, being free of original sin. What these figures indicate is that it is not too surprising that many young adults do not attend church on a regular basis in view of the fact that their knowledge of the truths of faith is so deficient.

An American book entitled, *Lost and Found: The Younger Unchurched and the Churches that Reach Them*, contains interesting information about young adults in that country.[7] Admittedly, the statistics it mentions were gleaned in a predominately Protestant culture, in a different country. Nevertheless, in general terms they are probably indicative of the situation in Ireland. Surveys have found that 80% of 20 to 29 year-olds believe God exists, and 70% consider themselves to be spiritual and are interested in knowing more about God. At the same time, 67% believe the church is full of hypocrites; 77% think

6. Press Release by The Iona Institute. http://www.ionainstitute.ie/pdfs/Press_Release_by_The_Iona_Institute_2Nov2009.pdf
7. Ed Stetzer, Richie Stanley & Jason Hayes (Nashville: B&H Publishing, 2009).

Christianity today is more about organised religion than about loving God and loving people; and 90% say they can have a good relationship with God without being involved in a church.

Those who wish to evangelise adolescents and young adults need to keep a number of points in mind. From a psychological point of view, adolescence is a time when young men and women move from being dependent on their carers, to become independent, and even rebellious, before embracing the interdependence which is characteristic of mature adult life. Developmental psychologists such as Piaget, Kohlberg and Fowler have studied adolescence and young adulthood from a number of overlapping points of view.[8] Erik Erickson's description of the eight stages of psycho-social development is particularly relevant. He maintained that, normally, adolescents and young adults tackle the fifth and sixth of eight developmental tasks, (i.e. a choice between identity and role confusion, and a choice between intimacy and isolation, respectively). The key virtue at these stages is fidelity in committed relationships. Carl Jung, one of the most introspective of psychologists, indicated that there was an important interconnection between personal identity and interpersonal relationships of an intimate kind when he said: 'One is always in the dark about one's own personality. One needs others to get to know oneself.'[9]

Knowing this to be true, John Paul II said something similar in FR 32: 'Belief is often humanly richer than mere evidence, because it involves an interpersonal relationship and brings into play not only a person's capacity to know but also the deeper capacity to entrust oneself to others, to enter into a relationship with them which is intimate and enduring ... what is sought is the truth of the person – what the person is and what the person reveals from deep within ... Human perfection, then, consists not simply in acquiring an abstract knowledge of the truth, but in a dynamic relationship of faithful self-giving with others. It is in this faithful self-giving that a person finds a fullness of cer-

8. James Fowler, 'Adolescence,' *Stages of Faith: The Psychology of Human Development and the Quest for Human Meaning* (San Francisco: Harper & Row, 1981), 69-77.

9. *C. G. Jung Speaking,* ed W. Mc Quire, & R. Hull (Princeton NJ: Princeton University Press, 1977), 165.

tainty and security. Human perfection, then, consists not simply in acquiring an abstract knowledge of the truth, but in a dynamic relationship of faithful self-giving with others. It is in this faithful self-giving that a person finds a fullness of certainty and security.' The adolescent's or young adult's ability to develop a satisfactory sense of human identity is largely dependent, therefore, on the depth and fidelity of his or her relationships, especially friendships. So from an evangelisation point of view, Christians need to foster a sense of non-judgemental friendship and belonging which will offset the individualism and loneliness which are common in modern life. Friendships are formed as people learn to empathise and share with one another within a context of growing trust, affection and commitment. When such a loving environment is provided, adolescents and young adults may be more open to relationship with the Lord and his kerygmatic message with all its ethical implications, (e.g. forgiving others in the unconditional way in which Christ has forgiven us). There is a saying I heard during my young adult years which helped me a lot at the time: 'I sought my soul, but my soul I could not see. I sought my God, but my God eluded me. I sought my brother and I found all three.' In other words, human relationships, especially of a loving and intimate kind, can mediate the presence and the merciful love of God, who was revealed in Christ's saving life, death and resurrection. As Gerald Manley Hopkins wrote, 'Christ plays in ten thousand places, Lovely in limbs, and lovely in eyes not his to the Father through the features of men's faces.'[10]

Some evangelists have discovered the value of praxis, especially where adolescents and young adults are concerned. Carol Gilligan has pointed out that, whereas the identities of females are mainly affirmed through relationships, those of males are mainly affirmed through tasks and activities. Exponents of praxis, therefore, would endorse a saying of Goethe: 'Try to do your duty and you will soon find out what you are.' Instead of beginning with issues of faith, Christian mentors can encourage young adults, both male and female, to engage in practical action such as volunteering to serve people who are less well off in

10. As Kingfishers Catch Fire, Dragonflies Draw Flame.

the developing world, or to participate in the kind of work that members of the St Vincent de Paul Society do in every parish in the country. Through their contact with the poor, the elderly, the handicapped and the marginalised, the eyes and hearts of adolescents and young adults are opened to the suffering of others and to the unjust structures of society that often oppress and discriminate unfairly against them. These realisations are food for reflection on values and meaning-of-life issues, in a way that often leads young men and women to ask religious-type questions. Adult facilitators can assist them to engage in theological reflection on their experience.[11] As a result, adolescents and young adults who may have been alienated from Jesus and the church may come into a new faith relationship with both and begin to pray from their hearts in a Christian way.[12] Alpha has a number of well-thought-out, and well-resourced courses which can help believers to engage in basic evangelisation of adolescents and young adults who are looking for unconditional meaning and hope.

Firstly, there is *Explore the Christian Faith: A Programme of Study for Students Aged 11-14.*[13] It deals with the same topics as the adult Alpha course but in a way that is adapted to the needs of young people. Although the talks are given by live speakers, there is a backup DVD which contains images, music, short films, and vox pops mentioned in the lesson outlines.

Secondly, there is *Schools Alpha: Taking Youth Alpha into Schools*. The course has been divided into three streams, Alpha-

11. cf Pat Collins, 'Experience and Belief in Theological Reflection,' in *The Broken Image: Reflections on Spirituality and Culture*, 118-31; 'Vincentian Praxis,' *Colloque: Journal of the Irish Province of the Congregation of the Mission* (Spring 2008), 493-5. Theodore Wiesner, 'Experiencing God in the Poor,' in *Spiritual Life* (1987). Siobhan O'Donoghue and Karl Nass, 'Vincentians in Action: An Interfaith Model for Civic Learning and Spiritual Growth,' *Journal of College & Character*, vol VII, no 6 (July 2006). Each year Wiesner's article is read by hundreds of students in De Paul University in Chicago to give them a Christian perspective on their social action. The article by O'Donoghue and Nass describes how the students reflect in a theological way on their experiences afterwards.

12. Pat Collins, 'Teaching Young People to Pray,' in *Beyond the Race for Points: Aspects of Pastoral Care in a Catholic School Today*, ed J. Matthew Feheney (Dublin: Veritas, 1999), 169-81.

13. London: Alpha International, 2008. See www.exploreforschools.co.uk

Lite, Alpha-Tech, and Alpha-Active. Like *Exploring the Faith,* this course is taught live rather than watched on DVD. There is a back-up DVD, however, which contains all kinds of video clips, and vox-pops. The course is also supported by *Alpha for Youth,* a very colourful manual in magazine form. As is usual with Alpha materials, the production values of both are very high.[14] *Plugged In –Youth Café* is another useful resource. It is backed up by a DVD which contains the contents of the six week course, including discussion starters and interactive prayer times. The DVD is accompanied by a detailed leader's manual. This series was designed to engage teenagers of today. The flexibility of the course means that it can be used for confirmation, youth groups and schools.

Thirdly, another course has been developed for use in third level colleges and universities. *Alpha for Students* is not all that different from the adult one. Each week, the talk which is given by a live speaker who looks at a specific aspect of the Christian faith, followed by discussion in the small groups. The emphasis is upon exploration and discovery in a relaxed and informal environment. This Alpha course usually lasts for 10 weeks, with a day or weekend away in the middle. Some courses are held over morning coffee or during a lunch break. However, most are evening courses which sometimes begin with pizza and a pint. Typically they last two hours and are held either in halls of residence, a student's flat, or some other venue. As with the other courses, *Alpha for Students* is backed up by excellent printed materials and a DVD. According to Alpha's own literature, courses are currently being run in 67% of British universities.

I am well aware that this brief section does not do justice to such an important topic. Gerard Gallagher has written a useful book which is well worth reading, entitled, *Are we Loosing the Young Church? Youth Ministry in Ireland from Vatican II to 2004.*[15] Another worth looking at is, *Cast Out into the Deep: Attracting Young People to the Church,* by Séamus Lynch.[16] The National Committee of Diocesan Youth Directors and the Commission

14. *Youth Alpha: Leader's Guide,* (London: Alpha International, 2008).
15. (Dublin: Columba Press, 2005).
16. Dublin: The Liffey Press, 2005. See also, Frank Mercandante 'Evangelising Teenagers,' *John Paul II and the New Evangelisation,* 197-204.

for Pastoral Renewal and Adult Faith Development of the Irish Catholic Bishops' Conference has published a helpful booklet entitled, *Called Together: Making the Difference*.[17] It aims to promote four goals: (1) To help young people grow, both in a personal sense and a spiritual sense. (2) To give young people the opportunity to experience and be disciples of Jesus Christ in their lives. (3) To inspire and facilitate young people to take an active role in the Catholic community. (4) To encourage the Catholic community to continually put aside any prejudices about young people and to recognise and empower their talents and energy.

When I was studying evangelisation in Detroit, our sociological lecturer Dr Michael McCallion spoke on a number of occasions about the importance of training Catholic youth workers. He pointed out that the church often says that young people are its pastoral priority because they are the Christians of tomorrow. However, the rhetoric is not always matched by practical action. How many full or part time paid youth workers are employed in our parishes or parish clusters? The answer is very few. Dr McCallion used to point out that in the United States, Protestant parishes spent, on average, nearly twice as much money on youth ministry as their Catholic counterparts. Judged by its effects, the available evidence seemed to indicate that it was money well spent. In Ireland we need to train youth workers who, among other things, will be able to engage in pre-evangelisation, basic evangelisation, and catechesis. Happily, the schools for evangelisation, which were mentioned in chapter ten, are mainly attended by young adults. There are also a number of groups that focus on the evangelisation of younger people such as Youth 2000,[18] Catholic Youth Care,[19] Pure in Heart,[20] National Evangelisation Teams,[21] and Jesus Youth, which is mainly working in the Indian community in Ireland.

17. The National Committee of Diocesan Youth Directors & the Commission for Pastoral Renewal and Adult Faith Development of the Irish Bishops' Conference (Dublin: Redemptorist Publications, 2009).
18. http://www.youth2000.ie/
19. http://www.cyc.ie/office-of-youth-evangelisation.html
20. http://www.pureinheart.net
21.http://www.netministries.ie/index.php?option=com_content&view=article&id=44&Itemid=54

Reports about child abuse have rightly led the church in Ireland to insist on the highest of standards for anyone working in the area of youth evangelisation. Firstly, they should read the national guidelines, *Safeguarding Children: Standards and Guidance Document for Catholics in Ireland.*[22] Secondly, they should read the specific guidelines of their own diocese about safeguarding children. Thirdly, they would be well advised to attend any child protection programme that may be put on in their diocese. When I lived in Detroit it was mandatory for anyone who worked with children. Fourthly, in Dublin, and presumably in other dioceses, anyone clerical or lay, who works with children, adolescents or vulnerable adults needs Garda vetting. Fifthly, in Dublin, and perhaps in other dioceses, any evangelists coming from abroad need a letter of accreditation from their superior, clerical or lay (e.g. the person's parish priest); police clearance from their own country; and a willingness to comply with the child protection policy of the diocese they are visiting.

Evangelisation by Means of the Mass Media

The Decree on the Media of Social Communications of the Second Vatican Council, entitled *Inter mirifica* (hereafter IM) maintains that:

- The church has a right to use those media which she considers necessary or even useful for the formation of Christians and for pastoral activity.
- The church has a right to own these media.
- Bishops and priests have the duty to instruct and direct the faithful on how to use these media.
- The media are to be used for the salvation and perfection of both believing Christians and of all mankind.
- The laity has the principal responsibility to animate the media with a Christian and human spirit.
- It is again the laity who are mainly to ensure that the media live up to God's providential purpose and the legitimate hopes of humanity.

22. It is available for viewing or download at, http://www. safeguarding.ie/downloads-1

Not surprisingly, Pope Paul VI appreciated the importance of the mass media in evangelisation. In EN 42, he wrote: 'In our age which is characterised by the mass media we must not fail … to avail of the media for the first proclamation of the message, for catechetical instruction and for a deeper study of the faith. When they are employed in the service of the gospel, the mass media can disseminate the word of God over a vast area and carry the message of salvation to millions of people. The church would feel herself guilty before God if she did not avail herself of those powerful instruments which human skill is constantly developing and perfecting. With their aid she may preach 'upon the housetops' the message which has been entrusted to her. In them she finds a new and more effective form – a platform or pulpit from which she can address the multitudes.' In EE 63, Pope John Paul II said: 'Given the importance of the means of social communication, the church in Europe must necessarily pay particular attention to the multi-faceted world of the mass media.'

Speaking on the occasion of the 44th World Communications Day in 2010, Pope Benedict XVI said: 'The spread of multimedia communications and its rich "menu of options" might make us think it sufficient simply to be present on the Web, or to see it only as a space to be filled. Yet priests can rightly be expected to be present in the world of digital communications as faithful witnesses to the gospel, exercising their proper role as leaders of communities which increasingly express themselves with the different "voices" provided by the digital marketplace. Priests are thus challenged to proclaim the gospel by employing the latest generation of audiovisual resources (images, videos, animated features, blogs, websites) which, alongside traditional means, can open up broad new vistas for dialogue, evangelisation and catechesis.'[23] The Pope leads by example. In spite of his advanced years, he has his own blog on the internet which is well worth visiting on a regular basis.[24] Although he talks about

23. Benedict XVI, 'The Priest and Pastoral Ministry in a Digital World: New Media at the Service of the Word,' http://www.vatican.va/holy_father/benedict_xvi/messages/comm.

24. http://thepopeblog.blogspot.com/ It is not clear if this is the Pope's own choice of material or selected by an editor on his behalf.

priests using the internet to evangelise, it goes without saying that lay Catholics can do likewise. Besides using the resources available on the internet such as Twitter, Facebook, GodTube,[25] and podcasts, the mass media also include such things as radio, TV, CDs, DVDs, magazines and the like which can be used, and sometimes are used for basic evangelisation.

John Paul also said in EE 63: 'Special attention should be given to choosing properly trained persons to communicate the message through the media.' Many years ago the Catholic Church in Ireland became aware of the need for media training. In 1967 the bishops set up the Communications Centre in Booterstown, in Dublin where clergy and laity received training which prepared them to work effectively in religious broadcasting on radio and TV. Unfortunately it closed years ago. Nowadays, Kairos Communications Ltd, which is located in Maynooth, engages in a number of similar tasks (e.g. training people to work in the media). Kairos runs a course on Christian communications and gives a Postgraduate Diploma to successful participants.

Basic evangelisation can be conducted by the mass media. As movies, like *Jesus of Nazareth* (1977) and *The Passion of the Christ* (2004) demonstrated, they can help to stimulate interest in the gospel, and can sometimes lead to genuine conversions or help to nurture men and women who have already come to have personal faith in Christ. In recent years a good deal has been written about the explicit and implicit themes, of a religious nature, in contemporary cinema. John C. Lyden's *Film as Religion: Myths, Morals and Rituals* examines films such as *Die Hard, The Godfather, Titanic,* and *Star Wars*.[26] More recently there has been a good deal of discussion about the way in which religion and spirituality are depicted in *Avatar*, which has been a worldwide box office hit. Films reflect cultural attitudes, both good and bad, to Christianity. That topic will be dealt with in the next section.

It is fairly obvious that no matter how realistic they are, the mass media such as cinema and TV are unable to create the same sense of belonging as live interrelationships can do. For

25. www.Godtube.com; www.tangle.com
26. (New York: New York University Press, 2003).

example, the whole Alpha course is currently being broadcast on God Europe, one of the religious TV channels. People can watch the talks and be inspired by their content, but surely something is lacking if there is no interaction with other people. The interpersonal context of enjoying a meal together, watching the talk on DVD in a group setting and then sharing and praying together, adds an important dimension to evangelisation. It is conducted by a community, within a community setting, with a view to adding new members to the wider Christian community. However, it is common nowadays to hear people say that they are Christians but feel no inclination to go to church. As John Wesley once observed: 'The New Testament knows nothing of solitary religion.'[27] We are called to fellowship with one another. It is not an optional extra.

Catholic TV and radio stations can be a means of evangelisation as many of those who watch or listen to EWTN are aware. Whenever I have tuned into EWTN on television it seems to be more interested in catechesis and apologetics than in basic, kerygmatic evangelisation. I think it would be true to say that it is highly unlikely that we will ever have a Catholic TV station in Ireland because it would be too expensive to run and because it is highly unlikely that it would receive a licence to broadcast. If Irish Catholics did make professional programmes on evangelistic topics they might be able to get EWTN to broadcast them on its network. United Christian Broadcasting (UCB) transmits in Ireland on the SKY satellite channel, number 214.[28] It sometimes focuses on the basic message of salvation. Recently, an interdenominational group of Irish Christians was granted a licence to set up Spirit Radio which began broadcasting nationwide in 2010.[29] Hopefully, it will be able to support and strengthen the faith of believers while helping unchurched and unbelieving listeners to come to have faith in Christ and his saving power by means of such things as teachings, interviews, moving testimonies, and good Christian music. It will also tell listeners about forthcoming evangelistic events such as Alpha,

27. cf Nicky Gumbel, *Alpha: Questions of Life*, 209
28. http://www.ucbireland.com
29. http://www.spiritradio.ie

Bible courses, and Christian conferences around the country. In Ireland, 3R Productions is a radio syndication service.[30] Every week it sends an hour long CD containing all kinds of programme inserts for possible inclusion by religious broadcasters on local and hospital radio stations around the country. The material covers topics of a social and religious nature such as, Irish and world church news, faith and doctrine, spirituality, social issues, and current events. Occasionally the inserts deal with basic evangelisation issues.

Many evangelisers know that recorded podcasts which are downloaded on to MP3 players, as well as recorded talks on tapes, CDs, and DVDs can play an important role in basic evangelisation. Even though they are not as good as hearing live talks within a community setting, they can be helpful to a person who wants to recall a live talk he or she has already heard. Recordings of this kind can be played in cars while driving to or from work, in the kitchen while doing the ironing, or on an MP3 player while out jogging or walking. There are companies that sell such CDs and DVDs, such as Éist, in Dublin.[31] As I know from the testimony of many people over the years, they have derived great benefit from such recordings. It is not uncommon for Christians to lend them to friends and neighbours in the belief that they too might find them helpful. To deal adequately with the media's role in basic evangelisation would probably need another book!

Evangelisation and Culture

Evangelisation as enculturation was mentioned briefly in chapter four. Pope John Paul II referred to this subject in FC 8: 'The whole church is obliged to a deep reflection and commitment, so that the new culture now emerging may be evangelised in depth, true values acknowledged, the rights of men and women defended, and justice promoted in the very structures of society. In this way the "new humanism" will not distract people from their relationship with God, but will lead them to it more fully.' He returned to the same subject in EE 58. Among other things he

30. http://homepage.eircom.net/~3rproductions/aboutus.htm
31. http://www.eist.ie

said: 'The proclamation of Jesus Christ must also reach contemporary European culture. The evangelisation of culture must show that in today's Europe too it is possible to live the gospel fully as a path which gives meaning to existence. To this end, pastoral practice must undertake the task of shaping a Christian mentality in ordinary life: in families, in schools, in social communications, in cultural life, in the workplace and the economy, in politics, in leisure-time, in health and in sickness. What is needed is a calm critical assessment of the current cultural situation of Europe and an evaluation of the emerging trends and the more significant contemporary events and situations in the light of the centrality of Christ and of Christian anthropology.' In their prophetic writings John Paul II and Benedict XVI have been great role models of what cultural evaluation and Christian enculturation involves. They have assessed the values and beliefs operating in the European Union in the light of the teaching of the scriptures and the church. They have also highlighted what is deficient or false, affirmed what is good, and proposed a constructive way forward. For example, Pope John Paul II has critiqued modern atheism in his Encyclical Letter, *Dominum et vivificantem,* and Pope Benedict has carried out a penetrating critique of modern capitalist culture in his Encyclical Letter, *Caritas in veritate.* Chapter two of this book was an attempt to engage in constructive criticism of postmodern culture from a Christian and evangelistic point of view.

The church has maintained that lay Catholics have an important role to play in the Christianisation of secular culture. In LG 31 we are told: 'The term laity is here understood to mean all the faithful except those in holy orders and those in the state of religious life specially approved by the church. These faithful are by baptism made one body with Christ and are constituted among the People of God; they are in their own way made sharers in the priestly, prophetical, and kingly functions of Christ; and they carry out for their own part the mission of the whole Christian people in the church and in the world. What specifically characterises the laity is their secular nature ... But the laity, by their very vocation, seek the kingdom of God by engaging in temporal affairs and by ordering them according to the plan of God.' In EN 70, Pope Paul VI identified the arena of the lay influence as 'the vast and complicated world of politics, society and economics, as well as the world of culture, of the sciences and the arts, of international life, of the mass media' as well as the more domestic areas of 'human love, the family, the education of children and adolescents, professional work and suffering.' In the national plan for evangelisation in the United States, the American bishops stated their third goal was: 'To foster gospel values in our society, promoting the dignity of the human person, the importance of the family, and the common good of our society, so that our nation may continue to be transformed by the saving power of Jesus Christ.'[32] As we know from the example of many committed Catholics in Ireland, lay people who are truly evangelised can have considerable influence in the areas where they work. Because the topic of enculturation is not the focal point of this book on basic evangelisation, nothing further will be said on this important subject.

Conclusion

We are called to evangelise, both by the Lord Jesus and the contemporary church. More specifically, the decline of Christian belief and practice requires a new evangelisation, one that aims to bring sinful human beings, especially the unchurched and unbelievers, into a liberating experience of the free gift of God's mercy and love as revealed in the saving death and resurrection of Jesus Christ. To respond adequately to this urgent need will require a major rethink by the whole church at the national, diocesan and parish level. To this end it would be very helpful if the Catholic Church in Ireland had,

1. A national plan of evangelisation similar to the American one entitled, *Go Make Disciples: A National Plan and Strategy for Catholic Evangelisation in the United States*.
2. A National Directory which could contain such things as, lists of the people, groups, courses and resources involved with evangelisation, together with addresses, phone numbers, websites, email addresses etc.
3. A national school of evangelisation which would provide fulltime and part time courses for adults and young people.

32. *Go Make Disciples*, pars.117-27.

As was suggested in chapter seven, to answer the church's call to devote all our energies to the new evangelisation will also require that we change our priorities and structures at the diocesan and parish level. Religious orders too need to re-prioritise in such a way that the new evangelisation becomes their principal concern in a manner consistent with their respective charisms. To date many of them have failed to do this to any great extent. Vocations will only come when they rekindle the fire of their evangelical enthusiasm in an energetic, innovative and outgoing way. Although the popes began to speak about the need for a new evangelisation in the mid 1970s, it is surprising, not to say a little disappointing, to see how many Catholics of all kinds have failed either to grasp the radical teaching of the church or to implement its demanding implications in a practical way. Hopefully, this book will help its readers, in some small way, to do both. Thankfully, lay people have already taken the initiative. Tine, a Catholic leaders network for the New Evangelisation, which was founded by Mgr Pat Lynch of the Céilí community in Kilbeggan, organises an annual conference, facilitates events such as the Creideamh mission in Galway (2009),[33] and helps groups that are interested in evangelisation to share a common vision, ideas, information, creativity and resources.[34]

Anyone who reads papal encyclicals will be familiar with the fact that they often end with a reference to the roles of the Holy Spirit and Mary the mother of Jesus. This chapter ends with words from Paul VI and John Paul II on the role of the Spirit in evangelisation and on the role of Mary. In EN 75, Paul VI wrote: 'It must be said that the Holy Spirit is the principal agent of evangelisation: it is he who impels each individual to proclaim the gospel, and it is he who in the depths of consciences causes the word of salvation to be accepted and understood. But it can equally be said that he is the goal of evangelisation: He alone stirs up the new creation, the new humanity of which evangelisation is to be the result, with that unity in variety which evangelisation wishes to achieve within the Christian community. Through the Holy Spirit the gospel penetrates to the heart of the

33. http://www.creideamh.org
34. http://www.tine-network.org

world, for it is he who causes people to discern the signs of the times – signs willed by God – which evangelisation reveals and puts to use within history.' John Paul echoed his predecessor's words on a number of occasions. In NMI 45 he wrote: 'The Spirit is the principal agent of the new evangelisation. Hence it will be important to gain a renewed appreciation of the Spirit as the One who builds the kingdom of God within the course of history.' In RM 21 he added: 'Through the action of the Holy Spirit the Good News takes shape in human minds and hearts and extends through history. In all of this it is the Holy Spirit who gives life.' In many ways these statements from recent popes bring us back to the theme of the first chapter, namely the inseparable relationship between renewal in the power of the Holy Spirit and effective evangelisation.

Mary the Mother of Jesus was the spouse of the Holy Spirit. Like the apostles and the 120 disciples she was baptised in the Spirit at Pentecost and exercised the gifts of the Spirit. Speaking in general of Mary's role LG 65, says: 'The Virgin Mary in her own life lived an example of that maternal love by which all should be fittingly animated who co-operate in the apostolic mission of the church on behalf of the rebirth of men.' Speaking in more specific terms, Pope Paul VI wrote in EN 81-2: 'A programme of pastoral action with evangelisation as its basic feature … is the desire that we rejoice to entrust to the hands and the heart of the Immaculate Blessed Virgin Mary … On the morning of Pentecost she watched over with her prayer the beginning of evangelisation prompted by the Holy Spirit: may she be the Star of the evangelisation ever renewed which the church, docile to her Lord's command, must promote and accomplish, especially in these times which are difficult but full of hope!' Although the scriptures do not tell us what she did after Pentecost, surely Pope John Paul II was correct when he said in one of his Wednesday teachings: 'In the newly emerging church Mary passed on to the disciples her memories of the incarnation, the infancy, the hidden life and the mission of her divine Son as a priceless treasure, thus helping to make him known and to strengthen the faith of believers.' In other words, like the apostles, she evangelised in the power of the Spirit. So it is not all that surprising that John Paul II said in NMI 58: 'I have often invoked Mary as the "Star of the New Evangelisation". Now I point to Mary once again as the radiant dawn and sure guide for our steps. Once more, echoing the words of Jesus himself and giving voice to the filial affection of the whole church, I say to her, "Woman, behold your children" (cf Jn 19:26)."

Recommended Reading

- Ed Stetzer, Richie Stanley, Jason Hayes, *Lost and Found: The Younger Unchurched and the Churches that Reach Them* (Nashville: B&H Publishing, 2009).
- Gerard Gallagher, *Are we Losing the Young Church? Youth Ministry in Ireland from Vatican II to 2004* (Dublin: Columba, 2005).
- The National Committee of Diocesan Youth Directors & the Commission for Pastoral Renewal and Adult Faith Development of the Irish Bishops' Conference, *Called Together. Making the Difference: A Framework Document for Youth Ministry in Ireland* (Dublin: Veritas, 2009).
- S. Dias, *Evangelisation and Enculturation* (Mumbai: Pauline Publications)
- Avery Cardinal Dulles, *Evangelisation for the Third Millennium* (New York: Paulist Press, 2009).
- Benedict XVI, 'The Priest and Pastoral Ministry in a Digital World: New Media at the Service of the Word,' http://www.vatican.va/holy_father/benedict_xvi/messages/comm.

SECTION FOUR

Epilogue

CHAPTER TWELVE

Some Controversial Issues

In EN 63, Paul VI wrote: 'Evangelisation loses much of its force and effectiveness if it does not take into consideration the actual people to whom it is addressed, if it does not use their language, their signs and symbols, if it does not answer the questions they ask, and if it does not have an impact on their concrete life.' In many ways that statement was the seed that later grew into John Paul's notion of an evangelisation that was 'new in ardour, methods and forms of expression.'[1] This chapter which augments the second, intends to focus on four of many possible cultural challenges that can arise when Catholics engage in basic evangelisation. The treatment here, though not exhaustive, intends to provide evangelists with a introductory understanding of just a few of the issues they may have to contend with.

Topic One: Postmodernism and Relativism

Secular culture is said to be *postmodern* in nature.[2] This world view maintains that, rather than being an objective fact, our knowledge of truth is subjective and at best probable, partial and provisional. Pope John Paul II described it in FR 91 in these words: 'The currents of thought which claim to be postmodern merit appropriate attention. According to some of them, the time of certainties is irrevocably past, and the human being must now learn to live in a horizon of total absence of meaning, where everything is provisional and ephemeral.' According to postmodernism nothing is absolutely certain. There is only an

1. Address to Council of Latin American Bishops in Port-au-Prince, Haiti (March 9, 1983), III: *Acta Apostolica Sedis*, 75 (1983): 778.
2. cf Pat Collins, 'Postmodernism and Religion' *Doctrine and Life* (Jan 1999): 22-31; Paul Lakeland, *Postmodernity: Christian Identity in a Fragmented Age* (Minneapolis: Fortress Press, 1997); Jim Leffel and Dennis McCallum, *The Death of Truth*, ed Dennis McCallum (Minneapolis: Bethany House, 1996), 199-214.

endless sequence of contexts and interpretations. Generally speaking, postmodernism is anti-authoritarian in outlook. It does not believe in all embracing explanations of life such as the one proposed by Christianity. Speaking about its wordview, Pope John Paul II said in FR 46: 'Its adherents claim that the search is an end in itself, without any hope or possibility of ever attaining the goal of truth. In the nihilist interpretation, life is no more than an occasion for sensations and experiences in which the ephemeral has pride of place.'

Pope Benedict XVI has referred to this attitude of mind as the 'dictatorship of *relativism*.' In his book *Truth and Tolerance: Christian Belief and World Religions* he quoted a line from novelist Umberto Ecco to illustrate his point: 'The only truth lies in learning to free ourselves from the insane passion for the truth.'[3] Is it any wonder that Benedict has stated: 'Relativism has become the central problem for faith in our time.'[4] Speaking about the characteristics of this approach to life he wrote: 'It defines itself positively on the basis of concepts of tolerance, dialectic epistemology, and freedom ... Relativism appears as being the philosophical basis of democracy, and is said to be founded on no one's being able to claim to know the right way forward ... a free society is said to be a relativistic society.'[5] Benedict also, quite rightly, says that New Age religion articulates a subjective type of spirituality which is suited to the age of relativism.[6] As I have written about this topic elsewhere I will say little about it here.[7] Suffice it to say that this pagan phenomenon, like a latter day Trojan horse, has insinuated itself into the thinking of many people in our society. For a number of reasons secularism, post-

3. San Francisco: Ignatius, 2004, 186.
4. Ibid., 117.
5. Ibid., 117.
6. 'New Age,' *Truth and Tolerance*, 126-9; Pontifical Council for Culture and Pontifical Council for Interreligious Dialogue, *Jesus Christ the bearer of the Water of Life: A Christian Reflection on 'The New Age.'* http://www.vatican.va/roman_curia/pontifical_councils/interelg/documents/rc_pc_interelg_doc_20030203_new-age_en.html (Accessed 2nd November 2009)
7. Pat Collins, 'New Age Spirituality,' *Spirituality for the 21st Century*, 106-13; 'The New Age Movement Evaluated,' *He Has Anointed Me*, 154-9.

modernist relativism and New Age spirituality pose a very real challenge as far as Catholic evangelisation is concerned. We will look at two of them here.

a) Catholicism and non-Christian religions

In his *Credo of the People of God* which was published in 1968, Pope Paul VI said: 'We believe that the church is necessary for salvation, because Christ, who is the sole mediator and way of salvation, renders himself present for us in his body which is the church. But the divine design of salvation embraces all men, and those who without fault on their part do not know the gospel of Christ and his church, but seek God sincerely, and under the influence of grace endeavour to do his will as recognised through the promptings of their conscience, they, in a manner known only to God, can obtain salvation.' In NA 2 we read: 'The Catholic Church rejects nothing which is true and holy in non-Christian religions. She regards with sincere reverence those ways of conduct and of life, those precepts and teachings which, though differing in many aspects from the ones she holds and sets forth, nonetheless often reflect a ray of that Truth which enlightens all men. Indeed, she proclaims, and ever must proclaim Christ 'the way, the truth, and the life' (John 14:6), in whom men may find the fullness of religious life, in whom God has reconciled all things to himself.' Christians believe that God has revealed absolute truth in and through the person and teachings of Jesus Christ and that he is the sole mediator between God and human beings (cf 1 Tim 2:5), and that there is no other name by which people can be saved (cf Acts 4:12). However, people in modern culture find those claims very hard to accept. They tend to see Jesus as merely one religious genius among many others such as Buddha, Lau Tzu, Zoroaster and Mohammed. Furthermore, when Catholics maintain that their church is the one true church which offers salvation to mankind on God's behalf,[8] many people,

8. Writing about the relationship of the Catholic Church to the many other Christian Churches and ecclesial communities, par 16 of *Dominus Iesus* says: 'This church [i.e. Roman Catholic], constituted and organised as a society in the present world, subsists in [*subsistit in*] the Catholic Church, governed by the Successor of Peter and by the bishops in communion with him'. With

including many Christians, see that claim as being arrogant, intolerant and unjustified. They consider all religions as valid paths to transcendence. Those who espouse the notion of the 'perennial philosophy' believe that there is one universal river of religious experience which expresses itself in and through the various wells of the world's great religions, from the non theism of classical Buddhism, to the theism of Judaism, Christianity and Islam.

In the year 2000, Cardinal Ratzinger published a Declaration entitled *Dominus Iesus, on the Unicity and Salvific Universality of Jesus Christ and the church,* in order to counteract these relativist views. While not denying the universal salvific will of God, the declaration argues that such a truth must be maintained together with the equally important truth that 'the one Christ is the mediator and way of salvation' for all. We do not know how the salvific grace of God comes to individual non-Christians. The Second Vatican Council limited itself to the statement that God bestows salvation 'in ways known to himself' (AG 7). 'At the same time, however, it is clear that it would be contrary to the Catholic faith to consider the church as a way of salvation alongside those constituted by other religions.' Accordingly, 'one cannot attribute to these [other religions] ... a divine origin or an *ex opere operato* salvific efficacy, which is proper to the Christian sacraments. Furthermore, it cannot be overlooked that other rituals, insofar as they follow from superstitions or other errors constitute an obstacle to salvation.' If a discussion about the respective merits of different religions arises Catholic evangelists would do well to remember what Cardinal Ratzinger said in par 22 of the Declaration, *Dominus Iesus*, 'Equality, which is a presupposition of inter-religious dialogue, refers to the equal personal dignity of the parties in dialogue, not to doctrinal content, nor even less to the position of Jesus Christ – who is God himself

---

the expression *subsistit in*, the Second Vatican Council sought to harmonise two doctrinal statements: on the one hand, that the Church of Christ, despite the divisions which exist among Christians, continues to exist fully only in the Catholic Church, and on the other hand, that 'outside of her structure, many elements can be found of sanctification and truth', that is, in those churches and ecclesial communities which are not yet in full communion with the Catholic Church.'

made man – in relation to the founders of the other religions.'[9] The church believes that all religions find their fulfilment in Christ. As John Paul said in NMI 6: 'Christ is the fulfilment of the yearning of the world's religions and, as such, he is their sole and definitive completion.'

A growing number of theoretical and practical atheists deny the existence of God. As John Paul II said in EE 9, there 'is an attempt to promote a vision of man apart from God and apart from Christ. This sort of thinking has led to man being considered as the absolute centre of reality, a view which makes him occupy – falsely – the place of God and which forgets that it is not man who creates God, but rather God who creates man.' But there is still a restlessness evident in the hearts of many of these postmodern men and women. As Pope Paul VI observed in EN 55: 'In the modern world, and this is a paradox, one cannot deny the existence of real steppingstones to Christianity, and of evangelical values at least in the form of a sense of emptiness or nostalgia. It would not be an exaggeration to say that there exists a powerful and tragic appeal to be evangelised.' Pope John Paul II said something similar in EE 45: 'Come over to Macedonia and help us!' (Acts 16:9). Even if it remains unexpressed or even repressed, this is the most profound and genuine plea rising from the hearts of Europeans today, who yearn for a hope which does not disappoint.' As was noted in chapter seven, modern day evangelists need to tune in to that nascent sense of inner poverty and need, and the ways in which it typically manifests itself in modern culture.

Although unbelievers are sceptical about religious claims based on authority, they are usually respectful when people claim to have had genuine religious experiences. As Pope John Paul II observed: 'People today put more trust in … experience than in dogma.'[10] A number of years ago Cardinal Ratzinger wrote something similar: 'Dogma without experience,' he observed, 'is dead, while experience without dogma is blind.'[11]

9. For an official Church summary of *Dominus Iesus* see http://www.memorare.com/reform/djsummary.html

10. RM, 42.

11. Cardinal Leon-Joseph Suenens, *Renewal & the Powers of Darkness* (Ann Arbor: Servant, 1983), x.

Because I have written elsewhere about religious experience I will say little about it here.[12] Rather than being talk or thought *about* God, it is a conscious awareness of the mediated mystery of the divine or the numinous. Arguably it is made up of four interrelated elements.

- Firstly, desire for some meaning or reality beyond one's everyday self.
- Secondly, attention to reality, such as the twin bibles of creation and the scriptures, in the belief that they can mediate transcendence.
- Thirdly, revelation, when desire gives way to conscious awareness of transcendence / God.
- Fourthly, a response which springs from, and expresses the revelation.

This fourfold pattern is quite evident in the story of how Philip the evangelist shared the kerygma with the Ethiopian eunuch (cf Acts 8:26-40).[13] The official's religious desire was evident in the fact that he travelled such a long distance to visit Jerusalem and that he was pondering the scriptures on the way back. His attention was manifest in forgetfulness of his surroundings and his reading of the prophet Isaiah. His moment of revelation occurred when Phillip explained that Isaiah was referring to Jesus, the Suffering Servant, who like the eunuch, was an outsider who suffered injustice, and died for the forgiveness of sins. The eunuch responded to what Philip proclaimed with faith and asked to be baptised. As a result he went on his way rejoicing. It seems to me that evangelists would be more effective if they were familiar with the fourfold dynamic of religious experience, and could identify and facilitate it in the lives of people they want to bring to the Lord.[14]

The importance of religious experience in modern culture would imply that, instead of preaching Christian truths to people

12. Pat Collins, 'Religious Experience,' in *Spirituality for the 21st Century: Christian Living in a Secular Age*, 37-64;

13. Pat Collins, 'Reading Scripture and Religious Experience,' in *He Has Anointed Me*, 160-7.

14. cf Pat Collins, 'Person-to-Person Evangelisation,' in *Gifted and Sent*, 160-7; 200-8.

in an objective way, it might be better on many occasions to share one's subjective experience of those liberating truths. Needless to say, all kinds of objective Christian truths which are implicit in such testimony can be mentioned, such as the universality of sin; the Lordship of Jesus; the free gift of his saving grace; the possibility of being filled with his Spirit of incomprehensible love etc.

Topic Two: The way of God versus the way of the world

In Rom 12:2 Paul wrote: 'Do not conform any longer to the pattern of this world, but be transformed by the renewing of your mind.' Clearly the apostle was contrasting two kinds of life, one which is moulded by worldly thinking and values and the other which is moulded by the thinking and values of the Lord. This notion was echoed in the Apostolic Fathers who often spoke about the two ways. For example, in par 5 of the letter of Ignatius to the Magnesians we read, 'For just as there are two coinages, the one of God and the other of the world, and each of them has its own stamp impressed on it, so the unbelievers bear the stamp of the world, but the faithful bear the stamp of God the Father through Jesus Christ, whose life is not in us unless we voluntarily choose to die into his sufferings.'[15] When he came to Ireland in 1979, Pope John Paul II referred to the conflict that exists between the ways of God and those of the world. At Limerick he uttered these prophetic words: 'Your country seems in a sense to be living again the temptations of Christ: Ireland is being asked to prefer the kingdoms of this world and their splendour to the kingdom of God.'[16] He spelt out what he meant. For example he mentioned the challenges that growing prosperity was likely to pose. He said, 'The Irish people have to choose their way forward. Will it be the transformation of all strata of humanity into a new creation, or the way that many nations have gone, giving excessive importance to economic growth and material possessions?'[17] At Galway he said to the youth of Ireland: 'The lure of pleasure, to be had whenever and wherever it can be found, will be strong and it may be presented to you as

15. *The Apostolic Fathers in English*, 104.
16. *The Pope in Ireland: Homilies and Addresses*, 78.
17. Ibid., 77.

part of progress toward greater autonomy and freedom from rules. The desire to be free from external restraints may manifest itself very strongly in the sexual domain, since this is an area that is so closely tied to human personality. The moral standards that the church … has held up to you for so long a time will be presented as obsolete and a hindrance to the full development of your own personality.'[18]

I was born at the end of World War II. Like all other people of my age I have witnessed a huge change in the mores of the Irish. When I was growing up, work was hard to find, wages were low, and people led fairly austere lives from an economic point of view. That all changed with the advent of the so called Celtic Tiger. During the years of prosperity we lost the run of ourselves. Greed tended to predominate, while many people became acquisitive and materialistic. As we now know, some people began to live beyond their means with disastrous consequences. In many ways it looks as if the Christian rule book was thrown away where business and sexual mores were concerned. There is a good deal of evidence to suggest that in recent years avarice and irresponsible risk taking predominated in the business world, and at the same time there has been quite an increase in recreational sex of different kinds such as, one night stands, viewing pornography on the internet, and recourse to prostitutes.[19] So it would be true to say that, where sexual morality is concerned, a large number of people of all ages seem to be going the way of the world. Psychiatrists maintain that about one in twelve in the population is suffering from a sex addiction of one kind or another.

One of the striking aspects of St Augustine's early life was the fact that he seemed to be addicted to sexual sin. We know

18. Ibid., 46.

19. There are many good books on this subject. One that I found helpful, was Miriam Grossman MD, *Unprotected* (New York: Sentinel, 2006). This psychiatrist describes how college health centres do a good job educating students about all sorts of health issues. They expect that, given accurate information, students will make responsible choices about such things as not smoking, wearing seatbelts when driving, taking exercise, avoiding trans-fats etc. The only exception is in the sphere of sexual health. She criticises universities for focusing almost exclusively on helping students to express

that he had a number of mistresses one of whom bore him a son. Although he was attracted by Jesus and his gospel, the prospect of having to give up his permissive sexual behaviour held him back. He described his dilemma as follows: 'It was, in fact, my old mistresses, trifles of trifles and vanities of vanities, who still enthralled me. They tugged at my fleshly garments and softly whispered: "Are you going to part with us? And from that moment will we never be with you anymore? And from that moment will not this and that be forbidden you forever?" What were they suggesting to me in those words "this or that"? What is it they suggested, O my God? Let your mercy guard the soul of your servant from the vileness and the shame they suggested! And now I scarcely heard them, for they were not openly showing themselves and opposing me face to face; but muttering, as it were, behind my back; and furtively plucking at me as I was leaving, trying to make me look back at them. Still they delayed me, so that I hesitated to break loose and shake myself free of them and leap over to the place to which I was being called – for unruly habit kept saying to me, "Do you think you can live without them?"'[20] Augustine went on to say… 'Thus I came to understand from my own experience what I had read, how "the flesh lusts against the Spirit, and the Spirit against the flesh".'[21] He explained: 'Because my will was perverse it changed to lust, and lust yielded to become habit, and habit not resisted became necessity. These were like links hanging on one another – which is why I have called it a chain – and their hard bondage held me bound hand and foot.'[22] It is not too surprising to find that in his

---

their sexuality without much restraint. The casual sex which they take for granted is the number one problem according to Grossman. She believes that sexually permissive trends on campus, especially the practice of hook-ups, are detrimental not only to males but in a special way to females. They often lead to incurable STDs like herpes and AIDS, abortions which can have harmful physical and psychological effects such as post-traumatic stress disorder; delayed pregnancy by means of artificial birth control until conception is virtually impossible; misguided sexual activities which can contribute to heightened levels of anxiety, depression, eating disorders and suicidal feelings.

20. Ibid., bk 8, chapt 11.
21. Ibid., bk 8, chapt 5
22. Ibid., bk 8, chapt 5.

Confessions he wrote, 'Grant me chastity and continence but not yet.'[23] Augustine tells us that the conflict between the desires of the flesh and those of the spirit came to a point of intensity when he heard a child recite a rhyme, 'Take and read, take and read.' Believing this to be a providential instruction of the Lord he opened his Bible at Rom 13:13 and read: 'Let us behave decently, as in the daytime, not in orgies and drunkenness, not in sexual immorality and debauchery, not in dissension and jealousy.' As Augustine said: 'I had no wish to read any further, and no need. For in that instant, with the very ending of the sentence, it was as though a light of utter confidence shone in all my heart, and all the darkness of uncertainty vanished away.'[24] Augustine became a Christian and led a chaste life from that time onwards.

Many contemporary people may be equally resistant to the gospel message because of a reluctance to change, especially their sexual behaviour. A number of points can be made about this. In *The Gifts of the Spirit and the New Evangelisation* it was suggested that basic evangelisation consists of four steps: (a) Proclamation of the Good News. (b) Demonstration of the coming of the kingdom either through deeds of merciful love, action for justice, or healings and miracle working. (c) Repentance as a response to justifying faith in the Good News. (d) Discipleship, which involves being taught about how to follow Jesus.[25] It seems to me that the issue of sexual behaviour only arises after the Good News has been proclaimed and has led to a metanoia, (i.e. a change in the person's image of God). Repentance is not a pre-requisite of accepting the Good News, but rather a consequence of it. There can be quite a gap in time between accepting the gospel in faith, repenting of one's sins, and changing one's behaviour.[26] This is where conversion of life comes in. Writing about this subject, Cardinal Razinger said in a talk on The new evangelisation: 'Whoever converts to Christ does not mean to create his own moral independence, does not intend to build his own goodness through his own strengths. "Conversion" (*metanoia*) means exactly the opposite: to come out of self-suffi-

23. *Confessions* (London: Sheed & Ward, 1945) ,bk 8, chapt 7.
24. Ibid., bk 9, chapt 12.
25. (Dublin: Columba Press, 2009), 18-9.
26. Raniero Cantalamessa makes a similar point in *Life in Christ*, 38.

ciency to discover and accept our poverty – the poverty of others and the sufferings of the Other, his forgiveness, his friendship. Unconverted life is self-justification (I am not worse than the others); conversion is humility in entrusting oneself to the love of the Other, a love that becomes the measure and the criteria of my own life.'[27]

It is important for evangelists to stress that chastity is not only attractive in itself, the Holy Spirit gives those who accept the Good News both the desire and the power to change their sinful and possibly addictive behaviours. I have been very impressed by the fact that when people become aware of the beautiful teaching of Pope John Paul II on sexuality, which is contained in his master work, *Man and Woman He Created Them: A Theology of the Body*, most of them find it very attractive.[28] In par 81 of *Evangelium vitae*, (hereafter EV) John Paul echoed his book when he wrote: 'At the core of the gospel ... is the affirmation of the inseparable connection between the person, his life and his bodiliness ... the meaning of life is found in giving and receiving love, and in this light human sexuality and procreation reach their true and full significance.' Christopher West, an American layman, has shared how the Pope's teaching helped him to move away from sexual irresponsibility. He has since written a number of books which explain John Paul's profound thinking in accessible terms, (e.g. *Theology of the Body for Beginners: A Basic Introduction to Pope John Paul II's Sexual Revolution*). Incidentally, it contains an interesting chapter entitled, 'Sharing the Theology of the body in a New Evangelisation.'[29] West has also made a number of CDs which explain and apply the Pope's teaching.[30] In Ireland an organisation called 'Pure in Heart' successfully promotes John Paul's message among young people. Evangelists can learn from their experience.[31]

27. Talk to catechists in Rome (2000).
28. Boston: Pauline Books and Media, 2006.
29. (West Chester, PN: Ascension Press, 2004).
30. CD by Christopher West, *Sexual Honesty: A Proposal to Engaged Couples About the Truth and Meaning of Sexual Love.*
31. http: / /www.pureinheart.net

Topic Three: Loss of a Sense of Sin

Explicit or implicit awareness of a sense of sin is a prerequisite for salvation because Christ died for the forgiveness of sins. But as Pope Pius XII famously observed: 'The sin of the century is the loss of a sense of sin.'[32] Why has the awareness of personal wrongdoing declined in contemporary society? Back in the 1950s Paul Tillich made perceptive observation about existential anxiety. He said that while all people at all times have been troubled by deep seated apprehension in the face of non-being, it has been evoked by different threats down through the centuries. In classical Greco-Roman times it was mainly evoked by the fear of inexorable fate and death; in the late middle ages at the time of the Reformation and the counter-Reformation, it was often evoked by the fear of guilt and ultimate condemnation; and in the postmodern era it is usually evoked by the fear of emptiness and meaninglessness.[33] There is a good deal of evidence of different kinds, such as Emile Dukheim's description of normlessness and Viktor Frankl's logotherapy, to indicate that in contemporary society people are mainly preoccupied by issues to do with meaning and values. As a result, they tend to overlook topics such as fate, sin and guilt.

Pope John Paul II provided an insightful answer to the question, why are so many people are unaware of their wrongdoing? In EE 76, he spoke about people's 'inability to see themselves as sinners and to allow themselves to be forgiven, an inability often resulting from the isolation of those who, by living as if God did not exist, have no one from whom they can seek forgiveness.' In RP 18, John Paul included a section entitled, 'The Loss of a Sense of Sin.' The following points constitute a summary of the Pontiff's main argument. Firstly, because of relativism, there is often a denial that there can be intrinsically illicit acts, independent of the circumstances in which they were performed by the subject. As a result, sin is no longer seen as an offence against a divinely revealed precept of an objective kind but rather as something that merely 'offends man'. Secondly, the human sciences can also weaken the sense of sin. For instance, psychologists

32. Radio message to the United States National Catechetical Congress held in Boston (26 October 1946): *Discorsi e Radiomessaggi*, VIII (1946), 288.

33. *The Courage to Be* (London: Fontana, 1969), 48-61.

can try to lessen feelings of guilt while arguing that many of our choices are in fact predetermined by unconscious factors. Sociology for its part often argues on similar lines by saying that bad behaviour is influenced by societal factors, so much so that the individual is declared not really responsible for his or her evil actions. Thirdly, due to an exaggerated emphasis on sin and the fires of hell in the past, the pendulum has often swung in Christian circles to the other extreme. There is a tendency not to recognise sin anywhere. Such an emphasis is put on the love of God that the possibility of any punishment due to un-repented sin is excluded. As John Paul observed, as a result of influences like these, modern men and women are threatened by a deformation and a deadening of conscience, which as GS 16 pointed out, is 'the most secret core and sanctuary of a person.' Some time after writing *Reconciliatio et Paenitentia,* John Paul returned to the subject of blindness to sin. He said, 'While the effects of sin abound – greed, dishonesty and corruption, broken relationships and exploitation of persons, pornography and violence – the recognition of individual sinfulness has waned ... In its place a disturbing culture of blame and litigiousness has arisen which speaks more of revenge than justice and fails to acknowledge that in every man and woman there is a wound which, in the light of faith, we call original sin.'[34]

After many years of pastoral experience, especially administering the sacrament of reconciliation, I have been surprised by the number of people, mainly those in a younger age bracket, who seem to have little or no awareness of their personal sins. For instance, a person might say, 'Father it is seven years since my last confession.' Then I'd ask, 'How do you think you may have fallen short in your relationship with God or your neighbour during that time?' Sometimes the penitent will reply, 'I do not remember doing anything wrong father. I try to be good to everyone.' Then I might go through a brief list of familiar human weaknesses such as holding on to a grudge, saying hurtful things to others, telling a lie, being dishonest, failing to attend Sunday worship, misusing one's sexuality and the like. Often the penitent will say, 'I don't think so, well maybe I said

34.Address to the American bishops on the importance of the sacrament of reconciliation. http://www.zenit.org/article-10090?l=english

some bad words!' It is hard to know why adults could be so blind to their own faults. I'd love to be able to interview their relatives, friends and colleagues to see if those who know them would agree that they never do anything wrong! While I give such penitents absolution because I believe that the very fact that they have come to the sacrament is some kind of admission of wrongdoing, nevertheless I suspect that having confessed in a superficial way they will only feel superficially forgiven.

In the early 1980s I trained to be a spiritual director in Boston, Massachusetts. My mentor at the time was Bill Connolly SJ.[35] On one occasion he circulated an unpublished article he had written entitled, 'Admission of Sin and the Experience of Alienation from God.' When I read it, I felt that it was not only perceptive, I felt that it had implications for those involved in basic evangelisation. Early in his paper, Connolly said, 'the words "sin", and "sinfulness", are not terms that describe directly the inner experience of many Christians.' The words say too little because they often connote an extrinsic transgression rather than one involving an inner attitude. They say too much because they are often associated with undifferentiated feelings of unworthiness. However, people frequently talk about experiencing a sense of alienation from God. This feeling of separation is reinforced by a desire to control their own experience. Deep down they suspect that if God were to address them they would have no control over what he might say. He could say anything, call them to anything. He could undermine their attitudes toward themselves, challenge their emotional preoccupation with their work, overturn their basic social assumptions, and so on. As a result they could be left without integration and confidence. To protect themselves, they try to control their experience of God and let him say only what they feel they can safely hear. They may as a result, hear nothing significant until they are willing to relinquish their control of the dialogue. People typically exercise

34. Address to the American bishops on the importance of the sacrament of reconciliation. http://www.zenit.org/article-10090?l=english

35. William J. Connolly & William Barry, *The Practice of Spiritual Direction*. (San Francisco: Harper & Row,1982); Madeline Birmingham and William J. Connolly, *Witnessing to the Fire: Spiritual Direction and the Development of Directors* (Kansas City: Sheed & Ward, 1994).

inner control by suppressing the awareness of feelings such as guilt, shame and sorrow, and by failing to express them in an open, honest way to God. Connolly remarked that, 'rarely do alienation and control succumb to an explicit realisation that one needs forgiveness. Rarely are they explicitly seen as experiences of sinfulness.' The contemporary person who tries to have a relationship with God seldom sees him or herself as offending God. After all, it is difficult to admit an offence in any relationship if it threatens the very viability of such a relationship. It seems easier to admit ignorance, inadvertence, or inability. For this reason, says Connolly, 'the person would rather put up with confusion or blankness than admit that he or she has offended God.'

A number of points follow from these insightful observations. Firstly, evangelists need to understand Connolly's thinking about the reasons why people fail to directly acknowledge sin, and the ways they indirectly acknowledge it, such as talk about alienation, a lack of a sense of meaning, integration or belonging. It is a striking fact that in chapter three of his Apostolic Exhortation, *The Church in Europe*, John Paul II spoke about people's search for meaning and hope, rather than for forgiveness of their sins. As Is 6:1-6 and Lk 5:1-11 make clear, it is in the light of the perceived holiness of the living God in Christ that we become aware of our sin. That notion is implicit in the words the priest prays in the sacrament of reconciliation: 'May the Lord who enlightens every heart, *enlighten yours to know your sins* [my italics] and to trust in his mercy.' Secondly, Connolly made the important point that sinners need to be secure in the knowledge that God loves them before they can feel safe enough to acknowledge their faults in a more explicit way. So often the evangelist has to accept that many people they converse with will be far from clear about sin. However, their unconscious sense of sinfulness may be implicit in their conscious longings for meaning, integration and inner peace which are rooted in a sense of alienation from God. The woman at the well of Samaria only admitted her sexual sinfulness when she felt secure in the acceptance and love of Jesus (cf. Jn 4:4-42). As Wis. 12:2 tells us, 'Gradually you correct those who offend; you admonish and remind them of how they have sinned, so that they may abstain from evil and trust in you, Lord.' As CCC 1432 says: 'Conversion is first of all a work of the grace of God who makes our hearts return to him: "Restore us to thyself, O Lord, that we may be restored" (Lam 5:21). God gives us the strength to begin anew. It is in discovering the greatness of God's love that our heart is shaken by the horror and weight of sin and begins to fear offending God by sin and being separated from him. The human heart is converted by looking upon him whom our sins have pierced.'

Topic Four: Who Will be Saved?

St Paul tells us that God desires 'everyone to be saved and to come to the knowledge of the truth' (1 Tim 2:4). According to the teaching of Jesus in Lk 8:12, those who take the gospel message to their hearts with faith will be saved. Nevertheless, he intimated in Mt 7:13-14 that only a minority of people would enter eternal life. 'Enter through the narrow gate,' he urged, 'for wide is the gate and broad is the road that leads to destruction, and many enter through it. But small is the gate and narrow the road that leads to life, and only a few find it.' In Mt 22:14 he added: 'For many are invited, but few are chosen.' In Gal 5:19-21, St Paul wrote: 'The acts of the sinful nature are obvious: sexual immorality, impurity and debauchery; idolatry and witchcraft; hatred, discord, jealousy, fits of rage, selfish ambition, dissensions, factions and envy; drunkenness, orgies, and the like. I warn you, as I did before, that those who live like this *will not inherit the kingdom of God* [my italics].'[36] St Peter stated that 'It is difficult for good people to be saved; what, then, will become of godless sinners?' (1 Pet 4:18). Cardinal Avery Dulles has pointed out that there was a virtual consensus among the Fathers of the church in the East and the West, together with the Catholic theologians of later centuries, that judged by these scriptural criteria, the majority of mankind will fail to make it to heaven.[37] For example, St John Chrysostom wrote these chilling words: 'Among thousands of people there are not a hundred who will arrive at their salvation, and I am not even certain of that number, so

36. cf Cardinal Avery Dulles, 'Who Can be Saved?' in *Church and Society*, 522-34.

37. 'The Population of Hell,' *Church and Society*, 387- 400.

much perversity is there among the young and so much negligence among the old.'[38] From a theological point of view we can look at the prospects that two distinct groups have of experiencing salvation, namely, Christians and non-Christians.

a) Will non-Christians be saved?

The notion that outside the church there is no salvation has undergone refinement and development in recent church history. In the second century the anonymous author of *The Shepherd of Hermas* wrote in chapter 53: 'For the sinners will be burned because they sinned and did not repent, and the outsiders will be burned because they did not know the one who created them.'[39] In 1442, the Council of Florence stated that, besides being a punishment for un-repented mortal sin, hell fire could be a punishment for people who through no fault of their own, were born as non Catholics, 'The holy Roman Church … firmly believes, professes and proclaims that none of those outside the Catholic Church, not Jews, nor heretics, nor schismatics, can participate in eternal life, but will go into the eternal fire prepared for the devil and his angels, unless they are brought into the Catholic Church before the end of life.'[40] At the beginning of the Second Vatican Council, Pope John XXIII read a profession of faith that included these words: 'I confess and hold the Catholic faith outside of which no one can be saved.'[41]

Over the centuries the understanding of that teaching was developed. It is interesting to note that Jesuit priest Leonard Feeney was excommunicated in 1953 for arguing, in a fundamentalist way, that baptism of blood and baptism of desire were useless, and so no non-Catholics would be saved.[42] In LG 16 we are told that non Christians, atheists, agnostics and members of other religions can, with difficulty, be saved: 'Those also can attain to salvation who through no fault of their own do not know

38. Ibid., 390.
39. *The Apostolic Fathers in English*, 246.
40. DS, 1351.
41. Peter Hebblethwaite, *John XXIII: Pope of the Council* (London: Geoffrey Chapman, 1985), 429.
42. The profession of faith of the Fourth Later Council of 1215 had stated that outside the church there was no salvation.

the gospel of Christ or his church, yet sincerely seek God and, moved by grace, strive by their deeds to do his will as it is known to them through the dictates of conscience ... But often men, deceived by the Evil One, have become vain in their reasonings and have exchanged the truth of God for a lie, serving the creature rather than the Creator.' It goes without saying, that although non-Christians can be saved with difficulty, Christians should make every effort to evangelise them.

b) What Christians will be saved?

All things being equal, however, baptised Christians have a better opportunity of salvation. Nevertheless, in Book 21 of *The City of God*, St Augustine rejected the idea that all the baptised are saved, or that all baptised Catholics are saved, and finally that all baptised Catholics who persevere in the faith are saved. Like St Thomas Aquinas, Augustine limited salvation to baptised believers who refrain from serious sin or who, after sinning, repent and are reconciled with God. It should be said that in more recent years a more optimistic view of salvation has been proposed in the writings of people such as St Teresa Benedicta of the Cross,[43] Karl Rahner,[44] and Hans Urs von Balthasar.[45] In pars 46 and 47 of his Encyclical Letter, *Spes salvi* (hereafter SS), Pope Benedict XVI seemed to endorse, at least in a qualified sense, the saving importance of a fundamental, transcendental

43. Edith Stein, *Welt und Person* (Freiburg: Herder, 1962), 159-62. Speaking of hell in SS 45, Pope Benedict wrote: 'With death, our life-choice becomes definitive – our life stands before the judge. Our choice, which in the course of an entire life takes on a certain shape, can have a variety of forms. There can be people who have totally destroyed their desire for truth and readiness to love, people for whom everything has become a lie, people who have lived for hatred and have suppressed all love within themselves. This is a terrifying thought, but alarming profiles of this type can be seen in certain figures of our own history. In such people all would be beyond remedy and the destruction of good would be irrevocable: this is what we mean by the word Hell.'

44. 'The Possibility of Eternal Loss,' *Foundations of Christian Faith: An Introduction to the Idea of Christianity* (New York: Crossroads, 1982), 443-4; 'Hell' in *Encyclopaedia of Theology: A Concise Sacramentum Mundi*, ed Karl Rahner (London: Burns & Oates, 1975), 602-4.

45. *Dare we Hope 'That All Men be Saved:' With a Short Discourse on Hell,* (San Francisco: Ignatius Press, 1988).

option for God: 'For the great majority of people – we may suppose – there remains in the depths of their being an ultimate interior openness to truth, to love, to God. In the concrete choices of life, however, it is covered over by ever new compromises with evil – much filth covers purity, but the thirst for purity remains and it still constantly re-emerges from all that is base and remains present in the soul ... Paul begins by saying that Christian life is built upon a common foundation: Jesus Christ. This foundation endures. If we have stood firm on this foundation and built our life upon it, we know that it cannot be taken away from us even in death. Then Paul continues: "Now if any one builds on the foundation with gold, silver, precious stones, wood, hay, straw – each man's work will become manifest; for the Day will disclose it, because it will be revealed with fire, and the fire will test what sort of work each one has done. If the work which any man has built on the foundation survives, he will receive a reward. If any man's work is burned up, he will suffer loss, though he himself will be saved, but only as through fire" (1 Cor 3:12-15).'[46]

So although there may be many sins that compromise and obscure a person's fundamental option for Christ, it can still be present beneath the dross of wrongdoing. Purgatory is a moment, out of chronological time, when people confront this painful and purifying realisation before entering the bliss of heaven. It has to be said that this view needs to be read in the light of what John Paul II said about the fundamental option in VS 67: 'It thus needs to be stated,' he wrote, 'that the so-called fundamental option, to the extent that it is distinct from a generic intention and hence one not yet determined in such a way that freedom is obligated, is always brought into play through conscious and free decisions. Precisely for this reason, it is revoked when man engages his freedom in conscious decisions to the contrary, with regard to morally grave matter.' That said, John Paul seemed to take an optimistic view where hell is concerned. He wrote: 'In Matthew's gospel Jesus speaks clearly of those who will go to eternal punishment (cf Mt 25:46). Who will these be? The church has never made any pronouncements in this regard ... The

46. SS 46.

silence of the church is, therefore, the only appropriate position for Christian faith. Even when Jesus says of Judas, the traitor, 'It would be better for that man if he had never been born' (Mt 26:24), his words do not allude for certain to eternal damnation.'[47] In any case, whichever understanding of salvation one adopts, whether pessimistic or optimistic, those who are committed to evangelisation need to be motivated by a Christ-like desire to seek out and save those who are in danger of being lost.

c) Contemporary notions of salvation

It has to be said that among those who still believe that there is a next life, there is a widely shared, but false, assumption that everyone will be saved because God is so merciful. As we have seen, especially in chapters four and five, it is gloriously true that God is merciful, but the Bible and the church clearly teach that God is also just. People ignore this vital truth at their peril. When I visited Africa a few years ago I was in an area where many members of a local tribe were HIV positive as a result of their permissive sexual practices. When the dangers of casual sex were explained to them by local nurses they refused to believe what they were told, presumably because it would have required them to change their behaviour in a way they were not prepared to do. Instead, they blamed their illness on the medicines they were being given at the local clinic. As a result, they made life so difficult for the nurses that they had to leave the area. Even though the men and women of the tribe rejected the advice of the Christian nurses and persisted in believing that there was no connection between their sexual practices and AIDS, they continued to be infected by the disease and to die from it's effects.

The current belief, that the way which leads to heaven is wide and that many take it in spite of their immoral behaviour, can also have disastrous effects. Firstly, it is contrary to the teaching of Jesus. Secondly, it diminishes human dignity by reducing a sense of personal responsibility and implying that no matter what people do they will by saved by a merciful God. Thirdly, if Christians believe that everyone is going to be saved

47. John Paul II, *Crossing the Threshold of Hope*, 185-6.

by God, no matter what they do, where is the motivation to carry out the great commission of our Lord by bringing the Good News to the ends of the earth? Fourthly, no matter what people believe, the objective facts remain the same, we have 'done what is evil *in your sight* [my italics]' (Ps 51:4) and all of us will have to account for our behaviour on the last day. As St Paul warned in Rom 2:5: 'Because of your stubbornness and your unrepentant heart, you are storing up wrath against yourself for the day of God's wrath, when his righteous judgement will be revealed. God "will give to each person according to what he has done." To those who by persistence in doing good seek glory, honour and immortality, he will give eternal life. But for those who are self-seeking and who reject the truth and follow evil, there will be wrath and anger.' Is it any wonder that Jesus said: 'The harvest is plentiful but the workers are few. Ask the Lord of the harvest, therefore, to send out workers [i.e. evangelisers] into his harvest field' (Mt 9:37-38).

d) Should Hell be mentioned?

In the light of these considerations, the question arises, should those engaged in basic evangelisation ever refer to the possibility of going to hell? Pope John Paul II said that some preachers, catechists, and teachers, 'no longer have the courage to preach the threat of hell. And perhaps even those who listen to them have stopped being afraid of hell.'[48] While it is important to talk occasionally about the fear of hell to Christians who have already been converted to the Lord, it seems to me that it should only have a minor place in basic evangelisation. It is a striking fact that the kerygma is positive in its orientation. It stresses the mercy and love of God rather than the fear of hell.[49]

That said, there is another point of view. When St John Vianney, the patron of all priests, was appointed Curé of Ars in

48. Ibid., 183.

49. It is important to understand the phrase, 'fires of hell' in a purely metaphorical way. In CCC 1034 we read: 'The chief punishment of hell is eternal separation from God, in whom alone man can possess the life and happiness for which he was created and for which he longs.' On the four torments of hell according of St Catherine of Sienna see Ralph Martin, *The Fulfillment of All Desire: A Guidebook for the Journey to God Based on the Wisdom of the Saints* (Stubenville: Emmaus Road, 2006), 52-54.

1818, there was a clear need for basic evangelisation. The religious formation of the families who lived there had been neglected during the French revolution and its aftermath. There were many other people in the parish who were ignorant of the truths of faith and led unspiritual, worldly lives. Surprisingly, instead of beginning by proclaiming the kerygma, the new curé seemed to focus on the fear of God in his inaugural sermons. He said: 'Christ wept over Jerusalem … I weep over you. How can I help weeping, my brothers and sisters? Hell exists. It is not my invention. God has told us. And you pay no heed … you do all that is necessary to be sent to it. You blaspheme the Name of God. You spend your evenings in the local bars. You give yourselves to the sinful pleasures of dancing. You steal from your neighbours. You do a world of things which are offences against God. Do you think that God does not see you? He sees you, my children, as I see you, and you shall be treated accordingly. What misery! Hell exists. I beg you: think of hell. Do you think that your curé will let you to be cast into hell to burn there forever and ever? Are you going to cause this suffering to your cure?'[50] The following Sunday he continued in the same vein. Having referred to the parable of the last judgement, he quoted the words of the Lord: 'Depart you cursed.' Then he went on to say, 'Cursed by God! How frightful a disaster! My children, do you understand? Cursed by God, by God who loves to bless! Cursed by God, who is goodness itself! Cursed without remission, cursed eternally! Cursed by God.'[51] With all due respects to the saintly curé of Ars, I do not think that many contemporary evangelists would feel comfortable with this austere, fearful approach. That said, when it seems appropriate, evangelists should speak about the possibility of eternal separation from God within the positive context of a proclamation of God's free offer of saving grace in Jesus Christ.[52]

---

50. Henri Gehon, *Secrets of the Saints* (London: Sheed & Ward, 1973), 26.
51. Ibid., 27. Vianney's mention of the curse is interesting in the light of what was said about the curse in chapter four on the kerygma.
52. Session 6, canon 8 of the Council of Trent said: 'If any one says that the fear of hell, whereby by grieving for our sins we flee to the mercy of God or refrain from sinning, is a sin, or makes sinners worse; let him be anathema.'

Conclusion

This book has been about basic evangelisation. However, it is evident from this chapter that the kind of apologetics which were mentioned in chapter four are sometimes necessary. As Pope St Pius X said in a letter to the French bishops entitled, *Notre charge apostolique*: 'Catholic doctrine tells us that the primary duty of charity does not lie in the toleration of false ideas, however sincere they may be, nor in the theoretical or practical indifference towards the errors and vices in which we see our brothers and sisters being plunged … whilst Jesus was kind to sinners and to those who went astray, he did not respect their false ideas, however sincere they might have appeared. He loved them all, but he instructed them in the truth in order to convert them and save them.' So while those involved in basic Catholic evangelisation need to be aware of the thinking and feelings that are common in modern culture, they also have an obligation to correct them in a sympathetic but fair way.'[53] This book ends with a prayer which expresses many of its key aspirations:

> Father in heaven, you so loved the world that you sent your divine Son to be our redeemer. I thank you that, not only have I been baptised and confirmed into his saving death and resurrection, I also have the inner assurance that my sins, though many, are forgiven and forgotten, not through any merit of my own, but by the free gift of your Spirit.
>
> You have not only invited me to forgive others as you have forgiven me, you have also commissioned me, together with other believers, to bring the Good News of your unconditional mercy and love to the unchurched and the unbelievers of our day. Lord Jesus we cannot bear effective witness to you without the energising fire of your Holy Spirit, which was first cast upon the earth on Pentecost Sunday. Help us to fan into a mighty flame the gift we have already received while expressing our gratitude for that gift by means of good works, especially that of bearing witness to the gospel.

53. cf Tim Staples, *Apologetics for the New Evangelisation*, 6 CD set (St Joseph Communications, 2004) http://www.aquinasandmore.com/title/Apologetics-For-The-New-Evangelization/SKU/8099.

Enlighten our minds and hearts to know how and when to proclaim this Good News in word and deed, even to the point of healings and miracles, so that we may astonish and amaze the profane and secular world in which we live. May your Spirit be so active in the hearts and minds of those we seek to evangelise, that they may be led by heartfelt longings for meaning and a sense of ultimate belonging, to open their depths to the transforming power of the kerygma.

Lord, you have said in repeated messages of a prophetic kind that a great age of evangelisation is about to be inaugurated by you, one which will usher in a new springtime for the church. Help me, together with other believing members of the Christian community, to become an effective instrument of your saving purposes in the world. Amen.

Recommended Reading

- Nicky Gumbel, *Searching Issues* (Eastbourne: Kingsway, 2004).
- Harry Blamires, *The Christian Mind: How Should a Christian Think?* (Vancouver: Regent College Publishing, 2005).
- Joseph Ratzinger, *Truth and Tolerance: Christian Belief and World Religions* (San Francisco: Ignatius Press, 2004); Benedict XVI, *Saved in Hope: Spe Salvi: Encyclical Letter* (San Francisco: Ignatius Press, 2008).
- Joseph Ratzinger, *Salt of the Earth: The Church at the End of the Millennium* (San Francisco: Ignatius, 1997).
- Avery Cardinal Dulles, *Church and Society: The Lawrence J. McGinley Lectures, 1988-2007* (New York: Fordham University Press, 2008).
- John Paul II, *Crossing the Threshold of Hope* (London: Jonathan Cape, 1994).
- Hans Urs von Balthasar, *Dare we Hope 'That All Men be Saved:' With a Short Discourse on Hell,* (San Francisco: Ignatius Press, 1988).

Index